Abayef
A Bridge Builder Between Faiths

Dr. Daniel Dana

Mazo Publishers

Abayef – A Bridge Builder Between Faiths

ISBN: 978-1-936778-86-7

Copyright © 2011 by Daniel Dana

Contact the Author:
d_dana777@yahoo.com

Published by:
Mazo Publishers
USA: 1-904-638-5397
Israel: +972-2-652-3877

Website: www.mazopublishers.com
Email: cm@mazopublishers.com

Editorial Consultant to the Author
David Herman

All rights reserved.
No part of this publication may be translated, reproduced, stored in a retrieval system, or transmitted in any form or by any means, electronic, mechanical, photocopying, recording or otherwise, without prior permission in writing from the publisher.

*To the G-d of Israel,
who has performed many miracles in my life
and has helped me understand who I am.*

❋❋❋

*To Marina, my wife,
who has helped me to develop my deep love for Israel.*

Contents

AUTHOR'S NOTE	7
ACKNOWLEDGMENTS	7
INTRODUCTION	9

Part One

    ROOTS   13

Part Two

    REVOLUTION   35

Part Three

    DOWNFALL   117

Part Four

    REDEMPTION   153

EPILOGUE   209

Appendix I

    SHIITE REFORMATION IN IRAN   211

Appendix II

    SHIITE LAW AND THE WEST   217

Author's Note

WHAT YOU READ IN this book is not fiction, but a true story. Over the past six decades I have lived amongst different religions including Shiite-Muslims, Muslims, Zoroastrians, Christians, Baha'i, and Jews. I have been active in the areas of politics and religion. I have concluded countless hours of research and have written volumes of research papers. All of my adventures have convinced me that the motion of democracy, liberalism and secularism for the first time in a Muslim country will not be possible unless there is first a cultural, global, reformation. During my research I concluded that Iranians, during the past 14 centuries, lost their national dignity and identity, and I believe that this happened again 30 years ago.

It is very clear to me that Iranian society today is ready for a cultural reformation and renaissance. Shiite Islam today is a major sect of Islam but was created by the original Iranian resistance. It has abused Islamic Ideals and Theology and is truly only a political sect. The children of those fathers, the original reformers and creators of Shiite Islam, have the right to reform Shiite Islam in order to heal society, minimize international terrorism and create a new, reconciled world.

Acknowledgments

IT IS MY GREAT honor to offer my acknowledgements to all of the Muslims, Jews, Christians and the many politicians who have helped me reach this very clear understanding. But beyond all I offer my deepest thanks to my dear brother Yaakov and his wife. He has helped me greatly with the editing and shaping of this book, and his wife has given up many evenings of being with, to allow him to do so. It is more than clear that without his help the next generation of Iranians would not be able to understand this message. I deeply believe that the 40 million Iranians who were born after the revolution will absorb the message of this book, more than anyone else, and use it to build a better future for themselves and their children.

Thanks to my good friends Prof. Ze'ev Maghen (Bar-Ilan University), Prof. Moshe Maoz and Prof. Moshe Sharon (Hebrew University,

Jerusalem), Rev. Jan Williem von der Houven (International Christian Embassy), David Herman, Meir Ezri (the first Ambassador of Israel in Iran) and the Iranian Community in Israel who helped me to be more mature in deep understanding of the valuable term of "Zion" and "Zionism".

Also deep thanks to many Iranians everywhere in the world either Jews, Christians, Zoroastrians, Baha'is or Muslims who have worked with me, shoulder to shoulder in the International Peace & Love Movement (PLIM) for more than 32 years, to prove that Israel is the twin sister nation of our beloved country Iran.

My deepest thanks go to my good friends Yakof Reichert and Chaim Mazo for their professional job in helping to prepare this manuscript for publication.

Introduction

TEN THOUSAND YEARS AGO a large group of Homo Sapiens were forced to travel south to Southern Europe because of the growing ice in the north. From Southern Europe these humans migrated over to the Middle East. These Homo Sapiens were called "Aryan." The most civilized of this group went to the area that is now known as "Iran," which is derived from the word "Aryan." The 19th century philosopher Frederick Hegel explained that today's civilization developed from those first people ten thousand years ago; the first fire, the first use of the wheel and the domestication of horses all originated in Iran.

Some of my people claim, as Hegel states, that our people's cultural-historical background dates back ten thousand years. Some of my people claim a history of 7,000 years, as Girshman the archeologist claims, that our first national army was organized seven millennia ago. There are those who claim that we only have 2,500 years of history, since King Cyrus our progenitor. But with all those claims we forget that our great grandparents, 60 and 70 years ago, did not hold identity cards nor did they record their dates of birth.

MOSES WAS NOT THE only biblical hero to be persecuted by a king, the Iranian icon King Cyrus was as well; however, the king who persecuted *him* was his grandfather – King Azidhag. King Azidhag was the last of the Median kings. Cyrus' mother, Mondanna, was a princess of the province Pars. The Medas family realm was located in what is now northern Iran, near Turkey.

One night King Azidhag had a dream that a beet would grow out of the ground and cover up his whole kingdom. This dream filled King Azidhag with fear and he asked his royal interpreter to explain the dream. The royal interpreter explained that a male child would grow up and destroy him. King Azidhag, not wanting to be overthrown, gave a royal decree to kill of all of the male children in the kingdom.

The King's daughter had recently given birth to a son and, because of her love for her son, the princess gave her son, Cyrus, to a man named Harpak. The princess showed her father a dead baby girl in her son's place. Harpak raised Cyrus in the mountains until he turned thirteen. When Cyrus reached the age of thirteen, Mondanna came to visit her son.

Cyrus' father was from Pars, a state in the center of what is today's Iran. After his mother's visit, Cyrus went to Pars to visit his father's clan. There he trained and studied. When he turned eighteen he came with a large army and conquered his grandfather's kingdom; with this act he united Pars with Medas. In 538 BCE King Cyrus captured the city of Nineveh, and in 536 BCE he gave the command to allow the Jews to return to Jerusalem and rebuild their Temple.

Because of the free and accepting policies of King Cyrus many Jews came to live in Iran, and there was a large community in Pars. Pars was the center state of Iran; Persipolis was its capital. King Cyrus divided the country into 127 provinces, as described in the Book of Esther.

As the capital city of Iran was in the state of Pars, Herodotus, Cicero and Xenophanes, ancient Greek historians, as well as de Tocqueville, in the 19th century, called these people Parsian – from Pars. Because of these historians, the generations came to know the people living there as Persians. In 1938, Reza-Shah ratified in his parliament that their country's name should be "Iran," to rectify the mistake of the ancient western historians.

WHEN KING CYRUS WAS recruiting his original army, many leaders of the Jewish community came with King Cyrus to Persia, because of their respect for him. For 25 centuries they and their descendants were living in Iran. There has never been any other country in the world to have such a deep relationship with the Jewish people, consistently, for such a long time. Their friendship continued until the Islamic invasion destroyed all that had been built, 14 centuries ago in 638.

King Cyrus is the father of human rights and the only non-Jew to be called "messiah" in the Old Testament. This is just as significant for non-believers as it is for believers. The same man that is a hero in the book of God is considered a symbol for human rights 25 centuries later, the symbol of the United Nations. I am proud to call this giant my father, and I hope to walk in his footsteps. All of humanity should be proud to receive his legacy, his sympathetic attitude towards other cultures and religions.

In the book of Matthew, three Magi, Zoroastrian religious leaders came to Bethlehem to visit the newborn Jesus. In the book of Acts the Iranian presence is clear as well. It is well known that the first Christian missionaries to China were Iranian. To this day those churches are called "Persian temples." We can see that, for all faiths, in the days of King Cyrus there was freedom to practice openly in Iran.

During the reign of King Cyrus there was great freedom of religion and choice in Iran. His policies paved the way for the greatest yeshivot, Jewish study houses, of antiquity, Sura and Pompadita, which thrived during the Sassanid period two and a half centuries later. In each yeshiva there was in excess of ten thousand students, a number unrivalled throughout history.

After King Cyrus opened the doors to Israel many Jews went back there, but there were many who remained in Iran as well. I believe that my forefathers were among those Jews who came to Iran during Biblical times and remained there. I believe that my family was one of those families to stay, but I did not know this until fourteen years ago. And this is my story.

Part One
Roots

My Grandmother

ONE OF MY EARLIEST memories was from when I was the age of four or five. It was during the month of Moharram, when special rituals are performed. Through these rituals worshipers mourn for the original Caliphate – the first Shiite leaders 14 centuries ago, who were beheaded.

One of these rituals consists of whipping oneself on one's back with a Zanjir, a hand-whip of chains. People will whip themselves until their back bleeds freely. In another ritual a person will hit himself on his head with a sword. After one or two blows the sword cuts through the person's scalp and blood begins to flow. The worshiper will then hit the fresh wounds with his hands to help the blood flow. It is thought that the person whose blood spurts from his head the farthest is the most faithful.

These rituals are performed by parades of people in the main streets of the city. While I was standing on the side of the road watching these worshipers, a drop of blood, which had spurted out from one man's head, landed upon my cheek. I understood that this blood was very special and holy, so I did not want to touch it.

A woman standing nearby came over to me, grabbed my head with her hands and licked the droplet of blood off from my cheek. While she still had her hands wrapped around my head, I remember hearing her telling my mother that that blood is the holiest blood. While I understood that the blood was holy, what that woman had done disgusted me. That experience was so traumatic for me that over the next few days I washed my face repeatedly trying to get it clean.

During this month a person can attain a level of such religious ecstasy that he will hit himself too hard and kill himself with his own sword. In order to prevent this from happening, a close friend or relative will stand behind the person performing the ritual and hold a wooden board. When this person sees that the sword has caused the worshiper's head to bleed, he will stop the next blow with his board and take away the sword. This way the worshiper will not accidently kill himself. The worshiper will then slap the top of his head with his hands in order to help the blood flow.

The devout that perform this ceremony are called Ghameh-zan. While the Ghameh-zan perform this ceremony, people will stand along the sides of the streets chanting and praying.

During that early period of my life I was filled with ambition and desire to become a Ghameh-zan. I saw this as the highest level of faith, and did

1946-Daniel (Jamshid Hassani) at 6 months old, with his mother, Talate and his father, Ahmad.

all I could to prepare myself so that when I turned eighteen I would be able to perform this ritual as well. The philosophy of the blood sacrifice in pre- and early Judeo-Christian philosophy is understood as a form of sanctification done in the Temple; it is seen as a form of self-purification and can be a very beautiful act. In Shiite Islam it has become an act of barbarism and the most hideous face of sanctification.

The concept of sacrifice has powerful roots. A man can dedicate himself to his God, to a greater idea, a greater purpose; however, a man who does so for Shiite Islam, I believe, is not normal. Fourteen hundred years ago Iran was at the height of its cultural golden age. It was the superpower of the ancient world; its only competition was Rome. The Islamic invasion brought Iran down, and since then it has never returned to be even a shadow of what it had once been. A person who dedicates himself to the ideas of the people who have destroyed his culture and his history is not normal.

From the age of 11 until I reached 15, during the month of Moharram, I had the job of Saghgha. While the worshipers would walk through the streets performing the self-flagellating ritual of Ghameh-zani, my job, as a Saghgha, was to hand a cup of water to worshipers. Because it is considered a special honor to be a Saghgha, parents would send their children out to do this job. The children my age would compete with each other to see who could perform this task better than the others.

THE HISTORICAL AND RELIGIOUS background of the rituals of the month of Moharram can be traced back 14 centuries to Hussein. Hussein was the third of twelve Shiite Imams and the son of Ali. Ali was the father of Shiite Islam and the cousin of Muhammad the prophet. Hussein, from Kuffeh, Persia, and Yazid, the Admiral of Sham, which today is know as Damascus, Syria, were competing with each other on two accounts. Publicly, they were competing for the Caliphate, the leadership of the Islamic society. Privately, they were competing for the heart of a woman, Oraynabe.

Oraynabe had a relationship with both men but was only interested in being with the more powerful of the two. She told Hussein that if he could conquer Sham then she would leave Yazid, the son of Mo'aviah, for him.

Hussein left Kuffeh with his army towards Karbala on his way to conquer Sham. Yazid sent a message to Hussein advising him that if Hussein challenged him that he would behead him. When Hussein reached Karbala, his uncle Shemr-Ibn-Zel-Jowshan, the commander of Yazid's army, met him in battle. Shemr's army cut off the water supply from Hussein's camp, and on the tenth of the month of Moharram, Shemr's army conquered Hussein. Shemr beheaded his nephew along with all of his men.

It is because of this that every year during the month of Moharram, specifically on the tenth of the month, these ceremonies take place. Shemr's army conquered Hussein's by cutting off the water supply; consequently the Saghgha's job is considered a great honor.

MY PEOPLE HAVE LOST their national dignity and have suffered throughout the past 1,400 years, since the Muslim-Arab invasion of Iran and Jerusalem in 638. It is our enemies who have written our history. Now we understand that our history does not go back farther than the veil of our grandmother or the hat of our grandfather: the stories that we heard sitting by our grandparent's feet as children.

My mother's mother was among those multitudes of Iranians who had suffered from having had a foreign religion forced upon them, fourteen hundred years ago. She never understood that it wasn't truly her religion.

1970-The entire Hassani family.

Until I reached 15, my grandmother did her best to educate me to become an Ayatollah, a Shiite religious leader; Ayatollah is Arabic for "sign of Allah."

Privately, when a Shiite family prays together, the women stand behind the men. My grandmother always chose to stand directly behind me, so that she could correct me with my prayers. Even though the men are seen as the leaders of the prayer service, she would do this. Despite having this religion forced upon her, she helped me grow to become a better Shiite.

Since the spoken language of Iran is Persian and the prayers are in Arabic, millions of Iranians do not understand what they are saying when they pray. My grandmother was one of those people; however, even though she did not understand what she was saying, she *did* know how the prayers were supposed to be pronounced. As one blind man helping another along the road, my grandmother would stand behind me to make sure that I was saying everything correctly.

The prayers in Shiite Islam are recited by heart, not from a text, and it is forbidden to stop in the middle. My grandmother used to listen to my prayers while she prayed softly, standing behind me. When she heard me mispronounce a word, she would raise her voice and pray louder so that I would be able to hear the word correctly, and then I could repeat it again correctly. She then would slow down her pace so that I would be able to "catch up" to her and we could continue praying "together."

I was 15 years old at that time. Day and night I studied, and five times a day I prayed. The procedures for praying in Shiite Islam are not as easy as in Judaism or Christianity. Before prayer we perform vozoo, a ceremony consisting of washing one's face, hands, arms, feet and legs. In addition, there are several articles one needs for one's prayers, which must be prepared as well.

We would perform vozoo even in the middle of the winter. We did not have running water in our house; our water was drawn from a fountain in a courtyard out front. There were times that I remember going out to the courtyard in sub-zero temperatures and having to break the ice covering the fountain in order to perform vozoo.

My grandmother always tried to be the best grandmother she could to me. One way in which she did this was that she was always trying to imbue the principles of the Ayatollah in me. In those days my grandmother taught me that part of the principles of our faith is that I must never eat meat with milk. My father used to marinade his meat in yogurt to prepare it for barbecuing. This always bothered my grandmother and she used to tell me that I, who will become an Ayatollah, should not do so.

I remember how she always had a pleasant look on her face. I remember how she was always friendly to everyone. I remember the two braids she wore, and how she covered her head with a white flowered Chador, a veil. It took me over 50 years to realize that that fundamental law, of not mixing meat with milk, was actually not a law of Shiite Islam at all, rather, it is a tenet of Judaism.

One day, during the autumn of 1960, I remember that I was standing in the halls of Bayandor, my high school, in the city of Khoramshahr in the south of Iran. It was on that day that I found out that my beloved grandmother had passed away. She died without achieving her goal: to see her grandson become an Ayatollah. She was filled with this burning desire and it consumed her. She wished that my mother, her daughter, would have these same dreams. But my mother did not.

During that period of my life I began studying the history of my nation. I became excited to learn more about the history of my people, of the generations, which came before me. As this feeling, this identification with my country's history grew, contradictions began to arise in my mind between my Persian heritage and the basic tenets of Shiite Islam.

More and more questions came to my mind and I looked everywhere for satisfying answers for these contradictions. I consulted with my teachers and my parents and anyone who might have answers to these pressing questions.

Some questions I asked were such:

The history of Iran claims that once we had the largest, richest and most comprehensive libraries and universities in the entire civilized world. We had the most advanced research in mathematics, science, medicine and even astronomy. How could the Shiite Muslim Arabs, who had conquered Persia during the seventh century, destroy those intellectual riches; books, libraries universities, and hospitals along with many other facilities? How can we accept their explanation that if the books which we are burning are congruent with the Koran then we don't need them because the Koran says it and if they contradict the Koran then we need to throw them into the sea because they are heresy?

Multitudes of questions came to my young mind. On the one hand, I wanted to continue believing in the tenets of the Shiite tradition, to which my grandmother so dearly held. On the other hand, I kept finding contradictions between Shiite Islam and my country's history and heritage. Anyone I asked, my teacher or my parents, would quickly silence my inquisitive mind saying that it is none of my business.

But these contradictions in my mind only grew stronger as I grew older. By the end of high school I no longer truly believed in Shiite Islam, in fact, I had become quite antagonistic towards that belief system. The reason why these negative feelings became so strong was because I could never find any satisfying answers. Any questions that I would genuinely raise were brushed away and I was told that I was being foolish.

A Self-Made Champion

My uncle, Khalu-Muossa, Uncle Moses, was a charming man and was very dear to me. We had a very close relationship because I was the son of his oldest sister. My uncle was a colorful man; he was a train conductor, a great athlete and he had many tattoos, all over his body. He was affiliated with an underground party called Toudeh, a leftist-communist party. Khalu-Muossa tried to mentor me and help me purge my mind of the teachings of my grandmother, his mother. He did this by training me to become a great athlete. He wanted me to be a champion for our nation.

As I reached the age of 17 I found that I was slowly leaving the teachings of my grandmother and leaning towards my uncle. I was very active in boxing, and I had become the champion of gymnastics for all of the high schools of the province of Khuzestan, the oil heart of Iran. Because of all of my successes and the difficult competitions I faced, the top sports newspaper in Iran, Keyhan-Varzeshi, wrote an article about me titled: "A Self-Made Champion." When my uncle saw this headline he embraced me and told me that I not only was a "self-made champion" in sports, but that he saw the potential in me that I could become a "self-made champion" throughout every aspect of my life.

In those days the war between Israel and her enemies covered the face of the media all around the world. It was a time of political conflict between the Arab-Muslim countries and Israel. The Egyptian ruler, Colonel Jamal Abdul Nasser, one of the builders of Pan-Islamism, had a burning desire to conquer the local province of Khuzestan, whose general population was Muslim. His reasons were not only for the sake of expanding his influence over all the Arab nations, but he also wanted to have a significant stronghold in the Persian Gulf. Colonel Nasser spread anti-Israel and anti-Western propaganda throughout the media and as a result he had many supporters in Khuzestan. He promised the Arab world that within 24 hours of his invasion of Israel he would push all of its inhabitants into the Mediterranean Sea.

When I was 17, early one morning in 1962, I arrived at my high school on my Russian bicycle and I met my fellow classmates in front of the school. I was wearing my high school uniform, which consisted of a navy blue shirt and grey trousers. My classmates were wearing the same uniform as I was and had gathered in front of the school. They were protesting and were chanting angrily "Behead Moshe Dayan! What a great circumcision that will be!" In those days it was illegal to express these strong pro-Islamic ideas, but my colleagues saw themselves as the avant-garde of Pan-Islamism. They went into the streets and invited anyone passing by to join them. I was looked up to; I was the champion of the state in boxing and gymnastics. They invited me to join them in their protest.

When I was between the ages of 14 and 15, my family moved from the city of Shahrood, which is in the northeast of Iran to the city of Khoramshahr, which is in the southwest of Iran. My father was an employee of the national railway agency and this move had been necessary for his job. During that period of my life, my views were gradually shifting from being Pro-Shiite Islam to Iranian nationalist.

There were two conflicting political agendas circulating throughout Iran in those days. The majority view was pro-Arab, pro-communist and pro-Nasser. The minority was pro-Iranian nationalist, which also happened to be pro-Israel. Iran and Turkey were the only two Muslim countries, out of the 54 Muslim countries that had membership in the UN at that time, which approved the founding of the State of Israel. The rest of the Muslim world, obviously, criticized Iran for this view.

What was the reason for these two Muslim nations to support the recognition of the State of Israel in 1948? Historically, Iran had always been an ally of Israel. Two thousand five hundred years ago King Cyrus was the only non-Jewish man to be referred to in the Bible as a messiah. In a similar light, the books of Ezra, Nehemiah, Daniel and Esther, all speak of a positive relationship between the Jewish people and Persia.

The second country, Turkey was led, at the end of the First World War in 1918, by Kemal Ata-Turk, Mustafa-Pasha, who was the first Turkish leader after the fall of the Ottoman Empire. He became the leader of the new Turkey; he was pro-western and, because of this, also supported the founding of the State of Israel.

Back then I did not focus on the political situation. My main interests up to that point in my life were my studies, my family, and my athletic competitions. However, I understood that Jamal Abdul Nasser wanted to conquer Khuzestan and separate it from the rest of Iran. This I understood would destroy Iran because 90 percent of Iran's oil is extracted from this area. So I felt that I could not join the chants of my fellow classmates.

My high school was built on a very narrow street, no wider than six meters in width; there were sidewalks on either side of the street for pedestrians. Leading up to the gate of my school there were massive stone stairs, and in the gate hung two massive wooden doors. When I reached the school and saw the protest, I immediately knew that I did not want to get involved. There were about fifteen students there. I picked up my bicycle and went past them to park it on the other side of the gate in the corner along with the other bikes of other students. As I took my books from my book-bag on the back of my bike, my friends asked me to participate and protest with them. When I refused their invitation they were surprised that their friend, the school's top athlete, most popular student in the class and who they all looked up to, did not want to participate with them. Nasty words were exchanged and in the nature of teenagers, a fight broke out. The fight lasted for about half an hour. I was a boxer but they threw stones and I was outnumbered. Despite being greatly outnumbered, I held my own until Mr. Pourkey, the headmaster, came and broke up the fight.

Mr. Pourkey was a very nice man and an excellent educator. He insisted that we recount what had happened accurately or he would involve the police. Several days later the government relocated my family from Khoramshahr to Ahwaz, 170 kilometer away. Ahwaz was the capital city of Khuzestan. It was only years later that I learned that the city and area around Khoramshahr had been burning with anti-Israel, pro-Islamic, sentiment.

The Military

I FINISHED HIGH SCHOOL IN the new city. At the end of 1963, I was drafted into the military. I was sent 550 kilometers away from home to a military base named Shah Abad-e Gharb. I was one of the first participants in a special army program: Sepah-Danesh – the army of science. The purpose of this program was to educate the illiterate in the remote villages across Iran. This program was started as part of the Shah's "white revolution," created to modernize Iran and increase the educational level of the areas, which were still third world.

The soldiers involved in this program went through four months of basic training. For the remaining 14 months of their compulsory army service, the soldiers were each sent to small villages. In their village the soldiers were responsible for setting up schools for the children during the day, and night classes for the adults to teach them about modern culture and how to read and write.

There were 201 high school graduates along with me on my base for the duration of the four months of basic training. During basic training there was much competition between the soldiers. We were not only competing to learn how to be the best teachers we could be when we finished our basic training, but we were also competing to be the top soldiers of the course.

At the graduation ceremony for basic training, out of the hundred soldiers of the course, three would receive the rank of three stripes on their shoulder. Seven soldiers would get two stripes and the rest would finish with only one stripe. This was not only important because of the honor and rank, but the higher-ranking soldiers received a higher salary as well. In fact, the soldiers with three stripes got double the salary of the soldiers with only one stripe. Because of my strong athletic background and the self-discipline which I had developed as a result of my previous successes, I was the top graduate and I received three stripes at the graduation ceremony.

I have very fond memories from those days. I had many wonderful experiences. The Shah introduced the participants of our program as his sons, and the villagers received us as such. The residents of the villages took the honor and responsibility of working with the "Shah's sons" seriously and welcomed us warmly. They made sure that all of our needs were met. The Shah understood that these were young boys and that many of them had never left home for such a length of time.

Since I was able to prove that I was a capable soldier, the army assigned three villages for me to work with. I traveled from one village to the next by horse. It was very exciting work for me. Every Thursday evening and Friday is the Moslem Sabbath and considered a holiday in Islamic society, much like the Western Sunday. On Friday I had time off and would go to the closest city to take a shower and prepare something to eat. In the villages there were no showers, the people bathed in the rivers. The nearest city was fifty kilometers away. Leaders of the villages came to the "big" city once a month, but many of the villagers had never seen a city in their lives and the farthest they had gone from home was only over to the village next to theirs.

One time, after going away for the weekend, I brought back with me a newspaper. It was the first time in history that a newspaper had ever reached that village. When I read the newspaper to them, I explained that what was written inside is what was happening in their country. They were very excited to hear about what was going on in the world outside of their own. Another time, I brought a radio. None of the villagers had ever seen a radio either before that. It was an exhilarating experience for us all, for them to hear the music coming out of the radio, and for me, to introduce them to such an experience.

My responsibilities did not only include teaching the villagers to read; I was also responsible for introducing them to the world outside their villages. I established a Boy Scout troop and recruited 120 boys. I taught them various sports including track, volleyball, soccer, and ping-pong. During my time in the army I taught over 150 villagers between the ages of six and sixty to read and write Persian.

During our training, our officers had drilled us on the importance of being respectful to the culture of the villagers. Unfortunately, not everyone was. One of my friends was killed for having an improper relationship with one of the village women. Several other misfortunes happened as well as a result of soldiers abusing their position. Despite these terrible stories most of the soldiers had many wonderful experiences. Over the fourteen months that I worked with the villagers I had the pleasure of watching the entire social structure, of how these villages governed themselves, evolve and mature before my eyes.

When I finished my military service I was not interested in returning home to Ahwaz, where my family lived. I had two reasons for this: The first reason was because of my financial situation. I did not have a good job, and if I was not earning I did not want to be a drain on my family. The other reason was because of my sister.

1950-Daniel with his sister, Mahin. Later in life, she was the first woman graduate of the Iranian Police Academy.

My sister, who was two years younger than I, had been accepted to university to study medicine. In those days it was extremely difficult to get accepted to study at university. Out of several hundred thousand applicants each year, only 150 are accepted to law, 300 to medicine and only 5,000 are accepted to university in total. I was too embarrassed to return home, not having a job, and with my younger sister already in her second year of medical school. Instead, I went to live in Teheran.

When I reached Teheran I joined a troop of acrobats so that I could support myself. For a while I also held a job as a waiter in a German cultural house. Despite working at two jobs, my financial situation was tight.

The Police

ONE DAY I SAW an advertisement in the newspaper geared for high school graduates who had finished their army service. The advertisement offered the opportunity to train to become a police officer. The advertisement explained that the recruits were to train for six months in the police academy, then were to work for two years in different divisions of the police force all over Iran. After they finished a two-year tour they would return to the academy for another six-month officers' training course.

I applied for the program and passed all of the exams. The top ten graduates, out of several hundred from the course, were invited to stay on for an extra three-month course. Those recruits were to learn self-defense, advanced weapons training, specialized motorcycle driving and the other specialized skills. The police provided this course to train officers how to be bodyguards for top officials visiting from other countries. I was one of those top graduates and was accepted to this advanced course.

For the first two years in my service I was the ideal model police officer. I was disciplined, I always looked sharp, and my superior officers were always satisfied with my work. Because of my athletic background and my drive to work hard I received many letters of recommendation and awards.

At the end of two years, when, as the advertisement had promised, we were supposed to be sent back to the academy to become officers, I saw that they were not planning to fulfill their promise and I protested. My superior officers would only promise that "next year" they would send me to officers' training.

It is not easy to protest the police system; however, somehow I managed. I became the exemplary troublemaker. I would often get drunk and I instigated many fights. My family was embarrassed by my actions; they thought that being on the police force was not becoming of someone from their family. When I acted up, that embarrassed them even more. The next year and a half was very difficult for me and I was sent to prison multiple times.

One of these incidents was while I was in charge of a radio station. I recall that it was the middle of the day and I had already gotten drunk. I was leaning back in my chair with my feet up on my desk when a captain entered the room. When a superior officer enters the room one is supposed to jump up and salute them; I did not, and he became angry with me. We fought, and I pushed his head through a window and his hand broke. I found myself in jail very quickly.

One day, the commander of my division, Colonel Ahmad Javan, invited me into his office. My file was sitting on his desk and was divided into two parts. The first three years in my record was filled with commendations and records of exemplary service. The second part was the exact opposite.

Colonel Javan asked me why this was so, what had happened to change my attitude? I explained to him that the police force had broken their promise and was destroying my future. They had promised that after basic training and the first two years of service, I would be sent back to the academy for the officers' course and now, three and a half years after finishing basic training, they still hadn't kept their promise.

Instead of challenging my accusations he told me that he saw in me the potential to channel my talents towards something much greater. He offered me the chance to prepare for the entrance exams for university as an alternative to the officers' course. Colonel Javan thought that I could do much more for my country if only I had the proper training. I accepted and for the next six months for 15 hours a day, I studied the material one needed to know to in order to pass the entrance exams. My studying paid off. At the end of those six months I was one of the few who were accepted out of the 850,000 applicants to the Law program at Teheran University.

On the salary of a police officer I could not afford the tuition fees of the university. For the first semester I was forced to borrow money in order to cover the costs. But for the remaining seven semesters I found a way so that I would not have to pay at all.

Teheran University offered a full scholarship to the top three athletes of each sport in which the university competes. In my first year of university I came in second place in gymnastics, and for my remaining years at the university I was the champion gymnast and received the full sports scholarship.

My schooling and the athletic competitions were not my only obligations at that time. I was still a full-time police officer and had to juggle everything else alongside that position. On top of that, during my second year of university I got married, and had two children. During those years I was very busy and, to say the least, these were very difficult times for me. I owed much to my wife, Guity, who was very supportive of me.

Colonel Javan was very supportive of my studies. In fact, when I showed him the newspaper clipping that I had been accepted to law school, he

1971-Daniel's first marriage to Guity. The wedding was held at Teheran University.

embraced me, as if I was his own son. However, even before I finished my first semester, Colonel Javan was transferred and replaced by a different officer, Colonel Ahmad Manteghi. Colonel Manteghi was strongly against my studying, and he did whatever he could to make my succeeding as difficult as possible; he would often send me out of town so that it would be difficult to attend my classes. Several of my fellow police officers were not pleased with me bettering myself and were quite jealous.

Before I had begun my studies I had been in an accident. During 1968, I was escorting a major-general from the Indian army, their Chief of Staff, from the city of Karaj to Teheran. The cities lie roughly 40 kilometers apart. I was riding at the front of the motorcade when, without notice, a car turned onto the main road on which we were traveling. It is amazing how in the space of a moment your life can turn completely. I smashed into the car head-on, and the entire upper-half of my left leg from my hip to my knee was completely shattered. It took several months for me to recover. As a result of this accident I had to get regular checkups. This turned out to be a blessing in disguise.

At one point Colonel Manteghi tried to make it impossible for me to continue my studies. He decided to transfer me to the city of Kerman in the southeast of Iran, 2,500 kilometers away from Teheran. If I could not get to my classes I would not be able to continue my studies. As soon as I heard the rumors of what Colonel Manteghi was planning for me, I went straight to the hospital. I met with my doctor and received a letter confirming that I needed to stay in Teheran. Because of my accident I had to be close enough to the hospital so that I would be able to check in regularly. I remember Colonel Manteghi's expression when I showed him that letter. Exasperation was written across his face, but he could not say no.

The Olympics In The Soviet Union

DURING THAT TIME THE Cold War was raging between the seat of communism – the USSR, and the bastion of imperialism – the USA. It was difficult for anyone to get proper documentation to visit the Soviet Union; for an officer it was practically impossible. While I was still an acting police officer, being the University gymnastics champion I was invited to participate in the Collegiate Olympic Games, which were to be hosted in Moscow from the 1st to the 25th of August in 1973.

In those days there were about 60,000 students in Iran. Out of all of those students a total of 50 were invited to participate in these Olympic games, myself among them. Ten of the students were from Teheran University. Of the 50 students invited, six or seven were gymnasts, but I was the only gymnast from my university. Aside from being the only gymnast from Teheran University, I was the only police officer to be invited to participate in these games. The problem was that it was completely forbidden for anyone from the military or police to go to the Soviet Union.

I simply saw this as another of the many challenges I had to face when dealing with the police; I was used to them by now. The ordeal of getting the proper permissions, passports and papers, took three to four months. While the police continued to reject all of my requests to participate in the games, my university gave me much support since it was a great honor for them to be represented there.

Fighting the police bureaucracy was like hitting a brick wall. Finally, the dean of Teheran University, Dr. Houstang Nahavandi, wrote a letter to the head of the Iranian National Police, General Assadi, explaining what an honor it would be for Iran to be represented in the games. Dr. Nahavandi attached to this letter an edict, ratified by the government and approved by parliament, that any national champion may leave the country, no matter if he is in the military, police, or any regular citizen, as long as there are no negative intelligence records against him.

The police finally consented, on condition that I go through special

Representing Iranian National University Gymnastics team in Moscow in 1973. Daniel was the captain of the team.

intelligence training. Their specialized training included weeks of special courses in the Russian language and a two-month course, given by the intelligence, teaching me how I was expected to act when I was there, and what I should look for to report back about when I returned home.

On my return I had written an eight-page report, which covered my experiences while I was there. I included inside my recommendations on the current social and political situation in the Soviet Union. My main argument was that the best policy for the Iranian government to take with the Iranian university students, who loved socialism and were strong advocates of the Red Revolution, was to send them to see for themselves. What this would accomplish is that they would see how the people there were crying for their freedom. I recommended that they should stop suppressing the lectures on Communism in the university; instead, they should expose it for what it really does. The suppression was only causing a stronger support base.

While I was fighting to get the proper permissions that I needed to participate in these Olympic games, my uncle, Khalu-Muossa, was very excited for me and extremely proud. I had an intuition that he wanted to share something personal with me. Finally, he opened up and he gave me two small bottles, no bigger than a few centimeters in diameter and he asked me to fill one of them with water and one with dirt. Khalu-Muossa had been born in Bukhara, now part of the Soviet Union. He felt such strong nationalistic ties to the land in which he was born that he wanted me to do this for him. When I brought the bottles back he kissed them and placed them on his shelf; they were his most prized possessions. He kept them not unlike one keeps one's religious ornaments.

Before the year 1813 all of the territories north of the Caspian Sea were part of Iran but in the protocol of Golestan in 1813, and again in the protocol of Turkemenchai in 1828, cease-fire agreements were made between Iran and then Russia. Seventeen provinces, which are now the five countries of Azerbaijan, Turkmenistan, Tajikistan, Uzbekistan and Gorjistan (Georgia), were lost. These countries were lost mostly as a result of the terrible influence of the Shiite leaders of that time. So really, my uncle was not a Russian nationalist at all, rather, a pure Iranian nationalist.

Zhandarm

(The official police units responsible for the territories outside of the city.)

DURING THE EIGHT YEARS that I was working for the police I must have sent over 150 letters of resignation. I wanted to leave because I wanted to work professionally as a lawyer, or even as a judge, when I finished my degree. The police offered me a job as a judge within the system, but I was not happy with that prospect. I wanted to open a private practice.

I could probably divide my police service in thirds. The first third lasted for two and a half years. During that time I was the model officer. The second third lasted for a year and a half. For the duration of that period I was a troublemaker, the complete opposite of my first few years.

For the last four years in my service I resigned myself to be tolerant of my situation. Because I was in law school I had to support my family and myself, so I had no choice but to stay. I wasn't really an officer in spirit anymore, however, I had no choice and they would not let me go.

This position of being a student of law gave me a special social status amongst my colleagues in the police force. I was greatly respected, both by my contemporaries and even by my superior officers. It was a big deal to be a law student, whether I remained in the force or not. Sometimes I used this influence for the good, but sometimes I abused this status.

We used to work in shifts of 36 hours on-duty and 24 hours off-duty. The 36 hours on-duty was divided into thirds. For the first 12 hours, we would patrol with our motorcycles on the highways and rural roads. For the following 12 hours, we served in the police station and dealt with administrative work. For the final 12 hours, we had to be in uniform in the dormitories, ready to be called at a moment's notice; but we could sleep for that time.

During the 24 hours that I was off-duty I had to take care of my studies, my family and my sports career. This was a very complicated period in my life, and it lasted for four years. At times this schedule was beyond my physical capabilities, and at times I would get angry. But I persisted because I understood that I needed to do this; this was the life I had chosen.

One morning, at 5 a.m., I received a message that I had to present myself to the Lieutenant General, Biuck Amin-Afshar, the head of the national police, in one hour's time. The main headquarters, where he was stationed, was 80 kilometers away. Lieutenant General Amin-Afshar had a reputation for being very critical and easily angered.

One way in which I abused the honor I received from being a student was that I had let my hair grow long. It is military regulation that everyone must keep their hair short, but my superior officers were lenient with me.

I quickly put on my jacket and left on my motorcycle to make my appointment in time. In the message calling me to this appointment they had failed to inform me that they were assessing my file in regard to my requests to be discharged. Along with the Lieutenant General there were two other generals from his staff with him. General Ruzbahni and General Ghavami. And with these generals were the two highest-ranking colonels of the police.

Emotionally I was in a very difficult situation; I had conflicting feelings flowing through my head on my way over to the main headquarters. I asked myself: "Why had they called me so urgently?" "Why hadn't they told me what this meeting was for?" With no explanations I could not properly prepare myself for this meeting. I did not have the correct uniform for meeting the Chief of Police, and my hair was long and a complete mess. But I had to be there, so I had no choice but to go.

In my mind, at the same time I was feeling great pride and arrogance. I told myself: "A Lieutenant General wants to speak with me?! That's nothing! I am a law student and a national champion! But, on the other hand, why hadn't they responded to my 150 letters of resignation?" Despite this general's bad reputation, I was fuming! Such a meeting with a high-up commander is usually set at least 24 hours in advance, so the officer could prepare and arrive properly attired.

Had I known that the top five commanders of the police had called this meeting in order to accept my resignation from the service, I would have been in a much better mood, and I would not have acted the way in which I had. But since no one had told me in advance what was going on, I was feeling defensive, and angry!

When I entered the room in which the meeting was to take place and saw all of the officers in the room I knew that they were there to accept my resignation. This made me even angrier. Had I known, I would have come prepared in my dress uniform and with a proper haircut! When I entered the room I was supposed to salute the Lieutenant General, the Chief of Police. Instead I barged in and took off my helmet and stood there without saluting.

The generals sitting in the room were in shock. Lieutenant General Amin-Afshar yelled at me: "What kind of officer are you? Which police force are you from?! Who checked your uniform this morning?!"

I answered that no one had checked me before I left. He ordered me to open up my "French," my military vest. He wanted to check to make sure that I was dressed according to regulation. In anger I tore open my French and a button came off and rolled across the room. The room was silent while everyone in the room watched the big metallic button roll across the floor. The Lieutenant General was livid, but the other officers did all they could to restrain themselves from bursting out in laughter.

Being in the state that I was in, Lieutenant General Amin-Afshar was afraid that I was going to attack him and immediately rang the buzzer on his desk. This buzzer calls in the officers from the outer office, he wanted them to come in and restrain me. Lieutenant General Amin-Afshar ordered them to shave my head and send me immediately to jail.

While he was yelling at me, I was shouting back at him: "The Shah said that the military should be educated. I have every right to study ... It wasn't you who sent me to the university ... I sent myself! You have no right to stop me! The final exams for my studies at university are coming up, and if you do not allow me to take them I will pour a gallon of gasoline on myself and set myself on fire. Everyone will know that YOU are my killer."

The General's personal assistant, Captain Salahshour, knew me personally. He tried to restrain me, and explain to me that they had convened in order to review my requests to leave; however, the damage was already done. I was sent straight to prison.

After a period of 10 days, Captain Salahshour came to visit me in jail. He asked me for a list of the books and supplies that I would need in order to study for my exams. Captain Salahshour told me that the Lieutenant General himself made this request. Lieutenant General Amin-Afshar requested that while I was in jail I be given everything I would need to study, and when the time for the exams come I might leave jail in order to take them. My family was very concerned for me, and asked me if there was any way in which they could help. I told them that the best way to help me was to leave me alone so that I could study. I used that time in jail to study for my exams.

Lieutenant General Amin-Afshar kept his promise, and I was allowed to leave jail in order to take my exams, as long as I went with two fully-armed prison guards. My colleagues and professors were shocked and amazed when I arrived. Normally, when I came to school I was well dressed. It was surprising for them to see me in the prison garb. Needless to say that it was not a natural occurrence to see prison guards around the University's campus. My colleagues were also baffled why the government would let a prisoner take his university exams. But I did and I passed them all.

After graduation I was released from jail, and Lieutenant General Amin-Afshar finally accepted my resignation. Immediately, I went and registered with the Iranian Bar Association. All law school students after finishing their degree have to study for another year in order to pass the bar exams. During that year, while I studied, I had to support myself. So, while I was studying for the bar exams I took a three-month course with the Iranian Tourist Ministry to become a licensed tour guide. For the rest of that year I worked for Air Express International, an Iranian tour company. My job with them was to guide Iranians around Europe, the

US and around the world.

While traveling around Europe I fell in love with Paris. When I finally passed the bar exams, I applied to continue my studies in the University of Paris.

Part Two
Revolution

France

IN THE MIDDLE OF autumn of 1977, despite not having any money or financial support, I arranged to leave Iran with my wife and two children. My son, Payman, was four years old, and my daughter Bahareh was all of two months. My wife, Guity, had just finished her degree in psychology, and so we both were interested in continuing our education to receive a doctorate in the fields in which we had studied.

As the national champion in gymnastics I had had the opportunity of meeting Her Majesty, Queen Farrah Pahlavi of Iran, on several occasions. On one of them she had promised me that if I wanted to continue my studies she would help me do so and she would cover my tuition. Aside from that, I had gotten an offer from Air Express, the tour company I was working with, to be their Paris representative. So I had these two means through which I would be able to support my family and continue my studies.

During the first six months of our living in Paris we had to deal with many different challenges. Aside from the usual things which one has to deal with when moving to a new country, like getting the proper documents in order, learning the language, finding a place to live, the political situation in Iran was getting very hot and was building towards the Shiite-Islamic revolution. As a result of these political factors, both of the financial arrangements which I had set up fell through. The government was going through a great upheaval, so Queen Farrah could not keep her promise. Air Express could not make good on their offer either. I was forced to get a low-level job at a factory in order to make ends meet. But both Guity and I were committed to staying in Paris, so we continued studying French while we worked to support our family together.

Millions of Iranians, like myself, lost a lot as a result of the Shiite-Islamic revolution. The Shah was a nationalist and was very proud. He claimed that he would rather have his hand cut off before he signed another colonial-based oil agreement. He also was very arrogant and would make comments like: "every blue-eyed person in the west should come to Iran to see how a country should be built." In those days, a group of Iranian nationalists under the leadership of the Shah were preparing the country to become the Japan of the Middle East. In many areas we were developing very quickly.

The Shah's arrogance angered the western countries. In 1979, President Carter at a meeting in Guadeloupe dropped his support for the

Shah and pledged his support to Ayatollah Khomeini. Because of Carter's betrayal we didn't even become the Bangladesh of the Middle East.

Throughout Iran many of the intellectuals preached about the communist nuclei of the world: China, the USSR and Cuba. They were eager to put into practice their leftist communist ideals. At the same time, the religious people, with the support of the Islamic countries of the area, including Syria, Libya, Saudi Arabia, and Iraq, among other Islamic countries, were against the Shah as well. There was a third group in Iran, during that period, who were pro-western, and they too were against the Shah. Much of the country was against the Shah and supported Khomeini.

While I was studying French I arranged everything I would need in order to get accepted to the university. This took about a year, but finally I was accepted to continue my studies.

In the current intense political atmosphere in Paris I found my childhood mirrored. On the day that Ayatollah Khomeini arrived in Paris to lead the Islamic Revolution against the Iranian nationalists there was an excited buzz throughout the university. Khomeini wanted to set up his camp in the Village Neuf Le Châteaux. My fellow students were strong supporters, and there were many heated debates throughout campus.

The atmosphere permeating the campus reminded me of my days back in the Bayandor High School from when I had been seventeen. None of my fellow Iranian students understood why I did not support Khomeini, and began arguing with me. I told them that they were supporting a devil, and many nasty words were exchanged. At that time others labeled the people who did not support Khomeini as "SAVAK" – Iranian intelligence agents. This title became a slur. The right, left and center were all against the Shah, but, as a result of my background in the police, my Iranian colleagues accused me of being from the SAVAK.

I was studying with two Iranian diplomats Sadeghi and Amir-Chupani, who, even though they were being supported by the government would not outwardly admit that they supported the Shah. I remember once one of them pulled me aside and told me that I had to stop being so argumentative, if everyone here supports Khomeini then it is foolish to be so vocal about my opposition. I answered: "If we do not stand up for ourselves, then no one will hear our voice."

These people were not the only supporters of the Shah who were hiding their views. I met an Iranian military man, Colonel Motallebi, in Paris. He had been sent by the army to study in San-Sir, one of the top military schools in the world. He was studying there so that he could reach the rank of General. However, despite his rank and situation, he too refused to be vocal about his true views.

Colonel Motallebi was my next-door neighbor; his door was no more than three meters from my own. We lived together in the neighborhood of Beaux Gronelle, approximately a five-minute walk from the Eiffel Tower. We lived on the 25th floor of a very tall residential building called Reflet. The Colonel and I were very close, and we used to lament together over the Revolution. The day after the Revolution, his entire approach made an about face. Just the day before we had talked about the Shah. The very next day he was a staunch supporter of Khomeini. I was livid. How could he betray the Shah? The Shah had made him who he was.

Colonel Motallebi left his home every morning at 5 a.m. to go to San-Sir. One night I waited up all night so that I would be able to catch him when he left in the morning. When he left his home I jumped out at him and with both my hands I ripped the officer's stars from off his shoulders. I shouted at him: "You do not deserve these! Go back to Iran where you belong with all of the other traitors!" We fought. No one reaches the level of Colonel in any army without being able to handle oneself in a fight, but I was the stronger of the two and beat him senseless. Many angry words were exchanged, some of them I do not want to repeat. After that fight we did not talk ever again. He avoided me as a mouse avoids a cat.

A number of weeks later he was called back to Iran, and because of his loyalty to the new regime he was given a very honorable position. Eventually they sent him back to Paris to finish his studies, but he died suddenly, shortly after his return to Paris.

Everyone was in shock when Khomeini took over Iran. This is just one example of the aftereffects. To explain this shock, try to imagine that one day Fidel Castro would come from Havana to the White House, take it over, and force all of the once free American citizens to attach a red star to their foreheads with a thumbtack. That was the feeling regarding what happened when Khomeini took control over Iran.

Another example of the shock that people were feeling at that time was what happened to Motallebi's sons. Colonel Motallebi had two sons. At that time, one was eighteen and the other was sixteen; they were both strong supporters of the Revolution, but the shock of the aftermath affected everyone.

When the colonel died, his sons did not send him to the funeral home immediately. They decided that it was not respectful for him to go before they washed him. This was not normal behavior. Their mother walked in on them, their father's body was in the bathtub and they were washing him. The police came, and everybody heard how these boys washed the body of their dead father at home.

ECCLESIASTES STATES: "A GENERATION goes and a generation comes ... and there is nothing new under the sun." (1:4-10) History repeats itself time and time again. In 638, after the Islamic invasion of Iran, the Arab invaders massacred thousands upon thousands of people and many young people were taken as slaves. One of the most well known of these prisoners was Princess Shahrzad (Sheherezade), one of the daughters of the Persian King.

Princess Shahrzad was extremely unhappy about what had happened to her dynasty and she wanted to take revenge. Because of her lineage, the Caliph Shiite religious leader threatened to kill her unless she told him a story. This continued for 1001 nights when finally the princess took her revenge. This story is well known in western culture and is told over through literature and music. The conquered Iranian people were not happy with their new situation. In fact, members of the Iranian resistance killed the first three Caliphs, along with tens of the first Imams, Shiite clergymen.

Another person who received a lot from the Shah's government, but then turned and joined the Islamic Revolution was my wife's cousin, Dr. Ibrahim Yazdi. Dr. Yazdi received a top scholarship from the Iranian government and studied for many years in the US. He became a well-known doctor of medicine at Massachusetts University. Before the revolution he became the official Persian-English translator for the US government, and there are rumors that he worked for the CIA. During the months leading up to the Revolution he was the top translator for Khomeini, and after the Revolution he became the first Minister of Foreign Affairs.

Guity's family, including her parents from within Iran and her cousin, Dr. Yazdi from the US, applied a great deal of pressure on me. They told me that this is the end. I was very upset by the people who held onto Islam with one hand and Iranian nationalism with the other. I felt that these people were hypocrites. But Guity's family insisted that we return home and stop being so open about our support for the Shah. From the beginning I knew that the Shiite-Islamic Revolution would not be good for my people. But little by little I saw that it was becoming a reality. Even so,

I became very angry with my in-laws for placing me in this situation.

Dr. Yazdi was an example of the penetrating power of Shiite ideology. He came from what was at the time the most civilized country of the Middle East; from there, he moved to the United States where he studied for many years. However, despite where he grew up and where he was educated, he became a staunch supporter of the Shiite-Islamic Revolution. When a Shiite Muslim goes to a country, they do not go there to take part in its culture and heritage; rather, the hope is to penetrate and eventually take over that culture and country.

Throughout my life I cannot remember a time when my father was ever the slightest bit political. During that period I was being pressured by Guity's family as well as by many other friends. They told me to worry about the future and show support for the Revolution, so that I did not jeopardize Guity or myself.

One day I received a letter from my father. When I opened it, I was surprised to see that the title of the letter was "Vive Shah, Vive Iran – long live the Shah, long live Iran." In the contents of the letter my father gave over advice saying it was important to take care of my family, not to be rash and risk the life I was building for myself. He knew what my beliefs were, and he went on to tell me that I should hold onto them, but now was not the time to speak out. Having said that, the statement made in the title of the letter, for me, was the strongest statement he could have made. My father never spoke about politics, despite being a descendant of the Shahsavan Clan. Shahsavan means "lovers of the Shah." This clan was very prominent and strong Iranian nationalists.

For three months before the Shiite-Islamic revolution, Khomeini resided in France. There he was able to freely gather support from the US and other Western countries, as well as plan and prepare for his revolution.

One day I was in the Parisian branch of Bank Melli, the Iranian National Bank. I was waiting in line, along with half a dozen other people for our turn for the teller. While we were waiting, two clergymen strutted into the bank and, completely ignoring the line, they went directly to one of the tellers. I remember this incident so clearly that I even remember the teller's name. Her name was Zhaleh Daftarian, who happened to be a good friend of my wife.

I was so angered by their complete disregard for the other people, who were already waiting, that I shouted out: "Hey that's rude! You have to wait in line like the rest of us!" I admit now that my language was probably more colorful than that, however their response was even worse than mine. I left my spot in line, grabbed one of them and pulled him to the back of the line. In doing so, his turban fell off and I even succeeded in injuring him. These clergymen claimed that they were entitled; they were working for the people. I said that they were only destroying our country, not helping it.

The police became involved; a disturbance such as this is unheard of in a Western Bank, especially in France. However, because of the current political atmosphere, strangely enough, the people who were in the bank at that time supported the clergymen's rudeness and not my objection. Mrs. Daftarian told me off. I remember that everyone there yelled at me. A number of months after the Islamic Revolution Mrs. Daftarian called me to apologize for her behavior that day. She had been Muslim at the time and a strong supporter of the Revolution. Today, I hear, she is one of the leaders of the Zoroastrian community.

Now-Rooz

IT IS NOT AN easy task to meet with an exiled monarch. The Shah and the Queen after the revolution left for Morocco. King Hassan, then the ruler of Morocco, had accepted them as his private guests and arranged an entire quarter of the city of Rabat for them to live in, plus his full protection. The supporters of the Shiite-Islamic revolution were interested in capturing the Shah and killing him, so the Moroccan security services had to be on high alert.

At that time, everyone around me, my family, my wife, my friends, diplomats, the military, colleagues in and out of the university, supported Khomeini; everyone, that is, except for me. My mother and sister in-law came from Iran, specifically, to tell me that I should stop "my nonsense" of supporting the Shah. The atmosphere had changed in Iran, and they told me that "things are better now." With all of this pressure coming from all around, I searched for a way out: a way to deal with these pressures and the stress that accompanied them, and a way to channel them positively. I decided to go and visit the exiled Shah and the Queen.

On the 21st of March 1980 at 7 p.m. my plane landed in Morocco. From the time I got off of the plane until six the next morning I was interrogated by the Moroccan intelligence. They had assumed that I had come in order to kill the Shah. They were sure that someone had sent me, that I had affiliations with one organization or another. They could not believe that I was against the revolution, with all that had gone on, that I still supported that Shah. Finally, after eleven hours of interrogation three people from the staff of the Shah came and took me to a special residence.

The residence was beautiful. A simple student like myself had never seen such extravagance with five-star-hotel sophistication. The suite, which I was brought to, had the most elegant furniture and a library with several hundred books. I was advised that I should not leave my room, nor could I contact anyone. The guards were very respectful, and I was so preoccupied with what I had come to do that I was neither aware of my surroundings nor that, in essence, I was a prisoner. But they gave me no reason to feel imprisoned. They told me that if I needed anything the servants would attend to my needs.

Over the course of the next 36 hours I stayed in that suite. I slept a little, since I had not had a chance on the previous evening. Twice the Shah's personal guards came and continued questioning me. They reviewed my background several times. When I was asked why I wanted to meet with the Shah, I told them that I came to bring the Now-Rooz gift.

The traditional Iranian calendar is solar, consisting of 365 days, similar to the Gregorian calendar. The main difference between the two is that the traditional Iranian calendar begins on the 22nd of March. It is an Iranian tradition that on the Now-Rooz, the New Year, people bring gifts to the king.

It was also a tradition that once a month the King would open his court to the people for anyone who wanted to bring a complaint or gift. During my interrogation I raised this point. When my athletic accomplishments were discussed during my background check, I noted that I had had the opportunity of meeting Her Majesty, Queen Farrah before, and that Her Majesty might remember me.

The next day, the Moroccan guards came and carried out a full-body search of me to make sure that I had not succeeded in hiding any weapons of any sort. A little while later, at about 3:30 in the afternoon, the Shah's guards came to the residence and escorted me to a black Mercedes waiting out front. They drove me over to the residence of the Iranian ambassador. Outside of the residence an Iranian flag was blowing in the wind. This was the first time in two years that I had seen that flag out in the open; I was moved to tears.

When I went through the front door I came to a great hall. Lining the walls were exquisite tapestries, paintings. There were also beautiful sculptures placed throughout the hall, all of them created by top Iranian artists. At the far end of the hall was another room. The ceiling was over three meters high, and there were a number of crystal chandeliers hanging from the ceiling and similar light fixtures mounted around the room. There was a fire roaring in a magnificent marble fireplace, the mantle covered with intricate marble carvings.

At one end of the room there was a small coffee table with two benches, one on each side. I was escorted by one of the guards to this table, and was seated with my back to the hall. On my way to the table the guard tried to convince me to support the Shiite-Islamic revolution. I was in shock, though I realized that this must be a final test to confirm where my loyalties lay.

At the other end of the room, 25 meters away, the Queen entered with her entourage. They crossed the room towards us. The guard who had come with me stood immediately and saluted her. The Queen took the seat across from me, no more than forty centimeters away from where I was sitting. A massive dog, which had been escorting her, came and sat by my feet. Every movement I made the dog watched with diligence. I found this quite unnerving. The Queen saw that the dog was making me uncomfortable, and when a servant came over to take our drink requests the Queen asked her to lead the dog away.

The Queen was very sweet and very sympathetic towards my needs. She first asked me about my personal background, my family and education. I explained to her how I was studying now in France. I described how, over the past few months, I had become extremely disturbed by the building Shiite-Islamic revolution, but also how not one of my colleagues, friends or family understood me.

WHEN MOHAMMED THE PROPHET of Islam, was on his deathbed the question of succession arose. There were four candidates for the Caliphate: Abu-Bakr – the oldest, Omar, Othman, and Ali – the youngest. According to the Shiite ideology Mohammed announced on the day of Ghadir-e Khumm that Ali should succeed him. The Islamic people did not like his choice since Ali was the youngest. The candidates went to Saqifeh Bani Sadr to stand before the Muslim leaders of that time to decide who would take over the Caliphate. This meeting is legendary in Islamic society.

It was decided that Abu-Bakr, being the oldest, should take over the Caliphate. He was very old, and after two years he died. Omar succeeded him and ruled for six years. Piruz Nahavandi assassinated him. Othman succeeded Omar. He lasted for eight years until he was assassinated too by Behzad Hamedani. Finally, Ali was the Caliph, as Mohammed originally had requested, but he was Caliph for only five and a half years, until Ruzbahan Khorassani assassinated him. All of these great men were leaders of the Iranian resistance.

At the time of the Arab-Muslim invasion, the Muslim leaders ordered that all Iranians be killed unless they accepted Allah and Mohammed his prophet. They ordered all children to be taken as slaves. All of the libraries were sorted through. If a book supported the ideas of the Koran, it was burned, since it was not needed anymore, and if a book was against the ideas of the Koran, it was thrown into the sea, being heresy.

Piruz Nahavandi, Behzad Hamedani and Ruzbahan Khorassani among many others are considered legendary Iranian patriots. They were all top officers of the Iranian Imperial Guard. They would not accept the tyrannical government which had forced itself on their people, and they gave their lives to try and improve their people's situation.

The summer capital of the Iranian dynasty was in the city of Tissfun. There, there was a great palace called the "White House." These legendary heroes asked themselves how they could allow such tyrants to live in their beloved White House? And so they went on their suicidal missions with the hope that their selfless acts might wrench the leadership away from the Arab-Muslims and return it to their own heritage. The invaders destroyed the White House and the surrounding city, and in its place built a city, which today is known as Baghdad, meaning "a gift from God."

I DESCRIBED TO THE QUEEN that during my service in the military, and while I was in the police, I received many awards for my marksmanship with a handgun. I wanted to offer her my services and go to Teheran to assassinate Khomeini and then commit suicide, as those legendary assassins had. The problem was that I had been out of Iran for so long that I didn't have any contacts there anymore, so I told the Queen that I would like her help to assist me in setting up the proper contacts to accomplish my mission. Aside from which, I wanted to ask her that in return for this service she take care of my two children.

I could see that the Queen was greatly moved. She got very excited and, while we were talking, she smoked cigarette after cigarette. I understood that she was extremely nervous with excitement. However, despite her excitement over my proposal, she turned me down. "We are not terrorists," she explained. She advised me to go home to my wife and children and to seek out patriots like myself to spread the truth about what this revolution really was costing our people.

I insisted that I was serious, if only I could do it myself, I would. But she refused. She invited me to stay with them in Morocco with her for as long as I liked. But I was beaten. I had come like a lion with a purpose, and now I felt like a pussycat with little hope left.

The Referendum And Its Consequences

On the 5th of April 1980, the 12th of the month Farvardin, the first month of the Persian year, a referendum was held for all of the Iranian people residing in Iran and abroad. This referendum was held to decide if they wanted to continue with the Shiite-Islamic Republic. On that day in Paris there were thousands of people lined up outside the Iranian embassy. One voted with a red slip to vote against the Republic and a green slip to vote in support. Ninety-nine percent of the Iranian people, in and out of Iran, voted green. I voted red.

After all that had happened to me, I was not in a good spiritual state on the day of the referendum. Coming out of the voting booth, I announced to the crowd outside that anyone who votes green is destroying themselves and their country. Because of my outburst I was physically restrained and thrown out of the embassy. It takes time in order for people to be able to realize their mistakes.

For the first year and a half that I was living in France I had to renew my visa every few months. In order to do so I had to keep my passport up to date. A few weeks after my return from visiting the Queen, I went to the Iranian embassy to update my passport. When the clerk reviewed my passport he noticed that I had been in Morocco and asked me why I been there. I didn't think that it was any of his business and let him know that. He replied that the only thing for an Iranian in Morocco is the Shah.

I responded that I had gone to visit the Shah, and that it was not any of his business. The clerk right then opened up one his drawers and placed my passport inside. He then insulted me and promptly dismissed me. I objected, what right did he have to confiscate my passport? I punched him in the face and I was arrested on the spot. It was because of that incident that I applied for political refugee status in France.

That was the first time that I was arrested in France. They interrogated me for many hours. What puzzled them most was why I, an Iranian, was so against Khomeini? At that time over 99 percent of the Iranian population supported him. I had also told them that my wife's uncle was high up in the government. It is understandable why they could not understand why was I so against Khomeini.

In an attempt to explain to them my position, I told them the following story. This story comes from the first historians of Islamic history and describes how, during the first Islamic revolution, the Arabs then behaved, back in 638. The historians describe how when the Arabs conquered a land, they would savage it and destroy everything around for fun. They conquered many magnificent lands and would bring destruction wherever they went.

One story describes how a group of soldiers found a woman and her infant baby. They grabbed the baby from its mother, threw it up in the air and when the baby came down one soldier drew his sword and skewered the baby on the end of his sword. Competitions such as this one took place regularly between the Arab soldiers.

The first days of the Islamic Revolution in 1979 aroused in my mind many similarities between the actions of the rising power and the warriors of the previous revolution. The word Abad, in Arabic, means life sentence, and the word E'edam means execution. The public prosecutor of Khomeini's government was a horrible man named Khalkhali.

It was reported in the newspapers that he declared that if a man worked against the revolution, he did not deserve a trial. Khalkhali would line up people, fifty at a time, and point at each individual in the line, and one at a time declare: "Abad, E'edam, Abad, E'edam…" and this way he would decide what punishment each person "deserved" for his treason. If someone objected, he would reply: "Do not worry, if you are not guilty you will be a shahida, a martyr, in heaven."

From that day until now it took 30 years for the Iranian people to understand that Shiite ideology negates the western values of democracy and the personal freedoms it perpetuates. That is why the Peace and Love International Movement (PLIM) believes that the Shiite ideology has to be reformed before Iran can attain the lofty goals which the western world stands for. The forty million young Iranians who were born after the Islamic revolution understand that Shiite ideology and pluralism cannot go hand in hand.

Tabarzin

OVER THE CENTURIES THE term "Tabarzin" has been well known to the Iranian people. The term originally referred to a battle-axe that had been used by King Nadershah-e-Afshar in the 17th century to defeat the Russian and British agents as well as the invading Afghani, Turks and Arab armies. The Shiite clergy corrupted the Safavid dynasty in Iran, leading it to become weak. As a result, the Afghans invaded Iran and ruled for several decades. The last Safavidian king crowned as his successor the Afghan leader, as advised by the Shiite clergy.

Nadershah-e-Afshar, the son of Rezagholi, was a simple soldier who had been born in the state of Abivard-e Khorassan in northeast Iran. After leading the Iranian army to conquer the Afghans, he assembled the clans at Dashte-Moghan in the northwest province of Azerbaijan. At this meeting he gave the clans the choice of either crowning the son of the last Safavid king, King Tahmasb, or crowning him as the king of Iran. The clans chose him.

The other reason why the term Tabarzin is well known amongst Iranians is because it was the name of the Iranian gunboat, which was captured by a group of young Iranian nationalists in August of 1981. The motivating factor behind the capture of the gunboat was similar to that behind Nadershah-e-Afshar three centuries prior. In both cases the country was under foreign rule: in the 17th century it was the rule of the Russians and British, and in the 20th century it was the rule of Shiite clergy.

First Attempts

DR. SHAPOOR BAKHTIAR HAD been the last prime minister of Iran before the revolution of 1979. During the revolution he had left for Paris, and I went to seek him out. I understood that being the previous Prime Minister he would be an Iranian nationalist. But after a few weeks of working with him, I understood that he had really, although unintentionally, been helping Khomeini bring the revolution all along.

In a declaration, he announced that during his time as prime minister, all of 37 days, he was proud of only three things that he had done. First, that he had facilitated the ousting of the Shah. Second, that he had freed all of the political prisoners – terrorists. And third, that he illegalized the

SAVAK, the Iranian Intelligence Agency. I told him that he should be put in jail for this list of things of which he was so proud. I told him that he had not been the prime minister of Iran; he had been Iran's destruction.

The Iranian army had been renowned for its loyalty to the Shah. Dr. Bakhtiar had broken this devotion down to the point that they were the ones who had thrown him out. The political prisoners who Dr. Bakhtiar had released, had been in jail for good reason. Most of them had been terrorists, how could he let them go free? In addition, the SAVAK had been the keepers of Iranian society, and he had cut off their power. I realized that I could not continue to work with Dr. Bakhtiar, and left to continue my search for other nationalists. Shiite activists assassinated Dr. Bakhtiar in 1992. It would seem that the snake had bitten the hand that had fed it back to health.

I understand that there had been minor corruptions and bureaucratic problems in the Shah's governmental system. It was clear that there were legitimate criticisms of his government. However, I do not believe that this means that it was legitimate to overthrow the whole system. As I observed what was happening in my homeland, I perceived that people were growing more and more extreme. These trends I saw paralleled in the Islamic invasion of 638.

Upon my return from Morocco, I did my best to develop contacts in the media. I hoped to express my views to the largest audience as possible. I was interviewed several times. With the current events in Iran and being a Masters student of law formerly from Iran, I was seen as a good person to interview. It was during my interviews, back then, when I coined the phrase: "The Second Islamic Invasion."

The Javan Youth, was the first Iranian paramilitary group, which I had established in Europe. We carried out several operations, which I will describe in the upcoming pages. Many of the names used in the upcoming chapters are pseudonyms. They were changed in order to protect the people involved.

The Founding of Javan

In the winter of 1979, in an Iranian restaurant in Paris, I asked a violinist to play the Iranian national anthem. When the violinist finished playing the anthem I called out "Long live Iranian Nationalism." This declaration was not appreciated by many of the other customers in the restaurant; however, it forged a relationship between the violinist and myself. The playing of the Iranian national anthem, along with the expression of support for Iranian nationalism, was unacceptable in Paris, then, for most Iranians since at that time were ardent supporters of Ayatollah Khomeini.

During the following weeks Khomeini moved from Neuf le Chateau, near Paris, to Iran. There, he and his supporters began to kill anyone who would oppose him, from the simple people to the most prominent. Gradually, his terrorist movement moved into Europe and his agents became part of Iranian diplomatic missions. Through this diplomatic apparatus international terrorism moved into the West and acted against the Iranian expatriate population in those countries as well.

Iranians who needed to visit their consular institutions were forced to follow Shiite religious requirements. Anyone who did not was attacked when they left their embassy. For example, Iranian women who did not wear a chador, the traditional head covering, were attacked. It was under these circumstances that Javan was created in Paris in order to protect the Iranian population there.

The violinist invited me to his home where he introduced me to other Iranians. This was a very special night for me: I had wanted to meet like-minded people. At that time, even my own family was against me in my opposition to Khomeini.

While the violinist and I were waiting for his two friends to join us, we spoke of current politics and the critical situation of our country, both internally and externally. After some time his friends arrived. One was a well-dressed, good-looking, tall man about 45. The other was an elderly Iranian lawyer with whom I was already acquainted. The violinist introduced me to the tall man as Major-General Oveissi, the son of the ex-Chief of Staff of the Iranian army. Subsequently, Islamic agents in Paris killed General Oveissi and his brother in 1980.

The cooperation and friendship between us four grew quickly, and General Oveissi introduced me to his father. The previous week, Major-General Oveissi had formed the nationalistic organization, Nehzat-e-Nejat-e-Iran – the Movement of the Free Iran. I was nominated as the youth and student leader of this organization. I later renamed it Javan.

IT WAS A MASS suicide. Over 95 percent of the people of Iran supported the revolution. But little by little I began to feel that I was no longer alone. My brothers were exceptional. I spoke with my two brothers and they joined my cause. Khomeini was massacring people in Iran and was breaking all of the promises which he had made at Neuf le Chateau. Iranians soon realized that he was not truly a spiritual leader, rather, an absolute despot.

Gradually, I found other young people, 18 and 19 years of age in the university. Little by little I was able to convince them of the destructive elements of the Shiite-Islamic ideology. Several months later a wave of people left Iran. These people had realized their mistake in supporting the revolution. Amongst them I found others who were ready to listen to what I had to say. I did my best to explain to them the reality of what was happening in Iran. Javan grew tremendously in opposition to Khomeini's despotism.

I worked with General Oveissi and his group for about a year. During that time I had many conversations with General Oveissi, insisting that other groups of young people, such as this one that we had cultivated, could be gathered in other cities as well. I said that we could train our members to train others. Potentially we could have 500 seed groups instead of just one. I believed that once we had enough people following us we could go either to Kurdistan or to Baluchistan, border provinces of Iran in the North and South. From one of these provinces we could infiltrate into the Iranian society and recreate our own society based upon our own beliefs.

His answer would always be the same: "Our plans have to be dependent upon the US foreign policy. It is in their hands." I became frustrated with him and accused: "You are simply an American puppet. If we want it to happen, we will have to do it ourselves. We cannot rely on the government that caused our downfall in the first place." These disagreements eventually led to my breaking away from General Oveissi.

After I ceased my work with General Oveissi I sought out Princess Azadeh, the leader of Iran-Azad. Princess Azadeh was the niece of the Shah and the only member of the Pahlavi dynasty left who was an activist. She was excited by my ideas and supported Javan. I worked with her for another year and a half. Later on I contacted Major-General Dr. Bahram Aryana. He had been the chief of staff of the Iranian army before General Oveissi. After retirement he moved to Paris where I found him.

The cooperation between Javan and Iran-Azad grew daily. During this time Javan set up branches in many countries and demonstrated daily in the capitals of those countries. Once we hung a sixty by fifteen meter national flag of Iran from the Eiffel Tower, despite the prohibition

1980-Daniel in Paris with Princess Azadeh, niece of the Shah.

from climbing the tower with such objects. We also coordinated several attacks against the offices of the Iranian national carrier, Iran Air. On another occasion participants chained themselves to the Statue of Liberty in Paris. Throughout this time many interviews were held with the mass media explaining the situation in Iran and how it was anti-Western and supported terrorism.

The young students of Javan tried to hold a dialogue with the followers of Khomeini as well as with members of the left. They attempted to explain why they were defending Iranian culture and history and why they believed that the current regime was wrong ideologically. From the first day, the young students tried to explain to their fellow expatriates that they were mistaken in their support of Khomeini and that they could rectify their mistake by helping to stop him.

Our students tried to explain to the Shiites and the members of the left how they were wrong. History has shown that prior to the Islamic invasion in the seventh century, Iran had been a leading nation in the fields of economics, politics, education and military. This position was lost only because of the Shiite conquest. Our dialogue with the left pointed out that although there were positive aspects to socialism, there was no need to become slaves of the Communists.

In the 1980s the University of Paris was the center of Iranian debate between both proponents and opponents of Khomeini's regime. These debates were always between the Shiites and the Left. Neither of these two groups could accept anyone to be Iranian if they did not hold one of these two positions.

I rented a garden in the woods some eighty kilometers outside Paris. There I trained my followers. During the day I trained them in basic military techniques and athletic activities. At night I read to them from various Iranian history books in order to deepen their sense of Iranian nationalism. In the center of the garden we dug a large pit and built a bonfire. Around that fire I told stories of Iranian heroes and the value of patriotism. I tried to present to them the Hegelian ideas about Iranians as the first builders of society. I preached how the roots of our monarchical system grew into the modern governmental systems of today's superpowers.

We believed that from this political platform we could change the situation in Iran, and we were interviewed many times by Western media agencies. The locals objected to what was happening. One local member of parliament complained to the Ministry of Interior Affairs that a paramilitary group was being created in Des Yvelines similar to what had happened at Neuf le Chateau. The local paper reported the presence of the paramilitary group in their area. Our answer to the media was that we did not have sufficient finances to live in the city, as the Iranian authorities had cut our support. As such we were staying there, where we could be supported so that we would not become involved with gangs in the city.

Many of the students had been forced out of the University of Paris by the Iranians who supported either Khomeini – the blacks, or the Communists – the reds. One Saturday, students from our camp marched to the university holding a three-meter flag, singing the national anthem and shouting the slogan: "Death to despots in Iran and whoever supports them whether reds or blacks."

Because of our extreme behavior the opposing groups retreated. These groups were afraid that, although there were only 27 of us, we were supported by many thousands outside, or, that we had the protection of the police or military. We marched from the main gates up the stairs to the front of the university buildings. When we reached the buildings we turned around and started handing out pamphlets and debating with the opposing Iranians. By this stage the reds and blacks had realized that our small group was alone and they attacked us. They figured that our small group were monarchists and supported the Shah. As a consequence of the struggle between the groups many were hospitalized.

The media, including many magazines and journals, reported our march. One result of our march was that the rejection of our political viewpoint on campus was finally broken. The reports sympathized with the students who had been injured, and in the eyes of the Iranians in France who did not already belong to a political faction, we developed a very positive reputation.

Amongst those who were influenced by our affirmative action and who sought an interview with our group was Dr. B. Aryana. A decade prior, Dr. Aryana had been the Chief-of-Staff of the Iranian army. After retiring from the army he moved to France to continue his education towards a PhD in law. He also received the Legion of Honor from President de Gaulle. General Aryana invited me to a meeting so that we could discuss Iranian politics. He asked me jokingly why I, as an ex-soldier, had not invited him to take part in our activities at Paris University.

This meeting opened a new stage in the evolution of our Javan paramilitary group. It led us to look towards Iran as our goal, and no longer solely to activities in Europe.

Azadegan

General Aryana's background was well known to many Iranians. He was nationalistic and had shown himself to be a heroic officer in the Iranian army. He had never been involved in any form of corruption, and was recognized as a highly intellectual officer with a good command of pre-Islamic Iranian history. General Aryana had written a number of books. He also often lectured on the subject of pre-Islamic history and how Shiite Islam had destroyed Iran.

Some years before the Islamic Revolution of 1979, General Aryana had retired from the army and moved to France because of his affinity with Napoleon. He completely disagreed with the Islamic Revolution because it was completely contrary to his ideals of nationalism. In 1980 General Aryana formed the Azadegan group. This group had a "Robin Hood" philosophy.

General Aryana insisted on the complete secrecy of the meeting, even though he knew of my association with Princess Azadeh. Many times I asked that his group be used within Iran against the Shiite-Islamic regime, and had discussed this with Princess Azadeh and General Oveissi. General Aryana had even assessed the possibility of staging the attacks from Egypt, Israel, Jordan or Morocco.

After a number of meetings with General Aryana, the General requested that I undertake a secret mission in Kurdistan, the northern province of Iran. He had previously asked other groups to undertake the mission but they demanded money to do so, and General Aryana was unwilling to pay people who should rather have been doing it for their country.

During this same period, a group of nationalistic Iranian air force pilots, led by Shapoor Bakhtiar, the last Prime Minister under the Shah, had attempted to organize a coup d'état. Unfortunately, it had been uncovered and hundreds of pilots had been assassinated. This had happened because of their lack of secrecy. This was why General Aryana was so concerned with maintaining secrecy relating to my mission in Kurdistan.

In those days many Iranians heard that a select group of sailors had come to France to receive a delivery of three gunboats, which had been bought by the Shah in 1975, and sail them to the Persian Gulf. Eleven gunboats had already been delivered to Iran but the remaining three were docked at Cherbourg. A number of paramilitary groups were investigating how the officers and men could be convinced to support the Iranian opposition and hand over the boats to them. However, no group had considered the possibility of actually capturing the boats after they had left port.

General Aryana's vision was to capture these gunboats and establish an Iranian government-in-exile on the boats; then to sail to the Persian Gulf and attack Iran from the south. At the same time another group would attack from Kurdistan in the north. The crucial point in this plan was that the Iran-Iraq war had recently broken out and the hope was that with the two-pronged attack on Iran, the Iranian army would desert and support the Government-in-Exile and thus bring about the downfall of Khomeini.

The Heroes Move Out

IN ORDER THAT NOBODY would suspect anything when the group moved out of Paris, each member had to fabricate a story of where he was going in a way that did not tie him in with any of the other members of the group. Since the middle of summer had already passed, many were able to claim that they were looking for work in the vineyards and orchards in the provinces and neighboring countries. Most of our members were between the ages of 19 and 25, and would normally have spent their time on the beaches vacationing. However, they were all motivated to do something for their country, and so these students joined the liberation army of General Aryana to do something for their compatriots.

We were driven towards restoring 2,500 years of Iranian cultural development to our people. Fourteen centuries ago our culture had been destroyed and again two years earlier, with Khomeini's rise to power our culture had been ravaged once more.

For practical purposes we believed that we had to sacrifice our personal ambitions in order to focus completely on washing away the shameful label of "international terrorist," which we carried because of the Shiite leaders in Iran. We had decided to create something new and pass on a very clear message to the next generation that self-sacrifice was required for the sake of culture. In addition, the fragmentation of the Iranian opposition both inside and outside the country was another motivating factor for our band; we hoped to unite them all.

In Iranian history there is a story that tells of the Iranian crown being protected by two lions. Only a hero could take the crown from the mouths of these lions. Our group wanted to be that hero that would save the crown of Iranian nationalism from the mouths of the two lions. We saw those lions to be the Communists, who supported the Iranian Left, and the United States and her European allies, who had supported Khomeini for their own benefit.

It took us two days from the time we left Paris until we reached Lacuna, a Spanish port on the Atlantic coast. On our way we passed Lyon, San Etienne, Pieronne and Tallis in France as well as Bilbao and Santa Dor in Spain. We realized that, because of the need for secrecy, that when we were in port we should not speak Persian nor should we move in groups of more than two. Similarly, we should have no Iranian items on us for the duration of our 2500-kilometer journey. Despite our natural desire to enjoy ourselves, our belief in the mission spurred us on to obey our orders of secrecy.

Appointment At The Statue Of Hercules

WE ALL SHARED THE responsibility of preparing everything that we would need for our trip: passport, visa and tickets. We had to do all this under the strictest blanket of secrecy. General Aryana requested that our top 20 men from Javan, plus myself, should be prepared to go to Kurdistan to take part in guerrilla fighting after our mission. The men were divided into three groups, each group with a leader. All contact with General Aryana was through these three leaders in order to minimize contact. The Azadegan headquarters in Paris covered all of the financial expenses of the three groups; they also acted as a switchboard for all commands to the leaders of the groups.

On our third day after leaving Paris, the 9th August, 1981, the three groups met for the first time at the base of the statue of Hercules in Lacuna for further instructions, which were relayed from the headquarters in Paris.

The statue of Hercules, the hero of Greek mythology, was made of bronze and stands on a concrete foundation in the middle of a park. From there he watched the approach of the 20 brave young men and one young woman. The young woman was one of two who had been involved in our demonstration at the Paris University where she had been badly injured to the extent that she would never be able to become pregnant. Despite this she came on the mission because of her very strong feelings for her nation.

This woman was an ardent supporter of the Iranian Palavan philosophy. This belief states that the savior of a nation can only fulfill his or her role through the combination of great physical and mental abilities. Under this philosophy there is no discrimination of the sexes. Two examples of this philosophy were Queen Azarmidokht and Queen Poorandokht who had reigned in Iran over 14 centuries earlier.

The three men, who were the representatives of the headquarters in Paris, had all been officers in the Iranian army under the Shah. Roozbahan, the youngest, was their spokesman. Roozbahan strongly believe in keeping to the strictest levels of secrecy in order to ensure the success of our mission. Kaveh, who had been one of the generals in the Iranian army under the Shah, also insisted that the success of the liberation army hinged upon the ability to maintain complete secrecy. He stated that General Aryana and his army in Kurdistan were awaiting the news of the success of our mission. The third man, General Vandidad, also advised us on security matters but was more like a father to us than a commander of troops. He also advised that throughout our journey we live in small villages rather than in cities and never to go around in groups of more than two or three at a time.

After agreeing to follow the commands that had been given, our contacts departed from us. Each member our group went on his own way. Although, due to the exuberance of youth, many of our members had trouble keeping their promises regarding the maintenance of secrecy or following the rules of contact. As a result, often, these rules were broken. Despite their enthusiasm and burning desire to do what they had promised and believed in, their high spirits and sense of enjoyment often got the better of them.

Ambition drove some of our group to try and lead the others to take care of what they did or said. In one way we can say that our group had become a family as a result of our mutual goal lying ahead of us.

The Admiral

OUR COMMANDER, THE ADMIRAL, had recognized several special qualities in me. Even though I had met the Admiral at the headquarters back in Paris, it was only in Spain that we had an opportunity to sit together and discuss the operation. Mutual necessity had bound us together and we came to recognize the need for each other. We scrutinized each other, and both came to the conclusion that the other was worthy of their position.

Our Admiral had been the Admiral of the Iranian navy under the Shah; and I was looking for the leadership qualities in the Admiral which would be required in a guerrilla operation. The commander was looking for qualities in me, in addition to my physical prowess, that would inspire and motivate our group to capture the gunboat. While this silent evaluation was in progress the Admiral remembered that General Aryana had said that, on his return to Teheran, he would raise a gold statue in the gates of Teheran in my honor.

In Spain we met in a small cottage-like restaurant. There, the Admiral and I had a meaningful discussion. Mainly, the Admiral asked me about the physical, mental and spiritual capacity of our men to cope with unpredictable events. He wanted to assess my responses as well as the responses of our group. The Admiral wanted to evaluate the group's reaction to the likelihood that the mission could end in death for some, or even all of them. The clear response of all was that we were children of Iran and were willing to die for country. Not one had any fear of death.

From the first day, the discussions in Paris between myself, General Aryana and the Admiral had been based upon going to Kurdistan and waging a guerrilla war together with the Kurds and the liberation army on Iran. However, now for the first time, the Admiral began speaking of the three gunboats, including their capacities and their tactical value. He also explained the psychological implications that would be engendered if they were captured and a Government-in-Exile set up on them. The ideal of dying in Kurdistan for my country suddenly disappeared, and instead the prospect loomed of becoming food for the sharks in the Atlantic Ocean.

I gradually realized that the operation that he had discussed with the Azadegan organization and General Aryana was completely different from the operation which was now developing. However, I assured myself that there was no difference where I died if I was dying for my nation or for an ideal. Despite the fact that I was totally confused, I agreed to convince my friends to be ready for such an operation.

During that discussion I was totally surprised, despite the fact that I was ready to undertake any operation for the sake of my nation. I was wondering how I could have been so misled. In such an operation there is a need for mutual trust, and the question as to how such trust could be missing was eating at my heart. The Admiral recognized this feeling in me but answered only in silence.

The Admiral knew everything about my personal background as well as the background of the Javan, and realized that he could confidently place the operation on our shoulders. We finished the last of our beers, embraced and left each other.

Some of the members of the group had already had some military experience in Iran. Without completing two years of military service no one over the age of eighteen could leave the country. Some of my men had extra experience in guerrilla warfare, having been partisan fighters after the Islamic Revolution. Everyone had had some training whilst with Javan. Despite this I was unsure how I could tell the group of the change in our mission, from fighting in Kurdistan to a naval operation capturing three gunboats.

There is an expression in Persian which says that if greatness, success and honor are in the mouth of the lion then one must not hold back from trying to take them out of the mouth of the lion. With this mindset we began to prepare for the operation.

The Salazon Fishing Boat

ALL OF MY COMMANDOS were surprised when I explained the change in the mission and asked many questions. Many of my men could not really believe that the mission was even possible; we would be up against better-equipped and better-trained sailors on the three gunboats. Despite these concerns my commandos had no intention of giving up, notwithstanding their surprise and shock because of the change of the mission. They were all full of energy, enthusiasm and burning desire, yet they also were puzzled why the Azadegan had not placed more trust in them, and had kept them in the dark as regards the true object of the mission.

Although inwardly they blamed Azadegan for this lack of trust, no one verbalized these feelings outright. Some did express concerns regarding the lack of preparation for the altered mission. Still, I did my best to encourage them that they would still be able to carry out the mission even in its altered form. A distinct atmosphere ensued as my men turned inwards. Each of them tried to work through their emotions and hurts, which had been brought about by the lack of trust and the new dangers relating to the mission.

On the following day we received orders to immediately move from Lacuna in the north of Spain to Cadiz in the south. Again, security had to be maintained during our journey of thirteen hundred kilometers. On our way we passed through Valadali, Kassariss, Valajio, Cordoba, and Seville. The journey had to be completed within 48 hours.

The coordinators of our mission had feared that the security of the group had been compromised. They thought that some of our men might have made contact with some other Iranians in Lacuna who were possibly members of the crew of the gunboats in port there. So, in order to avoid detection we had to go from Lacuna to Cadiz. Cadiz was the second port of call for the gunboats after they were to leave Cherbourg on their way to the Suez Canal and then continue onwards to the Persian Gulf.

Again, on this journey too, our group traveled in units of no more than three and we made our journey in short stages. Although this complicated matters it was quite a positive experience for all. In Cadiz we again met up with the Admiral and the support staff.

The Admiral and support staff had arrived in Cadiz prior to my commandos in order to prepare all the documentation and equipment and obtain as much intelligence information as they could. The support team had negotiated with the owner of a fishing boat, Petros, to hire his boat for three days on the pretext that they were a group of oceanography students along with their professor and assistant professor. They were scouting the area to assess the quality of the waters. The Salazon, a 20-meter fishing boat, was subsequently hired together with her captain.

On the second day after our arrival in Cadiz, we went out on the Salazon together with the Admiral. Finally, for the first time, the details and planning for the capture of the gunboats was discussed. During the briefing, the Admiral opened up a diagram of the Tabarzin on top of the engine cover of the Salazon. There we all paid rapt attention to the description of the gunboat together with its personnel while the Admiral explained how the gunboat was to be captured.

The attack required that our commandos be divided into three groups, each with a leader. The Admiral explained that the first group, led by myself, would have to board the gunboat from the Salazon while disguised as Spanish custom officers. After capturing the officers on the gunboat, the second group, who had remained below deck on the Salazon, would board the gunboat and capture its arsenal. The third group would follow and capture the remaining sailors.

The odds were against our attack's success. Our 21 commandos were mainly students, while their crew of 31 were professional sailors on board a gunboat. Also, the sailors were familiar with the surroundings on the gunboat whereas our commandos had never before been on such a craft. Furthermore, there was a large arsenal on the gunboat whilst our commandos had only limited weaponry. Finally, emotionally, the sailors were defending what was their own while our commandos were attacking "blind."

These points were at the forefront of our minds. Discussions between my commandos and the Admiral, who was the only one with relevant experience, revolved around this imbalance in skill between the attackers and those who will be attacked. The debate was not only over the technology of weaponry but included all the "what if's" relating to our mission. Despite our precarious position, my group remained highly motivated. The only ray of hope in our minds was that we knew that four of the members of the Tabarzin would be cooperating with us.

The plan required the four on the Tabarzin to create a situation where the gunboat would report a technical problem to the other two gunboats and would then heave-to. After the capture of the Tabarzin, we would radio to the second gunboat in the squadron, the Khanjar, and request that she wait for them. At this point we would board and capture her. The same strategy would then be employed against the leading gunboat, the Neyzeh, which we would then also capture.

One question we could not answer was that while we knew that there were four crew-members on Tabarzin who would cooperate with our commandos, were there any on the other two gunboats who would cooperate? Another question prominent in our minds was how the second and third gunboats could be captured with fewer commandos than the amount used to the capture of the first. Some of our commandos would have to be left behind to guard the prisoners so not all would be available to capture the other boats. Finally, how would 21 "amateurs" be able to control the, almost, one hundred professional sailors who would be taken prisoner? These were some of the questions bothering the commandos for which the Admiral could not provide answers. The commandos were left to trust in their beliefs in order to overcome these problems.

Added to all these problems were the conditions on board the Salazon. She was a typical fishing boat painted in orange and green. Everything on board was untidy with equipment and tackle lying all over the place. Petros was a typical large Spaniard, with a red face and very pleasant. He was happy to spend three days with a group of students instead of spending time fishing. It was a lucrative situation for him and he enjoyed spending the time with his clients who were neither fish nor fishermen. While sailing his boat he spent much of time talking to the students as well as listening to the radio and his Spanish music.

At lunchtime on the first day he joined us for lunch. We provided him with some very good cognac. During this time, he increased the volume of the music as everyone enjoyed it. I dived into the sea from the top of the cabin and some of the commandos, including Cheko and Shirmard, followed me. I did this mainly to reassure one of the students, Sardar, who, after learning of the new goal of the mission, had become very fearful since he could not swim.

After lunch, since the Salazon was sailing close to international waters, the Admiral again opened the diagram of the gunboat we were going to capture and tried to reinforce what he had already said. He also assigned tasks to specific members of the group. While this was going on, our group had to pretend to follow our study of the ocean and we took water samples and brought them back for analyzing. Vishtasb and I were playing the roles of assistants to the professor – the Admiral.

The "professor" tried to explain every aspect of the mission to the "students" and assigned numbers to every part of the plan. He then questioned us on the numerical points to ensure our understanding. Sometimes the answers were amusing due to my commandos' lack of understanding. This, together with their natural youthful characters, led to much laughter.

At one point during this time of fun the Admiral suddenly pointed to a point in the sea several kilometers further on and announced that in two days time, Tabarzin would be waiting for us there. He insisted that from the moment that I put my foot on Tabarzin to the time that the Salazon separates from the gunboat should not take more than 30 seconds. He repeatedly tried to explain how the three gunboats were to be captured. He also added the fact that before the third group would reach the Salazon, they were to tie up Petros, destroy all means of communication and leave him with twice the amount of payment that had been agreed upon.

Shortly before sunset, the Salazon returned to port and our group separated from Petros with very good feelings. Immediately we split up and returned to our accommodation with strict instructions not to drink or go out but to sleep and make sure that we are completely rested for the following day. I, along with some of the other leaders, demanded that we meet with the support team in order to arrange for the purchase of Spanish Customs uniforms.

Vishtasb, Dadyar and I were given the money to go out and buy the items. We also each received seven gas pistols and their ammunition along with black holsters as well as the gas which could render a person unconscious. The support team emphasized the importance of keeping the guns safe and not to arouse suspicion with the police. The three of us then bought the necessary items and distributed everything amongst our group. However, I did not really trust the gas pistols so I went out and bought myself a dagger as well.

Sardar was not only a non-swimmer and unhappy with the operation, he became even more upset when he was issued a uniform and a gas pistol. He wanted to leave the operation but I was able to convince him stay on.

At approximately midnight, I received a message from the Admiral via a member of the support team. The message was that the gunboats were leaving Cadiz a day early and, as such, the mission would have to take place the next day and not in two days from now, as originally planned. The messenger added that Vishtasb and Dadyar had already been informed and that the members of the group had to be prepared. Everyone was to meet at a specific place at 07:30 the following morning.

Salazon – Part 2

ON AUGUST 9, 1981, the sun, bringing the heat into the room, woke me even before my alarm rang at 5:30 a.m. After a few seconds I jumped out of the bed and began to do fifty push-ups. These were not ordinary push-ups as they were done on clenched fists and with one foot over the other. I continued my regular morning regiment with fifty sit-ups, shadow boxing, kickboxing and other athletic activities.

I then woke Shirmard and Cheko with a sharp poke, as they were sharing the room with me, and I washed up. We had already packed and were ready to leave the hotel. We each had our own backpack with the items we would require for the mission as well as all the remaining items, which we were planning to leave with the support team. After leaving these items with the support team, we made our way to the Salazon.

Everything was going according to schedule as the church bells rang out eight times as our group of 21 arrived at the Salazon. The general atmosphere of the city was normal, its inhabitants went about their daily routines; they had no clue that these small groups of two or three Iranians, whom they passed, were on their way to do something great for their nation. In contrast, the young people were bursting with enthusiasm despite the many doubts and questions floating through their minds relating to all the changes, which had occurred to the mission.

The support group was waiting a few hundred meters before the Salazon in order to take any unnecessary items we had from us. As the items were handed over there were many hugs and an overall sense of concern from the support group as we went off to an uncertain future. Yet, all their actions had to be restrained so as not arouse any suspicion amongst the onlookers.

An Endless Beginning

THE PRESSURES OF THE previous days were hanging heavily on the shoulders of Sardar. Although he had taken part in many previous operations with Javan, the current situation had become more than he could handle. Not only was the anticipation of the upcoming operation weighing heavily on him, but also the rest of the group was making fun of him. It was clear that Sardar was suffering under this load.

As we neared the Salazon, Sardar began to cry and asked me that we leave him behind, since he did not feel that he was well enough trained to go on such a mission. Thousands of times he promised to forever remain silent regarding the mission. All this pleading affected all the others who agreed and said that they should leave him behind. I was adamant, though, that he accompanies us. When he was handing over his items to the support group he fell and refused to walk. I eventually decided to discuss the matter with the Admiral and told Sardar to wait for me next to a water tank until I returned.

The hearts of the remaining 20 commandos were filled with enthusiasm but still, they were very conscious of the one-sided battle ahead of them. All their previous experiences had been merely those of a Boy Scout troop, in contrast to their upcoming battle against hardened professionals, the limited effectiveness of their gas pistols against live ammunition. Everyone boarded the Salazon and hugged the Admiral who was waiting for them there. Petros had had such a good time the day before with theses "oceanography" students that he was very happy that his second day was beginning.

I took the Admiral aside and quietly spoke to him about Sardar's condition. The Admiral's answer caused me to catapult out of the Salazon and run to Sardar. None of my commandos knew what had passed between the Admiral and myself, or what transpired between Sardar and myself, but shortly after Sardar and I returned to the Salazon together. It was not even 8:20 when the Salazon left port and sailed off to an unknown destination.

As we sailed out of Cadiz the members of our group bade farewell to the city where they had spent the previous three days. Petros was busy with his job sailing the Salazon whilst he watched the "professor" speak to his "students," though he could not understand what was being said. Had Petros really thought about it, he would have realized that what the "professor" was saying to his "students" could not have been a simple lecture because of all the emotion and body language that he was displaying.

The Admiral actually said: "You are the young people, the builders of your nation. Therefore you can think only of victory and, clearly, you have to know that your bravery, your intelligence and your speed will be the elements essential for your victory. You have to know that your future will be evaluated by today. Today the eagle of power is sitting on your shoulders. Your burning desire will be self-fulfilling. Do not be impatient. Put all anxiety far away from you. Put aside all doubt and be one hundred percent positive that you will be successful. Be sure that the success of our nation is in your hands today. Therefore we begin our operation today in the name of God and the glorious history of our nation."

After this introduction, the Admiral later added: "As your three leaders explained to you at midnight last night, the three gunboats, Khanjar, Neyzeh and Tabarzin, are leaving port today due to unexpected circumstances. As such, we had no option but to carry out the operation today. I trust every single one of you and I believe that together we will be successful in today's operation."

I asked Shirmard and Cheko to take care of Sardar and to explain to him that nothing special would be asked of him, but because of security considerations, he could not be left alone, he would be protected. At this stage the Admiral began to re-enumerate the steps of the operation but without assigning any tasks to Sardar. Vishtasb and Delavar, the two other group leaders, opened the diagrams of the gunboats and again studied all the points of the operation. Several new questions arose which were answered by the Admiral. This continued until the operation was completely clear in the minds of the commandos.

The Admiral tried to minimize the danger of the operation and emphasized that the four members on the Tabarzin would assist as much as possible. Therefore, if they followed orders and the plan of battle, the chances of success would increase and the possibility of failure would decrease.

He took out three strong pairs of binoculars, he kept one and handed one each to Vishtasb and myself. He explained that with the binoculars we could observe the squadron leaving the port of Cadiz and see when the Tabarzin would stop to wait for them in international waters. He stated that he was convinced that they would never have a need to use their gas pistols.

He repeated that the first group, under my leadership, would be dressed as Spanish Customs Officers when we approached Tabarzin. We would not be able to make any mistakes and would carry the major burden for the success of the operation. The commander of the gunboat, together with his two officers and the ship's engineer, would receive the group of "Customs Officers" and be ready to assist them. The major point of concern would be any unforeseen circumstances, which could arise in relation to the other members of the Tabarzin, which would have to be handled with imagination. In the hypothetical case that any conflict arose it would have to be dealt with immediately.

At this point I became suspicious, already twice they had hidden information from me. I took note of these suspicions as the Admiral continued with his explanation.

The first group would have to clear the way completely for the second and third groups. The second group would have to immediately open the arsenal and arm all of our commandos. The third group would have to tie up Petros and disable the radios on the Salazon and then board Tabarzin. Working along the two sides of the gunboat, they would have to ensure that all the members of the crew had been found and taken prisoner. Vishtasb was made responsible for removing all evidence of us having been on the Salazon. As such, he would be the last to leave. He also had the task of explaining to Petros that the action was not a gang action but an act of national resistance. After much repetition the plan became clear to all the members of the group.

After his explanation the Admiral asked if there were any further questions or points of uncertainty. Nobody said anything except for Pashutan, a member of the first group. He asked, jokingly, whether he could have the head of Khomeini after the operation. Namdar asked when they would be back in Teheran. Such joking countered any feelings of fear that still lingered in our minds.

Finally the Admiral stated that after the capture of the Tabarzin, her commander would cooperate with the group in the capture of the other two gunboats. The Tabarzin would radio to the Neyzeh asking for technical assistance. When she came alongside the other boat the commandos would board and capture her. The same plan of attack would be used against the Khanjar. After the capture of the three gunboats, the center of command would be established on Tabarzin and everyone would follow the commands issued by the Admiral, who would be on board. Any of the sailors who were not prepared to cooperate with the liberation army would be handed over to the representatives of the Islamic regime in

Casablanca, Morocco.

The Admiral added that the gunboats would be recognized as the seat of the Iranian government-in-exile and would proceed to the Persian Gulf. Together with General Aryana, who was fighting in Kurdistan, we would induce the national army, which was fighting against Iraq to support the liberation army and thus close the bloody dossier on Khomeini.

With the conclusion of the Admiral's speech, Mehrafzoon and Zarnegar helped Vishtasb to serve glasses of cognac to all the members of the group. A full bottle was given to Petros with the hope that he would get drunk. The Admiral raised his glass and proposed a toast to the success of the mission and the liberation of Iran. The entire group, including Nahid, the woman of our group, drank the cognac and immediately followed me in the singing of the Iranian national anthem. Some of the young people were visibly moved by the singing of the anthem especially at the end when they all shouted out, "Long live Iran". I added that it was an honor to die for one's nation and that no fear existed in our midst.

In this atmosphere, Sardar, who was anxiously standing alone to side, realized that he would have to change. He asked himself whether the young teenagers who ran into the minefields to clear them for the following army or this young group of commandos were the true fighters for national dignity. With this battle going on in his heart he did not fully realize that those who were fighting for Khomeini were fighting for evil and Satan whilst those fighting against Khomeini were fighting for God.

Whilst the two groups had comparable encouragement, one was fighting for the glory of the nation, reconciliation with other nations, and goodness whilst the other group was fighting for Shiite Islam, beliefs that are completely irrelevant to Iranian culture. Shiite Islam was fighting against reconciliation, compassion, mercy and the mutual respect of all nations; whereas us commandos were fighting for these principles. Sardar was caught up in the 14 centuries of Shiite Islam in which Iranians had lost their golden ages, reputation, universal values and had become labeled as uncivilized and terrorists and could not rise up again. He began to see that through what he was watching then, a change was going to affect.

While Sardar was undergoing this internal battle, he was listening to my words to the rest of the group: "There is the beloved land of our fathers, the land where our fathers fell; the land where our children shall rise to bring back the valuable culture which has been destroyed. We must not forget that today, through this operation in which we are involved, we are joining yesterday with tomorrow."

The members of the group believed that I, as a 34-year-old, was a shining example of patriotism amongst them. My athletic and military background had earned me a special place amongst my compatriots. Shirmard was 26 years old and the second member of the first group. He was a tall and slender, a very strong man who had been a boxer and had undergone two years of military service as a tank commander. Dadbeh, Cheko, Pashutan, Atashdel and Mehrafzoon were the other five members of the first group. All had athletic backgrounds and held a personal loyalty to me; they always acted as one.

Delavar led the second group. He was 29 years old and a martial arts expert with a pleasant face. He had left Iran clandestinely after fighting against Khomeini. The other members of his group were Tiztak, Rahyar, Azarpa, Tooraj, Koohyar and Payman. The group had been active in Javan and had much paramilitary experience.

Vishtasb led the third group. He was 30 at that time. Vishtasb was the son of General Aryana, and had been an officer in the Iranian army. He exhibited more experience than one would think for a man of his age. The others in his group were Namdar, Dezhkhu, Sardar, Apratat, Nahid and Yavar. As with the second group, the third group had been members of Javan and had paramilitary experience.

During the operation the Admiral would have to take cognizance of what was happening both aboard Tabarzin as well as on board the Salazon. As such he did not tell the commandos when he would be leaving the Salazon and boarding Tabarzin. A very sensitive point in the operation was that none of the commandos had any experience as sailors and, as such, any mistake could be catastrophic. The most dangerous time would be the boarding of Tabarzin as the two boats were not equally out of the water. If a commando should fall between the two boats it would be the end of him.

Three Shadows

THE SALAZON WAS SAILING further out towards international waters. The passengers on board had said and asked everything that was necessary and were quietly waiting for the great event that was about to take place. Petros, after consuming much of the cognac, had become very mellow. All the items needed for the attack had been packed away. The area on which the diagram of the gunboats had been laid out had been cleared away and a light snack had been served on it. The Admiral was talking quietly with various members of the group while he frequently searched the horizon for sight of the awaited gunboats.

All of the members of the third group were dealing with their own internal tensions while trying to put on an outward appearance of calm. Vishtasb, as an experienced person and leader of one of the groups, was trying to help them to be calm and relaxed. I mainly kept to myself and went over the plan of battle and his responsibilities. Nahid was very confident and was supportive of the other members. She was thinking of Artemiss, the Persian woman admiral who, with one million soldiers, attacked and conquered Greece in the third century BCE.

Pashutan was the most vociferous and strongly encouraged the others through song and battle-hymns. Mehrafzoon, the youngest of the group, who had many times climbed to the first position in martial art competitions in his country, was quiet but very enthusiastic. Dezhkhu was trying to encourage the others in their inner battles. Atashdel was telling jokes in an attempt to lighten the atmosphere.

Cheko was more serious than others of his age and kept close to me. None of the other commandos had developed as close a relationship with me as he had. Cheko, Shirmard and I had been the original three in Paris who had begun the struggle against the Shiite regime.

Rahyar, the son of a former Colonel in the Iranian army, had a strong military mentality and was also a good friend of mine. He had brought many new members to Javan. He was also in the habit of keeping close to me and was very proud of what the group was about to do. He looked on it as a gift to his father who was then in an Iranian prison. He had first come into contact with Javan when he attended a meeting addressed by Erique Rulo, a reporter of Le Monde Diplomatique, who was justifying the Islamic Revolution of Khomeini. Nine of the members of Javan had arrived and disrupted the meeting with much shouting and chanting: "Long live Iranian nationalism and death to Khomeini and his followers."

That had been the first time that Rahyar had heard such a slogan being shouted and it was something, which he had long yearned for. He found in me an emotional and spiritual protector.

Vishtasb suddenly clapped his hands and everyone gathered around him. The Admiral and I, who had been on the other side of the Salazon, had seen the three shadows appearing on the far horizon and had we informed Vishtasb. Vishtasb shouted out: "In the name of God and Iran we are beginning our operation ... prepare yourselves."

I went down with the first group went into the Salazon and we changed into the Spanish Customs officers' uniforms – Khaki short-sleeve shirts and trousers and white shoes. After a few minutes we reappeared on the deck. On our belts we each carried a gas pistol. The pistols looked like revolvers. We carried extra gas capsules in our pockets. Each of us had a small backpack, but the second group carried ours, so we could keep the appearance of customs officers. I carried my dagger in the back of my belt.

Although Petros was partly drunk, he was completely taken aback. Vishtasb and two other commandos restrained him. The other commandos went down into the Salazon to change into uniforms of the Iranian Liberation Army. These uniforms were similar to those of the first group, but without any insignia.

Vishtasb gave Petros another large glass of cognac and Petros fell asleep; his hands were tied. The Admiral took over command of the Salazon and sailed her towards international waters and towards the three gunboats whilst following their progress through his binoculars.

I was on the deck of the Salazon with my team and the Admiral was in the wheelhouse. Vishtasb and the remaining two members of the group went below to change their clothing. We saw that the third gunboat had stopped as planned while the first two carried on. The Salazon accelerated into international waters and approached the third gunboat.

As the Salazon approached Tabarzin my heart began to beat faster. Everyone knew that this was the time when we would open a new chapter to the history of our nation. The Admiral quietly encouraged the members of the first group. Each member of the group was spread out over the Salazon preparing himself emotionally except for two, the Admiral and myself, we were together speaking quietly to each other. Cheko was laughing and continuing with his jokes.

The Admiral and I handed our binoculars to the other members of the group to give them all an opportunity to see the Tabarzin, which was now only a few hundred meters away. They noted that there were only six members of the crew on the deck of the Tabarzin.

From Cadiz to Casablanca

"Atashast In Bang-E-Nay-O-Nist-Bad
Harkeh In Atash Nadarad, Nist Bad"

"The Voice Of The Flute Is Fire And Not Merely Wind
Whoever Has Not Known This Fire Has Never Lived"

Pir-e Balkh (Mowlana)
13th-century Iranian poet and philosopher

THIS WAS THE BURNING fire in my heart and the poetry on my lips as I, the first, jumped onto Tabarzin. Both the commander of Tabarzin and our Admiral were experienced sailors and knew how to bring the boats together to maximize the chances of our success. With only a few meters between the two boats the Admiral, in half broken Spanish and French, explained that they were Spanish Customs Officers and requested permission to board Tabarzin.

In an instant I was aboard Tabarzin, and I followed closely by Cheko, Shirmard, and Rahyar. Within seconds the remaining three men of our first group were also aboard.

A bearded man wearing civilian clothes was standing on deck. He suddenly saw the second and third groups boarding from the Salazon and shouted: "Iraqis, the Iraqis! The Iraqis are attacking us!" He ran to the hatch to tell the rest of the crew who were below decks. As he ran his camera fell into the sea.

While I had been on deck, before, with the Admiral and he had showed me the gunboats through binoculars, he pointed this man out to me. He explained that this man was well trained, and a political agent of Khomeini. He told me to disarm this man as soon as I could because he would be the most dangerous to our mission's success.

When I saw him, as we boarded Tabarzin, I immediately realized the danger if this man were able to reach the others below deck. With no further thought I attacked him with my dagger just as the man reached the hatch leading below and fell through it. I was able to get in one blow with my dagger, cutting his shoulder. I then closed the hatch and stood on it for a few seconds and ran back up the ladder to the bridge of Tabarzin where I believed I should be in order to supervise the operation and see to the capture of the crew who were above-deck. Espahbod, the captain of Tabarzin, shouted to me that I should have remained at the hatch, as that was where the danger was. I then turned around and jumped down the three meters to the top of the forward gun and then directly leapt on to the deck and ran back to the hatch.

While my first act had been foolish, I complicated the situation even further by opening the hatch and jumping down below deck with only my dagger as a weapon. In the hatch the political agent was waiting for me and attacked me, but in defending myself I managed to cut his finger and nose. Within seconds, Cheko, Shirmard and two others, now armed with Uzi's and Kalashnikov's, appeared at the hatch and ordered the crew to surrender.

By this time, Mehrafzoon and the group under his control had checked the rest of the deck and, after opening the arsenal, had armed all of the commandos. Only I, who had been below deck, remained unarmed. Immediately the other six of the first group joined me, and took control over the 26 prisoners. At that point I no longer needed my dagger. The crew of Tabarzin was still under the impression that the attack had been carried out by well-trained Iraqi commandos.

Vishtasb and two of his group cleared all evidence from the Salazon that we had been there, cut all communications on board, left Petros tied up with double the payment of what had been promised to him in dollars. They boarded Tabarzin and set the Salazon adrift.

From the time that I first set foot on Tabarzin to the time that the two boats separated, it took less than 35 seconds.

Now, under the command of the Admiral representing her real owners, Tabarzin began to make way and to follow the rest of the squadron with the objective of carrying out the rest of the plan to capture them. The "boy scouts" who had fought for their ideals in Paris were now fighting with proper arms and feelings of pride welled up in all of us. We were drunk with victory and all of us "students" believed that, with the capture of Tabarzin, we were now capable of changing the destiny of our nation.

At this time Delavar and Zarnegar took on the role of protectors of the Admiral and became inseparable from him. With their gas pistols replaced by Colt Forty-Fives and with Uzi's at hand they had stationed themselves on the bridge together with the Admiral.

I, along with my team, was guarding the prisoners in the crew's quarters below decks. Another group of three commandos was in the engine room keeping an eye on the navigator, one of the collaborators, who was running the boat's engines.

Espahbod, the Iranian commander of Tabarzin, Shirowzhan, the Gunnery Officer, Azadan the First Lieutenant, and Chabokran, the boat's engineer, were the four members of the crew who had assisted our capture of the gunboat. They were all accompanied by at least two commandos in order to keep an eye on them as well as to protect them from the rest of the crew.

These four men will never be forgotten for what they did in the fight of Iranian patriotism against the Shiite invaders. They will always command the respect of the Iranian nation and will always be objects of our praise.

After the completion of the first stage of the operation they continued to assist the newcomers as much as they could. Both sides realized that they had all risked their lives for the sake of their country. The sailors realized that my commandos had no experience with sailing and tried to give them a crash course in running the gunboat and using its equipment. Both sides believed that together they were fighting against the Shiite-Islamic extremists who had insulted the dignity of their nation and its universal reputation.

After less than three minutes sailing, the Admiral left the bridge. Together with Delavar, Zarnegar, Apratat, Dezhku, Kuhyar and Nahid, he went below and inspected the prisoners. On the way from the bridge the Admiral congratulated all the commandos on the success in the first stage of the operation and encouraged them to continue to protect the fruits that they had already obtained.

When the Admiral reached the prisoners, some of them recognized him as having been the previous commander of the Iranian navy and stood at attention. Others refused to do so. However, all of them now realized that Iraqi commandos had not carried out the operation, but rather by the Iranian opposition. Up to this stage the commandos had not spoken in front of the prisoners and so had not given away their identity. Through the prisoners' reaction to the appearance of the Admiral and his associates it was easy to discern which of them were happy with this situation, and which were not. After almost a year and a half of the Islamic Revolution, many were still loyal to the previous regime. A hatred of the Shiite-Islamic regime was apparent amongst several of them.

Under these circumstances the Admiral began to speak to his ex-sailors – now prisoners. He spoke as a good father and Admiral:

"My dear children! As your ex-commander and father I salute every one of you. I wish you and your families all the best. You are the children of the Iranian national army, as we are. But each of us knows that over the past year and a half something has happened in our country, which does not benefit our nation. Now, as members of the National Liberation Army under the command of General Aryana, my friends and I have come to your house, as we believe that it is also our house. This ship is the legal territory of any Iranian who loves his country.

"Many of you know me personally. You also know General Aryana as a respected officer in the Iranian national army. First, I would like to apologize that over the past few minutes we have caused you anxiety. But you must remember that we are on a battlefield fighting for the dignity and glory of our nation. Remain calm and be sure that none of us will harm you. All of us must realize that over the past year and a half the Iranian national army, as with the Iranian culture, have been destroyed by the anti-Iranian Shiite Muslims. We are all soldiers and know when we have to attack and when we have to defend. This is why I want to advise you that we are your friends and not your enemies. We are all in the same battle. We are fighting for the protection of peace and love and not for retaliation and violence, which are the fruits of Shiite Islam. Therefore please realize that the conflict between one of our commanders and one of you was not as a result of hatred but as an act of war.

"Every single one of you has to ensure that you do not try to come into conflict with our people. I understand that some of you are probably not happy with what has happened and are not happy with our ideology. Democratically I respect this. The real Iranian army has never been concerned with differing ideologies but, while respecting them, has fought for national prosperity, dignity and harmony. Therefore the current situation can follow the same policy and understand each other and work towards the same goals. Therefore we must cooperate and help each other to reach the main target of individual freedom.

"In this National Liberation Army, from the oldest, General Aryana, to the youngest, possibly one of you, every single one of us must understand that the future will be built with our hands. Take care of the newcomers to your ship and try to cooperate with them. Realize that, whilst they are not professionals like you, their motivation is no less than yours. The situation of Iran is like a rope, which only needs patience to be untangled. Soldiers of the Iranian army, the flag of Iran has fallen to the ground and the enemy has trampled it in the dirt. You have to cooperate with these young people to raise it up again."

During the Admiral's speech everyone was silent. They were greatly challenged as they remembered that this man had been their commander in pre-revolutionary times. Many conflicting feelings were being experienced. Some of them were very happy with the situation as they were against the revolution; others were angry as they supported it. Many were asking themselves why they were not able to express their feelings whether positive or negative. What was the source of their fear that was stopping them from expressing themselves? Many also asked themselves why they had no freedom of choice in the matter. Possibly some were also asking themselves when this fear and lack of freedom of choice had actually appeared in their nation. They realized that it had started from the time that the strange religion had been introduced and that they, themselves, had come under its power through the leadership of the country.

Shiite Islam had prevented them from experiencing the freedom for which they longed. Some realized that it was up to them to help create the situation where freedom of choice would again exist. Some were considering whether they had been following the evil principles of the religious leaders rather than the positive principles of the true Iranian culture; they were balancing the consequences of following these two principles.

When the Admiral finished speaking he called for questions. A fat, non-commissioned officer very rudely asked where they would be going and what would be their final destination. The Admiral quietly answered that their final destination would be Iran. Then a short officer with a red face and fat cheeks and an olive leaf and star on his shoulder and an Ispahani accent, asked what the fate of the sailors captured would be. The Admiral answered that anyone who was prepared to cooperate were welcome to join the National Liberation Army. However anyone who was not prepared to cooperate would be handed over to the diplomatic staff of the Islamic Republic at the first port.

After that another young non-com with a sickly complexion, which was sitting with his knees drawn up, very quietly asked where General Aryana was at that time. The Admiral told him that General Aryana was on his way to Turkey, close to the Iranian border. A middle-aged man with a short beard and a paunch who was leaning on the corner of the table and who was wearing the apron of a cook asked whether the Iranian Liberation Army would deal with the two other gunboats in the same manner. The answer was that eventually it was hoped that the same good relationship would not only exist with the other two gunboats but also with all the Iranian army and navy.

Unknown Flies On The Horizon

SUDDENLY, WHILE THE ADMIRAL was replying to the prisoners' questions, Delevar who was on the bridge with Zarnegar, heard several helicopters approaching Tabarzin and called down to the Admiral to come up to the bridge. In fact Espahbod, who was at the wheel, also saw the approach of the helicopters on the radar. The pilots tried to make contact by radio. Instead of using the intercom, he asked Apratate to go down and ask the Admiral to come up urgently. He realized that the operation, which had only just finished and was supposed to be secret, was known to the Spanish and that they had come out to investigate. Espahbod believed that everything that had happened could not be taken as a violation of Spanish law because it had occurred in international waters.

The negotiation between the Admiral and the helicopter squadron was very respectful and he explained that what was happening was a private Iranian matter. As a commander of the Iranian navy he had the authority to take command of the gunboat. The National Liberation Army had not contravened any Spanish law and that the boats were on their way home. Satisfied, the Spanish pilots left after wishing him well and hoping that his mission would be successful.

During the time that the Admiral had been speaking to the helicopters, the commandos realized that something strange was occurring. The prisoners were also surprised. The presence of the helicopters created an unusual atmosphere on board the gunboat. I was in charge of guarding the prisoners and avoided answering the prisoners' bombardment of questions. I didn't know the details of what was happening but I also found the presence of helicopters very strange. I recognized the danger of the situation and the possibility of a counter-attack from my prisoners. I thus positioned myself with my back to the bulkhead where I could see all of them and had my machine gun ready. Meanwhile, Nahid, Atashdel, Rahyar, Kuhyer, and Azarpa were helping me below decks. Turaj, Tiztak, and Payman were on the foredeck.

The First Retreat

TABARZIN WAS SAILING FAST on the Atlantic Ocean just outside the Spanish border. We had to make sure that the frequency of the radios stayed the same so that we would be able to stay in touch with the two boats in front of us: the Khanjar and Neyzeh.

As we continued, Espahbod, the commander, understood that his faithful commandos had even more difficult tasks ahead of them, even though they had already passed the first test successfully.

The barracks of the naval officers of the gunboat was in the bow of the ship. We used these barracks as a makeshift jail. The Admiral's next challenge was to figure out how to come up alongside of the other two gunboats.

The other three commanders, Espahbod, Shirowzhan and Azadan, were to act as technical officers in order to assist Vishtasb in order to coordinate this next maneuver. After the capture of Khanjar, Vishtasb would be in charge of the prisoners on that ship. Chabokran would take care of the engine while I, along with my commandos, would attack the third gunboat and pull off the same procedure that we had in order to take over Tabarzin.

Kuhyar, one of the commanders, rushed over to me while I was taking care of the current prisoners and informed me that the second attack was about to take place. Aprotat relieved me and watched over the prisoners, so that I could prepare my commandos for the next attack.

We would have to repeat the same operation that we had already successfully carried out, when we transferred from the Salazon to Tabarzin. But now we would have to do the same thing from Tabarzin to the Khanjar. In order to do this we had kept our radio frequency on the same channel as the other two boats. We planned to tell the boat that we were having technical difficulties and ask if they could allow us to board so that we could get the right machinery to fix our motor.

For our transfer from the Salazon to Tabarzin we moved in three groups of seven. Now, for the next transfer, we planed to pull off the next step with only two groups; the first group would stay on the Khanjar. After capturing the Khanjar we planned to transfer its armory over to Tabarzin. For the final attack, to capture the Neyzeh, we would only have seven men.

The Admiral, from his room, called over the radio to the Khanjar but he did not receive an answer. He hailed them several times. He told the Khanjar that Tabarzin was having technical problems and asked if it could slow down so that we could come up next the boat and get supplies to fix our engine.

All groups were ready to attack the second gunboat. The Admiral continued to call the Khanjar but it still did not answer. Finally we received an answer from the Khanjar, the voice on the other end of the radio answered: "We heard your discussion with the helicopter and we know what has really happened to Tabarzin. We will not cooperate." When we heard their answer, our hearts sank. We had not changed the radio frequency to answer the Helicopter and the other boats had overheard what we had done.

The Admiral tried again, but this time from a different angle. He tried to explain to the second gunboat what our overall plan was, in order to appeal to their patriotism. Yet, he still was not successful. We understood, at that point, that our plan had collapsed. The other two boats went off towards the Persian Gulf, and we returned towards Morocco.

The Lull Before The Storm

THAT ENTIRE TIME WE had been traveling at full throttle on all four engines. When the captain, Espahbod, had he received the negative answer he commanded that we turn off two of the engines and our gunboat slowed down. The crew understood that something had changed.

We were 21 commandos in total and we split up into teams of three so that every part of the ship was controlled by one trio. Six were in charge of the prisoners, three where in charge of the barracks and another three the cafeteria. Our "commandos" were really only university students.

At the very top of the gunboat, in the wheelhouse, we set up a command station. From there Espahbod, the captain, sailed the ship along with two his assistants. They had been on the ship prior to our attack. The captain's assistants would bring messages back and forth between the captain of the ship and the rest of the men.

Since our success in the first part of the operation, this was the first time that anyone had time to speak with one another. Several of us went to explore the gunboat to see what facilities the ship had; we were not sure for how long we would be on Tabarzin.

At that point we had to regroup. We had two problems: first, we had prepared to capture all three boats and we only had one; second, our three contacts in Spain had been arrested and we could not contact them. We had to figure out what our next step would be.

As we became more and more familiar with the gunboat, our appreciation for our Shah grew. The power and strength of this gunboat was overwhelming. We were mere students and had not been privy to the inner-workings of our navy. We understood that these ships were quite advanced and that the Shah had bought these gunships with great wisdom.

After much deliberation and assessment of our situation we made the decision to cross through the strait of Gibraltar to Morocco. We knew that King Hassan II, the king of Morocco, had a good relationship with the Iranian nationalists and that the Shah's son was currently there. Even though we only succeeded in capturing one of the gunboats we decided to continue with our original plan. The opposition would declare statehood from Tabarzin.

While we were working together we discussed how far we had come. We were all students and except for myself, previously, none of us had had any significant military experience. How far we had come! Back in France we had only worked on minor operations. Now, even though we had not completely succeeded, we were pulling off a massive operation.

Sardar, who had been upset this entire time, began to calm down at this point. When I had forced him to come over with us to Tabarzin he had been a complete wreck. But now that the atmosphere had calmed down he began to as well.

The Admiral asked Vishtasb to bring the cook of the captured crew and his assistant to meet with him. We were 53 people on this boat and we needed to be able to eat while we were at sea. Our plan was to restock within several days, however our quest was to be much greater and we would need a chef. And we needed to be able to trust our chef that he would not poison us.

When the chef and his assistant arrived, they recognized the Admiral and were very respectful. The number one top lesson in the military is respect for your superior officers. Still, they were very suspicious. He was an admiral, but he was also from the resistance and fighting against them. The Admiral took the chef and his assistant into his quarters and spoke with them at length. I do not know what was said behind closed doors. However, the chef remained with us for over a week and was very faithful.

After 20 minutes, once we realized that we had lost the other gunboats, the Admiral came to speak with the prisoners. I was guarding them at that time, along with my top two men. The Admiral spoke to them with confidence as the former Chief of Staff of the Iranian navy. He also spoke with them with sympathy, as a father might. The Admiral was a very personable man, and he was passionate about our cause.

He explained how the Iranian National Liberation Army was waiting in Kurdistan, by the Turkish border; that once we came around we would establish a new government on this boat and that much of the Iranian navy was waiting to join us.

I observed the reactions of the captives and observed that their views varied. There were some that greatly identified with the Admiral's message of hope and building a better future. There were others in the group who were against his ideology and were quite angry. A third group identified with him; yet, were weary, since they were concerned for their families and friends back in Iran.

As the Admiral finished, he asked if anyone would like to ask any questions, but there were none. After he left, my prisoners began murmuring amongst themselves. I could see that they were planning something. I yelled: "You are prisoners, you must be silent or I will plant 18 grams of lead into your head." And there was silence. I then continued calmly: "If anybody would like to speak with the Admiral again it can be arranged, in here you are my prisoners and I insist on silence."

One man arose, I saw by his uniform that he was an officer. The man's name was Captain Sedri and he requested to speak with the Admiral. With my radio I called in three of my men who then escorted him to see the Admiral.

Captain Sedri is the model of what is an extremist. It was in fashion at that time to follow the communist ideology. It was seen as being the pinnacle of intellectualism. In Iran at that time if one supported communism one also supported Shiite Islam. Those two parties walked hand in hand: fascism and communism.

Captain Sedri had several demands. First, when I boarded the Tabarzin I came across a soldier immediately. I saw that he was about to sound an alarm. With my knife I attacked him. I cut his ear, his nose and his finger.

Captain Sedri wanted to know when we would be able to let them off the boat so that they could get proper medical care for the wounded soldier, as well as return to Iran. In addition, he had several other demands as well.

The Admiral was able to accept some of his demands but I saw, when he returned, that he was not happy. I could see that at this point Captain Sedri realized that the former captain of Tabarzin was cooperating with the Admiral and he tried to attack the captain's assistant, Azadan. My men saw immediately what he was doing, put him down and took him back to join the other prisoners.

When the Admiral heard what had happened he ordered my men to take Captain Sedri to the mess hall instead of back to the other prisoners. The Admiral entered with two of my men along with two of the officers from the gunboat. The Admiral sat Captain Sedri down in a chair in the middle of the room by one of the tables and he pulled up a chair beside him. The Admiral then had one of his men bring over two glasses and a bottle of Cognac and poured himself and Captain Sedri a glass. He understood that Captain Sedri's animosity could be potentially damaging to our operation.

The Admiral, calmly and in a very friendly, fatherly tone spoke to Captain Sedri: "You are a prisoner. There are very specific international laws about how you are supposed to act. We are your captors and can make your life very difficult. I advise that you let go of your animosity." The Admiral then called in Azadan as well and sat him down next to Captain Sedri.

He called for another glass and spoke with them both. "I would like you two to put your differences aside." He continued: "You are brothers, you trained together, you fought Iraq together. It would be a shame to destroy that over something so trivial." The Admiral did not succeed in reconciling the two, but he did succeed in defusing the situation and minimizing the resentment between the two.

The Imperial Guard Officer

THE TWO OFFICERS, AZADAN and Captain Sedri, both had a feeling of shame. I did not know which one was more shameful. When Sedri attacked Azadan he spoken such terrible words, despite presenting himself as an intellectual. I have never heard such horrible language used before. But all of my men and one young woman, Nahid, my commandos were 100 percent convinced that this communist was collaborating with the black army which labeled us as evil terrorists. We saw Sedri as the symbol of our enemy. He is the one who destroyed our country.

We told our prisoners that our first port-stop would be Casablanca. They were surprised but understood that this was because the son of the Shah was living there and the king of Morocco, King Hassan II, had a very good relationship with the Pahlavi dynasty. Our prisoners understood that they had lost the gunboat and requested that we deliver them to the Moroccan army to send them back as military prisoners.

The chef had planned the menu for that day, to prepare Chelaw-Kebab, a traditional Iranian dish. After negotiations with the Admiral the chef was told to continue with his planned menu. At the Admiral's command, the prisoners ate first and then the commandos. It was wonderful for us all: our first time eating since we had captured the boat.

After lunch the sailors sent a message to the Admiral that three of them wanted to speak in private with him. One of them was dressed in a blue one-piece uniform and the other two wore their regular navy uniforms and had their ranks on their shoulders ostovar-yekom, three up and two down. They spoke with a southern-Iranian accent. I was familiar with this accent because of the years during my childhood when I had lived in the south of Iran.

Five commandos went down to the prison to bring these men up. These soldiers spoke critically with the Admiral. How could they obey the commands of a group of students? They understood that among their captors there was myself, who they thought had been an imperial guard, and the Admiral, who had been the Admiral of the Shah's navy. Aside from those people, they understood that the rest of my commandos were students.

While I had not ever been part of the imperial guard they assumed that I had. In their eyes the guard were best-trained military men. My men must have told them this in order to scare them and when they saw my level of training that only confirmed this story.

These prisoners complained that it was wrong for them to have been captured by a group of students. How could this be? How could he, a former admiral of the navy be working with a group of students? They continued to badger the Admiral with several complaints about their conditions as well.

The Admiral replied that they are the ones who should be ashamed.

They are the ones who supported the Islamic Revolution and as a result a group of students captured their gunboat. He told them that when the boat docked in Casablanca they would be set free. He continued that they might see his commandos as students. However, they are members of the liberation army of Iran and must be treated with respect. Aside from which, they are prisoners and must act accordingly. Afterwards he sent them back to the other prisoners.

Later on, the Admiral told me that one of these sailors had offered his services to train our men how to use the gunboat. The Admiral told me that we have to be very careful with them, despite that they may act in a friendly manner. They are very professional and it would be easy to mess up the entire gunboat by dropping a small key into the correct spot.

My commandos were trying hard to be friendly with their prisoners. They felt that since they are all Iranian, if they treat the prisoners well they might be able to convince the prisoners the come join them. I told them that they have to be careful and treat them as prisoners for they will not hesitate to take advantage of even a small mistake.

Footprints On The Back Of The Cannon

Espahbod was a very sharp naval officer with over 20 years experience. He had much experience from fighting in the Iran-Iraq war. He was one of the top experts in the navy for this type of gunboat. For five hours he was sailing and controlling Tabarzin when the three representatives came to speak with the Admiral. Espahbod overheard their discussion. When the prisoners left the captain's room, Espahbod called the Admiral over to his station to show him two single footprints on the back of the cannon in front of him.

The wheelhouse was on the highest level of the ship, elevated over two meters over the top of the cannon and over two meters away from it. The cannon itself was over two meters in height from the deck of the gunboat. The controls for the ship were situated off the wheelhouse in front.

The cannon itself was rounded and covered with oils and condensation such that it was very slippery. The only way for those footprints to appear there would be for someone to jump from the controls area, by the wheelhouse, a distance of two meters by two meters and then again a similar distance onto the deck.

Espahbod had overheard the Admiral saying that I had not been a member of Special Forces. He was interested in speaking with the Admiral about me and so Espahbod called him over to the controls to show him the two footprints on the cannon.

Espahbod told the Admiral that during the first 30 seconds of the attack he saw me board the boat and attack the naval officer that had been at that time on the deck. After he saw me attack the officer, the officer ran to a hatch on the deck and had fallen inside. Espahbod then explained that I had run up to the controls by the wheelhouse. He was afraid at that point that the wounded man would warn the other soldiers so he told me to go back down immediately and take control over the other soldiers.

Instead of running down the stairs again, I understood that time was crucial, I decided to jump. I ran to the controls, leapt over the side onto the cannon and jumped again, from there, onto the deck beside the hatch that the wounded solder had fallen into. In one second I had made that jump.

When Espahbod had seen this he looked away, fearing that I had killed myself. However when he looked back to see my crumpled body on the deck I was not there. I was already in the hatch. Espahbod told the Admiral that if he could not see the footprints on the cannon then he would not have believed that I had just done this feat.

The Admiral was extremely excited. He called Vishtas to call for me. When I came to them they grilled me about my life's story. How could I have done such a thing? Only an acrobat could do things like that. In fact, I had been an acrobat.

A Parisian Cold Winter

WHEN I REACHED ESPAHBOD'S office, the Admiral introduced me warmly to him. He called me over to the deck with the controls and showed me the footprints I had left behind. He told me that my jump had been extraordinary.

Espahbod told me that after he had seen me jump, he had looked away expecting me to have leapt to my demise. When he turned back to look for my body he was shocked to see that I had already jumped into the hatch. He asked: "Is it possible that you could show us again how you did that?"

I looked down at the distance of the jump and looked back to him and I answered: "that would be absolutely crazy to do. However, if I were presented with the right circumstances again, I could do it a thousand times more." One cannot express the feeling of patriotism that I feel. My love for my country flows along with my blood, giving life to my whole being. Under the right circumstances I could fly.

It was a warm and intimate discussion; we were sitting and he offered me a cup of tea. The Admiral asked about my background, my childhood, and how I became the man that I was. He asked about my political activities before and during the Shiite-Islamic revolution and what it was that caused me to be involved.

I spoke with them about my father's tribe, Shahsovan, which means in Persian-Turkish "faithful men to Shah." His tribe was known for their patriotism. Their support for the Shah and nationalism is legendary. My great-grandfather was the head of the tribe. I explained that actually my actions are not extra-ordinary since my patriotism flows through my blood. The Admiral himself was half Persian and half Turkish and he was interested in learning more about my Shahsovanistic background.

The main root of the affiliation between the Shah and Iran is connected with what Fredric Hegel explained, that Iran was the home of the first civilization on earth. Since those ancient times, 2,500 years ago, the Shah had been the central coordinator of all religious, social, political and military activities. The Shah was the central leader for all these areas. This idea is the seed still living in the hearts of Iranian patriots. However, if the Shah would abuse his station or there had a true need for social change then that must be taken care of.

I told them how in 1974 I was a graduate of Law from Teheran University, I had already passed the Bar exams and I had been the Iranian national university champion of acrobatics. My wife had finished her degree in psychology and we had moved to Paris in order to continue our education there in 1977.

I recalled to them that when we had arrived in Paris it was in the middle of winter and very cold. Leaving the airport I had Payman, my son of four, on my shoulders and Bahareh, who was only two months old, in my arms. Guity was carrying our bags.

For the first week we rented a small room in a cheap hotel in the Latin Quarter in Paris. I had looked for a small flat for us to live in and a way for us to study the language. I had been in France many times, since I had been a tour guide, and I had a basic knowledge of the city. I had a friend, Hushang, who had been my good friend during our studies in

Teheran University. He had arrived in Paris a year before we had and he offered to let us stay in his home until we could find a home of our own. He said: "you have two small children and little money, how long can you continue to live in that hotel and pay so much?"

Two weeks later I found a flat. That first winter was very cold and it was difficult for us. I continued to tell them about other experiences I had had in Paris specifically about my neighbor the colonel who had turned against the Shah after the revolution. I also told them about Dr. Ibrahim Yazdi and how, later I traveled to Morocco and had the privilege to meet Her Majesty, Queen Farrah.

The Heroes Of The Persian Gulf

ONE OF OUR 31 prisoners, a young, small man, about 30 years of age, was the communications and radar expert of the team. He had a sickly look about him and a yellow face. He spoke calmly and quietly with an accent from the south of Iran. At times I felt that he was sympathetic towards me and I felt that he wanted to communicate something to me. Several times I spoke with him. I asked about his family, his health. I told him that if he needs anything I could try and arrange it.

He explained to me about the mission of the gunboats. He said that the sailors that were selected to bring these gunboats went through a rigorous selection process. Not only did they have to be top sailors, but they also went through psychological and intellectual testing as well. He told me that the sailors there on this mission were the elite of the Iranian Shiite-Islamic Republic Navy. It was so important that the best be chosen because these gunboats were tactically crucial for the Iran-Iraq war, which was raging at that time.

Financially this mission was very beneficial to them. These soldiers were receiving much compensation for this mission and they had received extra training in navigation as well. Many of them bought gifts while abroad for their family and children. He spoke generally about their experiences.

Sadly, he explained about one accident that had occurred. When they had been in the Persian Gulf, MIG-23 fighters attacked them, the Russian equivalent of the American Phantom-16 fighter. They were sailing two gunboats, the Rostam and the Azerakhsh. He had been on the Azerakhsh. Both were very similar to the Tabarzin. While they were out they saw that a squadron of MIG-23's from the Iraqi air force were coming to bombard them.

He told me: "We were sailing when I saw the MIGs coming. I immediately told my superior officers. We quickly ran and put on our helmets and vests. As the MIGs dived they opened fire on us and with our machine gun we returned fire. On the first pass our firing had no effect, but on the second pass we hit one of the MIGs and in plummeted into the ocean in a ball of flames."

Everyone was overjoyed that they had successfully brought down one of the MIGs. But their elation did not last. The MIGs came by a third time and the sailor told me that their boat was torn in two, as if it were a box of matches. Half of the boat was thrown up into the air and he was thrown overboard. He had been badly wounded but alive. "When I hit the waters I immediately removed my helmet and vest so I would not be weighed down. I knew that I was alive, but I was in total shock I watched the half remaining of my gunboat sink into the depths of the ocean." he recalled.

"I had been injured. While I was floating in the sea, I lost consciousness several times from the pain of my wounds. I would wake up immediately and then lose consciousness again. The salt of the sea in my wounds was overwhelming. When I was able to regain enough focus to open my eyes again, I saw that the other gunboat had been destroyed as well."

"I called out to my friend Samandar, 'Sandi, Sandi' to see if he had survived. We had been right next to each other when our boat had been hit. After several calls I heard him call back. I looked out over the sea and saw him trying to swim, as I was. We found a way to reach each other and continued to call for other survivors. A third person, Issa, had survived as well. The three of us continued calling but no one else had made it. We were three out of 44 people, and we were the only survivors.

"After a while we helped each other remove our boots, which were weighing us down, and we removed our belts and attached them together so that the waves would not separate us. We fell in and out of consciousness and it became dark, night. All I remember next is waking up in the Bushehr Air Force Hospital with my family around me." He and his two friends had been floating for 40 hours before they were rescued.

He continued: "I know that you are a champion of Iran. My friends and me are as well. Damn our government that has separated us. We should be fighting shoulder to shoulder for Iran's freedom rather than fighting against each other."

The Arrest Of Roozbahan

ALL OVER THE MEDIA stories were coming out about the gunboats, which had disappeared in the Mediterranean Sea. Three Islamic-Republic Iranian gunboats had been incognito. Two had been found but one, Tabarzin, was still missing. There was word that it had been captured. The Islamic Republic refused to comment. Members of the Spanish helicopters of the border control, which had witnessed the actual events reported on what they had seen. But since then there had been no more word.

The Spanish police suspected that the people who had captured Tabarzin had cohorts in the area and began a search for anyone who might be collaborating with the rebels. After capturing Tabarzin, we lost all contact with our contacts back in Cadis. Roozbahan, the leader of our overall operation along with the two generals, had not heard from us and assumed that we had failed. In defeat, they arranged to bring our belongings with them back to France. They packed up everything in a blue Citron station wagon and began the 2000-kilometer journey back to France. The problem was that the police knew that whomever was helping us would have come from France, and seeing their French license plates, they captured Roozbahan and the generals easily.

They were taken into custody and brought back to the station for questioning. For hours they were grilled, why had they come there? What were they doing in Spain? Roozbahan and the generals were well accustomed to these tactics, being military men. And they understood, based upon the techniques being used, that the police knew more than they let on. But they would only answer that they were there on vacation.

Finally the inspector gave an order to check their car. In their car they found the possessions of 21 different students along with wads of French and American currencies. If these people claim to only be vacationing then why do they have all this in their car? Here they are, three political refugees from France in Spain with the possessions of 21 Iranian students and more money than most people earn in a year. With the stories coming out over the media at that time, Roozbahan and the generals could not contest the accusations against them. They were arrested and transferred to the jail of another city.

At the new jail they were interrogated again. With the current circumstances they agreed to cooperate and report all of the details of their operation. But they would only consent to this on the condition that they could contact their headquarters back in France and find out what was happening. The prisoners were of the highest class in France and they were not accustomed to the accommodations that the jail provided. While they were physically uncomfortable they were quite worried as well. They felt responsible for the young men that they had sent out on a dangerous mission. As far as they knew, all of them had been captured and would be killed on their return to Iran. Aside from those feelings of guilt they were worried for their own lives. If they were handed over to the Islamic Republic they would be hung.

The interrogator asked them to sign a confession of their connection with the "pirates" who had captured the gunboat. Roozbahan and the generals refused, they insisted that before they signed anything they needed to contact either their men on the Tabarzin or their contacts back in France. They were sent back to their quarters. The next day, their fourth day in custody, they were called in to be interrogated again. This time, however, everything was different.

When they entered the office of the interrogator there were several men there. There were two translators: one from French to Spanish and a second from English to Spanish. In the corner was a young well-dressed man with a leather briefcase. In the center of the room was an official-looking man with white hair who was the chief investigator of the Spanish police and had come from Madrid especially for this case.

The investigator told them that the young man in the corner was a lawyer sent on behalf of the government to represent them. He continued that he had brought the translators because he wanted to make sure that everyone understood each other completely. But still Roozbahan and the generals insisted that they would not sign anything without contacting their own lawyer in France first. The evidence was pointing to them clearly. But they understood that if they sign they are looking at a minimum of 20 years imprisonment on the charges of pirating. Aside from which they were very concerned about the young men that they had sent, as they thought, into the jaws of the wolf.

The interrogator threatened that if they do not sign a confession their case would be sent to the Justice Department of Spain and tried in the High Court. But still, they refused as long as they were not allowed to contact their own lawyer or their men on the gunboat. The interrogator sent them back to their quarters for another night.

The next morning, on their fifth day in detention, everything had changed, yet again. The head prison guard ordered Roozbahan and the generals to shower and shave, and prepare themselves for another meeting. At that meeting the entire atmosphere had taken an about-face. While on the day before the room was so tense that you could see the tension radiating with your eyes, on the fifth day everyone was relaxed and happy.

The same lawyer and translators were there and the chief interrogator informed them that their belongings were to be returned to them and they were free to go. Roozbahan and the generals were in shock. What had happened over night? They were asked to sign that if they returned to Spain they would inform the Spanish police before they came and they were sent on their way. On their way out the interrogator told them that Tabarzin had negotiated with the French government for asylum and had returned the boat to the naval officers of the Islamic Republic who were on their way to Algeria to meet the other two gunboats.

Casablancan Investigators

THE ADMIRAL, ALONG WITH the 20 men and one woman, were all motivated to do something for their nation and country. While, later their act was called "terrorism," ideologically they were trying to provide the opportunity their people needed to break free from the Shiite-Islamic Regime. Even though their original plan had been to capture three gunboats, and they had only captured one, they still believed that they could achieve their original objective and establish an opposition government onboard.

Our first goal was to reach Morocco. Morocco was important for several reasons. First, The King of Morocco, King Malek Hassan II, had been a good friend of the Shah and identified with a monarchial governmental system. We believed that it would be a strong alliance for us where we would be able to coordinate our attack from there. The other reason for landing in Morocco was that the son of the Shah was currently residing there. We wanted to instate him as the next Shah, so we needed to his cooperation as well.

Before we had left the international waters into Morocco we informed our prisoners that we were going to stop off in Morocco. They were not pleased. Many of them protested. They feared that a monarchial system would not be sympathetic to them. The Admiral promised them that he would request from the authorities that they be sent directly back to Iran. That relaxed them. But he continued, admonishing them, "you are military prisoners. It is not becoming of you to act in this way. This is not a negotiation and our informing you of our plans is a courtesy on our part."

At the break of dawn we came close to Casablanca. There was a calm breeze and the weather was warm. We could see the lights of the city and the spotlights, for the navy, were two pillars illuminating the skyline. The Admiral ordered the crew to clean up the ship and make it presentable. "This will be our first contact since capturing the Tabarzin," he said. "We have no way of knowing what the reactions will be and we have to make sure everything is in order."

Along with several commandos I was in charge of the prisoners. Our responsibilities included accompanying them whenever anyone needed to relieve himself and make sure that their basic needs were taken care of. Zarnegar and Delavar, along with two other commandos, were in charge of taking care of the captain's room. Azadan and Shirowzhan were officers from the original crew who were cooperating with us. They were working with Espahbod. Vishtasb and Nahid were coordinating communications between the different parts of our crew and brought supplies to all who needed.

These 53 people, the Admiral, 21 commandos and 31 sailors were filled with anxiety. We had no idea how our act of patriotism would be accepted. Every person was busy, each with his or her own task and no one was idle. Still, tension permeated the ship. Even the prisoners were affected.

It took over two hours of communicating with the port of Casablanca to get our answer through. We sent out the message: "This is the Imperial Iranian gunboat Tabarzin. We would like to enter your waters and dock at your port."

It took so long to communicate since our vessel was no ordinary boat. Politically, we were a hot potato. To assist us would have serious political international implications. Over the radio we were passed on from one person to the next until we reached someone of enough authority to do something. It had been only that morning that the king, with the head of the army, had decided what he would do if, and when, we came. Only later on we had found out that this operation was being compared in the media with Israel's Cherbourg and Entebbe operations.

On the 27th of June in 1976, a group of George Habash hijacked an airplane leaving from Ben Gurion and was supposed to travel via Athens to Paris. These terrorists brought the plane to the Entebbe Airport in the Congo, near Uganda. On the 4th of July, Colonel Yonatan Netanyahu, the brother of Benyamin Netanyahu, along with a unit from the Israeli Special Forces arrived in the airport in Entebbe. Within 90 minutes they successfully saved the hoFs, over 200 passengers from all over the world, with only four casualties.

Prior to the Israeli Six-Day War in 1967, President Charles de Gaulle made a deal with Israel to sell it several gunboats, the same model as Tabarzin. After the Six-Day War, because of his pro-Palestinian sentiments, President de Gaulle decided not to deliver the final four gunboats, which had already been paid for. There were many negotiations back and forth, but in the end he refused. On December 24, 1967, under the command of General Mordechai (Mika) Rimon, a unit of naval experts captured these gunboats, from the Cherbourg Naval Port. They were welcomed as heroes when arrived in the port of Haifa on the 26th of December.

We were unaware that our operation had been compared with these. These comparisons were based on the international sentiments at that time. The implications were neither negative nor positive for us. Personally I felt that this was positive, they were both operations that were necessary in self-defense. However, from an Islamic point of view, it is never positive to be compared to Israel.

We contacted the port with three requests: Our first request was that we deliver 26 captives from our gunboat to them, and we requested that they send these prisoners of war back to Iran. We were not sending all 31 because five members of the original crew had opted to remain with us. Our second request was that they supply us with food, water, fuel and spare parts for the Tabarzin. We made it clear that we were fully willing pay for everything. Our third request was that we would like to send out the message to the media that we are Iranian freedom seekers, and all Iranians who would like to join our cause and join the government-in-exile are welcome.

We understood that it would take a while to receive a reply for our request since it involved the entire chain of command, and every message we sent had to go through many channels before it reached an authority who could make the decisions. After several hours we finally received a reply that they would agree to our requests and that they were sending a military ship out to meet us and escort us to the port.

At this point we were unsure how we would be received. From our own point of view our operation was an act of self-defense. A tyrannical government had taken our country, and we were acting against them to take our home back. We took all pains to make sure that no one was hurt during the operation, and only one person had been. But we were unsure how others would see what we had done. It could just as easily be seen as an act of terrorism or piracy.

The Admiral ordered all hands on deck. As the escort was coming for us the Admiral arranged a special ceremony, where we raised the Iranian national flag. Everyone saluted and it was a very moving experience for us all. The prisoners heard over the radio what was happening and many were upset, but they had no choice. As we finished raising the flag a Moroccan ship came and escorted us to port.

As we approached the port we saw that all along the dock of the port there were cannons lined up pointing in our direction. That, in itself, was nerve-wracking enough, but when we reached the dock we were asked to dock between to gunships, each one three times our own size. After our escort ship pulled away another gunship pulled up next to our own so that our position was completely enclosed. And we realized that, at that point, there was no way out for us.

Once we were docked completely we heard over a loudspeaker a call for the Admiral to come off the gunboat. He left along with the captain and two other officers. Several Moroccan generals were waiting on the dock to negotiate with them. Before he left the ship, the Admiral called for me and told me: "I do not know what is going to happen now. I am leaving you in charge of Tabarzin. It is your home and your responsibility now. You are a soldier and it is your trench and last refuge." He continued that when any of our commandos are visible and on the deck they must not be armed. With the prisoners or anywhere else beneath-deck we could go with our weapons; however, onboard we must leave them aside. This had been one of the conditions negotiated with the Moroccan Authorities.

The anxiety levels of our prisoners rose. Each one began to prepare the gifts that they had bought for their families. Many were friendly with us and discussed with us what they feared might be the reaction of the military court once they returned to Iran. This alone was good reason for fear. But many understood that the situation was not normal. They saw that we would not go topside with our weapons. This unstable situation added more to the anxiety levels.

Zarnegar received a message from the Moroccan military that everyone on board, commandos and prisoners, must leave the gunboat, one by one.

Each person would be escorted by two Moroccan soldiers and brought for interrogation, then returned to the ship. But even before they began their personal investigation a group of Moroccan soldiers came on board to tour the ship. After they had scrutinized our ship they sent for us, one by one: first the prisoners, then our commandos. This entire time we still had not heard back from the Admiral and we were, obviously, not happy.

The interrogation techniques of the Moroccan soldiers were very aggressive. The original crew of the ship, our prisoners, was upset by their techniques and the atmosphere grew even tenser. The members of the crew were afraid that the Moroccans would use whatever knowledge they had gained from the interrogations and sell it to the Iraqis.

It had been over 10 hours and we still had not heard from the Admiral or Espahbod. Each member of our crew and each prisoner was taken one by one to be interrogated. The ship was crawling with Moroccan soldiers. Our morale was down, and sinking deeper fast. I assessed the situation and understood that I had to intervene or we would lose all control.

I gathered the entire crew, along with the prisoners and spoke. I told them how I admired them all; even though we were on different sides, they are all my people. I explained that we were all in this together. Then I spoke about our common history: Iran. I tried to outline the highlights of past 2,500 years of our joint history. I spoke about the greatest and most patriotic events that had formed our great nation. As I spoke I saw in my audience's eyes recognition of identification. I was not anymore just an imperial guard to them; I was a lawyer and a thinker. I tried to instill in them that this event, that they are part of, will go down in history books.

There were many questions in many different areas and issues. As I answered these questions, one by one, I was able to give a positive impression and diffuse much of the tensions that had built up. I tried to instill in them optimism. As a good father, good soldier and good neighbor, you will return home.

Out of the fifty-tree people investigated by the Moroccan soldiers, aside from the Admiral, I do not think that anyone was interrogated for the length of time that I was, two and a half hours. They asked me about every detail of my past: my childhood, how I began Javan, my experiences in France. When I told them about the previous time I had been in Morocco, they became very interested. They were very thorough, but never did I feel the aggressiveness that the crew had complained about. They were very respectful the whole time.

Stockpiles Of TNT

AT THAT TIME AN International Conference of Islamic Countries was taking place in Morocco. We predicted that, as a result of the Son of the Shah staying in Morocco and their monarchial system which lead the country, would support our goals. However, it would seem that that was not powerful enough to contest with the conference. Many of the crew-members were not happy with the investigators and the anxiety levels among the commandos rose: it had been over ten hours since we had last heard from the Admiral and Espahbod.

I personally did not feel this anxiety, despite my two and a half hour interrogation. I did my best to diffuse the tensions. During my investigation I was asked: "Last time you were here you promised that the next time you come, you would apply for a visa. Why didn't you apply for a visa before you came this time?" Of course this question was not asked in total sincerity. It was the investigator's way of letting me know that nothing could be slipped past them. Still, my response was fully patriotic: "I go where I am led, my country calls for me to be here, and I have returned." I continued: "As long as one of my people are alive, the Shiite-Islamic leaders in Iran with be plagued with troubles."

The general living conditions of the people on Tabarzin was becoming more and more difficult by the hour. Not only because of the interrogations and the absence of the Admiral, but also because the crew had understood that they would be leaving soon. They had prepared their possessions and every moment of delay elevated their stress levels even more.

My commandos' patience was being tested as well, every time they had to go on deck they had to relinquish their weapon to a friend. This added much to the stress levels as well. To compound the situation after several hours we did not have enough fuel for hot water for showers, and only a few hours after that we ran out of cold water as well. I placed restrictions on the water usage so that we would be able to last as long as possible.

The Moroccan soldiers were not helping our situation. Now that they had interrogated everyone on board many more questions came to mind, and they continued to call people to continue their questioning. We had captured this ship, and they were boarding as if it were their own. They insisted on checking every nook and cranny, over and over again.

One of the crew's officers, Captain Sedri, who had been wearing a white dress-uniform when we first arrived, but now his clothing was wrinkled and not clean-shaven, was poisonous to the crew. He spoke out often and picked many fights with my commandos. I took him aside and did the best I could to calm him down, with hope that if I won him over, the rest of the crew would fall in line.

I delivered my post of watching over the prisoners to my best commando and I invited the officer to the mess hall to talk with me. We sat by a window, each on a different side of the table and we looked out at the dock. I brought over some fruit and a bottle of Cognac. We were alone, and I poured him and myself a drink. I wanted to create a friendly atmosphere.

I told him: "The nature of a cobra is such that when he is on his way home, he goes straight. But if he is out attacking, he spirals up and sways back and forth in order to confuse his prey." I explained that just as a snake has two natures my commandos and I are the same. I explained that the cannons that we saw out of the window are immaterial; he is not the only professional soldier.

The first glass I poured him relaxed him a bit and the second even more. By the third glass he had completely relaxed and finally opened up to me and began to talk. By that time the Admiral had been away for almost 30 hours. He said that we are all prisoners. He said that he appreciates our patriotism and identifies with our cause, but it is like we went to put on mascara and poked out our eye in the process. Aside from which, the interrogations were disastrous. Who knows what classified information was handed over to the Moroccans?

I was anxious, he was right, and I decided to give him a chance to talk. I asked him what he would do in my shoes. He thought for a few minutes and then said: "If your heart is strong enough I recommend that you blow us out of the water."

He continued to explain that the weapons stockpile is stored just on top of the engine and fuel tank. If I were to place a 5-liter gas can on top of the weapons room, cut a hole in the side and then shoot it, it would explode the whole ship immediately. That, in turn would be a strong enough explosion to blow up the ships surrounding us; and who knows what damage that would do to the rest of the city, and how many lives it would take. He recommended that I send a short note demanding the return of the Admiral and Espahbod within forty minutes, or I would blow us all out of the water.

I poured him a fourth shot and sent him back to the rest of his crew. I wrote the message and sent it the Moroccans officials. I then lifted the catwalk to our ship and declared that we would not allow anyone to board our ship anymore. It was Iranian territory, we had captured it, and any attempts to board would be seen as an act of aggression and we would respond to the attack.

I kept most of the crew out of my plan, except for my closest friends. After I had sent the message I saw the officer again and noticed that, for the first time, he was smiling. Everything was ready. We understood that either they would agree to send back the Admiral within the allotted time, or we would accept our role as soldiers, and die for our country.

In the wheelhouse we set a timer for 40 minutes, but by the time 22 minutes had passed, the Admiral and Espahbod had returned; however, those 22 minutes were not quiet. The Moroccans sent messengers to negotiate with us, but we held our position and would not allow anyone on board. They tried to negotiate more time, but we held to our 40-minute ultimatum. We refused to budge from our terms and before 22 minutes had passed the Admiral and Espahbod were back on board Tabarzin. Everyone cheered. In the name of the Iranian National Liberation Army, we had won this battle.

The Admiral embraced me and told me that I had performed a miracle. And when I returned to where we kept the prisoners, I turned to the young officer in white and said: "Thank you for your advice." But with my eyes I challenged him: "You've created a fire without any smoke. Are you brave enough to do the same on your return to Iran?"

The Admiral collected us and explained to all: "You did a wonderful job until here, and we have passed another test. Now your task is doubled, though, you must take careful watch over the prisoners because now they will be extremely upset. They will not be returning home yet." We all went on our way and prepared to disembark from the port.

Dismemberment

WITH THE RETURN OF the Admiral and Espahbod there was a returned sense of optimism. The Admiral spoke over the loudspeakers, his words were directed towards the prisoners: "We are all soldiers, we are all fighting for the same side. It makes no difference which side you believe you are on. We are compatriots; whether you are fighting for a piece of land, or a gunboat. We thank you all for helping us reach this far, and helping us successfully complete our mission to this point. We must continue further, and would appreciate your further cooperation for the rest of our mission."

The feelings amongst the crew and commandos differed. It was clear that the prisoners were not pleased. We had told them that they were going to be returning home from Morocco, and they had already prepared their belongings. Our crew, on the other hand, was relieved to finally be leaving port. The entire time we were docked we had felt like prisoners ourselves. We knew that they had completed one part of the journey, and were pleased to be continuing with our mission.

The Admiral continued to explain that he had negotiated to receive supplies from the Moroccan government, however, since they did not want to get politically involved, they would not take the prisoners. Shirowzan and Azadan began to prepare the ship to receive the supplies. There were special pipes that had to be arranged to receive water, and others to receive fuel. We also got two boxes of handcuffs. The Admiral knew that the prisoners would not be pleased and we would need extra precautions for this next leg of our journey.

It was well past midnight when the great engines of Tabarzin began to turn and we finally departed from the deck. The Moroccan officers shook hands with us and we left. At the final minute, before we left port, several men with cans of paint came to Tabarzin and painted over its identification number. Its number formerly had been "320" and the soldiers erased the "3" for security reasons. Also when we entered Algerian national waters we exchanged our Iranian flag for an Algerian flag. A Moroccan navy ship escorted us to the straight of Gibraltar and from there we were on our own.

While we were on our way to Gibraltar the Admiral explained to me what had traversed during his time with the Moroccans. He explained to me that while he was there he was essentially a prisoner. He had full access to many luxuries, but he could not go as he pleased. If I hadn't made my ultimatum, he would still be there now.

However, while he was there he had many opportunities for negotiation. He had arranged for all of the supplies that we had received. Also he contacted the other opposition leaders in order to try and gain support for our mission. Among those leaders there were many wealthy individuals; however, they saw our act as an act of terrorism and would not support us. We decided, from that point, that our last hope, was France and we continued into the Mediterranean Sea. The Admiral also warned me that we have to keep a close eye on the prisoners. Now that they were not going to be returning home, they would be very difficult to deal with.

Some of our prisoners, psychologically, were trying to convince themselves that they were military prisoners. Consequently, they did not feel that it was their business getting involved in the political aspects of their situation. Others saw themselves as political prisoners and were extremely angry that we were not leaving them in Morocco. These prisoners did not want to be associated with our goals and saw their continuing with us as a threat to what they stood for.

For hours and hours I stood with the prisoners. By that time I felt that I could read their minds. I saw that many of the prisoners, however they saw their situation, were mentally preparing themselves for the interrogations that they would be going through with the intelligence agency on their return to Iran. I guarded in shifts of two hours on guard and one hour off guard. While I was off duty I discussed with the Admiral and Espahbod our situation. The Moroccan officers had interrogated everyone on board and we were trying to figure out what they were planning to do with this information. One scenario which we had came up with was that the Moroccans would sell the information about our whereabouts to the Shiite-Islamic government, and the gunboats which we had tried to capture, would be waiting for us in ambush.

As we reached the Gibraltar Straight and entered into the Mediterranean Sea we discussed what our next step should be. As we saw it, we had two options ahead of us. We could continue south, to the right, and follow along the North-African countries until we reached Egypt. Or we could continue north, left, past Spain to France.

We felt that Egypt might support us because before 1979 Egypt and Iran had been very close; also, Sadat had been a close friend with the Shah. On the other hand, we were afraid that the other two gunboats might be waiting for us in the Algerian territorial waters. We also knew that Libya was against us and we would have to be careful if we were to go that route.

We felt that France might support us because shortly before our operation took place, the foreign minister of France had been assassinated in Beirut. We knew that as a result of this, François Mitterrand, then the president of France, was on very bad terms with the Shiite-Islamic Republic.

When our prisoners heard that we might be going to Egypt many became very upset and fearful. They knew that Egypt was not on good terms with the Shiite-Islamic Republic and did not think that the government would be sympathetic to their cause. There were several who even threatened suicide or to sabotage the ship. Their hysteria tipped the scales and we decided, finally, to go to France.

While we were discussing our plans I remembered a letter that had been written one hundred and eighty years before. Napoleon Bonaparte had written a letter to the Shah of that time, Fath-Alishah. In his letter he wrote that while we, the Europeans, were still living in jungles, you were ruling a major part of civilization of Earth. This letter today is in the Louvre in France. And when we finally decided to go to France, I remembered those words. During Napoleon's time, Russia was trying to influence northern Iran, and England was trying to influence southern Iran. Because of this, France became interested in Iran as well, and showed respect to its rich history via this letter of tribute.

The Storm

SEVERAL HOURS AFTER ENTERING into the Mediterranean Sea Espahbod brought to our attention a storm, which lay in our plotted course ahead. We understood that we would have to prepare, and make sure that our crew and our prisoners were well taken care of.

As our journey continued, and I got to know the crew better, I understood that we had, not one, but two storms ahead of us: one outside the ship, and the second inside – from our prisoners. I understood that they were extremely angry with us, but even more, with their crew-members who had joined us: Espahbod, plus three officers and two engineers.

Espahbod contacted me over the radio and requested that I place the prisoners in handcuffs. The prisoners were shocked; we had not treated them so poorly until now, what had changed? Once all of the old crew was properly detained Espahbod came into the room.

Espahbod explained why he had decided to join the Iranian National Liberation Army and explained that he believed that everyone in his crew should join them as well. He continued telling them that a storm was up ahead and requested that they cooperate, whether they are in support or are against this operation, since the boat belongs to them all, and everyone's life is at stake.

His speech touched my heart. I saw in the prisoners' eyes that many were touched as well, including the young officer who had helped me regain control of the ship from the Moroccans. However, not everyone felt as I did. One officer jumped up, the same one, which I had injured when we first boarded the ship, and he shouted: "Why don't you just kill us?" This officer had been a representative of the intelligence agency of the Shiite-Islamic Republic.

Espahbod responded: "We didn't give you your life, just to take it away. We are brothers, and military men. You have lost the last battle and are our prisoners, but we have treated you well. However, if you do not keep to our rules we will have to take measures to ensure the safety of our crew. We have decided to go to France. We will deliver you to the French authorities and they will send you back to Iran. Until then we request your cooperation and hope that you will accept our apologies for having to handcuff you."

After Espahbod left the prison he ordered Shirowzan and Azadan to prepare the ship for the storm. A rope had to be tied through poles around the perimeter of the deck, so that people who had to be on deck would have something to hold on to, and would be able to maneuver around. Also, everything on the deck had to be moved to the afterdeck, at the stern of the ship and tied down. This was a very big job and the storm was approaching fast. We also moved all of the prisoners to the living quarters in the stern, which were more secure. Finally, we all wore life preservers, crew as well as prisoners.

The waves were growing bigger and bigger. Anyone who went on deck had to wear a heavy bright yellow raincoat. This way if anyone fell overboard they would be easily seen. With the coming of the storm, everything grew dark. The waves threw the gunboat around like a box of matches. This made it difficult to get any of the essential tasks needed for running a gunboat done. It was hard just to stand in one place, let alone guard our prisoners.

Several members of the crew and prisoners developed motion sickness and began throwing up. Whoever was not regurgitating, and had any medical training, took care of those unfortunate crew-members that had fallen ill. I did not know how many had grown sick. I am sure that no one was spared from feeling ill at all, whether they were able to keep down the bile or not.

I saw my crew falling left and right. I knew that we were vulnerable and if I did not act fast the prisoners might overtake us. I was able to make my way to the ladder, which led to the upper deck and I wrapped my arm around the vertical pole of the ladder. It was in this manner that I was able to stand on my feet and keep my gun ready. I ordered three of my commandos to do the same with other poles around the room and we were able, in this way, to maintain control.

Some waves were higher than our ship and there were times that we were in a valley with great liquid mountains surrounding us, threatening to collapse over us, burying us under tons of brine. I stood guard over our prisoners for eight hours until the storm subsided. During this time I was called up to the bridge several times. I knew that if I were thrown overboard there would be no way I could be found. But I gave regular reports to the Admiral. I assured him that the prisoners were being carefully watched and that there was nothing to worry about.

It was especially difficult for the prisoners as they were still handcuffed. Because of this when they were sick we had to clean them up, bring them medicine, bring them to the bathrooms and at the same time guard them. Espahbod exclaimed that he had never seen such a strong storm and feared that it would tear our little gunboat in two. But finally, the night came to an end and everyone came out of it, more or less, in one piece. Even so, the storm raged on.

Potatoes Of Salvation

ONE OF THE SECRETS of good sailing is the potato. When the sea becomes too rough, even for the most weathered sailors, they turn to the potato. Why? Baked potatoes are a fantastic remedy for seasickness. Baked potatoes have the ability to calm an upset stomach even during the most difficult storms. Our chef had prepared for us baked potatoes and everyone on board was eating as much of them as they could.

But to call someone a potato, in the navy, is a great insult. Potatoes have no roots. It serves the purpose of a root of its plant, but it does not have visible roots itself. To call someone a potato is to say that they have no roots, that they are not anchored. It is saying that that person does not have the ability to accomplish anything, nor are they grounded in any real beliefs. We overheard from our prisoners their murmurings, how we are potatoes with no roots trying to save our country.

The waves were so high that they sometimes covered the head of the gunboat. The waves threw the boat in the air many times. Even the professional sailors were sick to their stomachs. One minute you could find yourself sitting and the next minute you could be flying through the air, as another wave dropped out from under our boat.

We were using the dining hall as a makeshift infirmary but getting the sick there was a very different story. Espahbod made it clear that anyone who needed to go from one portion of the ship to another was taking their life into their own hands. If someone would fall overboard, we would not be able to save him or her. Despite this, it was important to transfer the very sick in order to give them proper medical attention. I was faring better than most, so that responsibility of transferring people to our sickbay had fallen onto my shoulders.

The tensions were high and many arguments broke out between the sailors and my commandos. Each side would blame the other for the situation that we were currently in: on a ship in a storm, somewhere in the middle of the Mediterranean. The sailors claimed that we were destroying a wonderful empire that was being built, and my commandos would retaliate that they had pledged allegiance to a system of beliefs that was foreign. The term hot potato was thrown around several times: a hothead, with no roots. The debate continued using historical references, each side bringing support or rebuking the other side from their heritage. My commandos would charge the sailors of being like Pol Pot, mass murderers, and no care for their history. The sailors would rebuke that we were fascists and racist.

For the duration of the storm, over six hours, our arguments raged: among ourselves, between our people and our prisoners and between nature and us. Finally after six and a half hours the storm subsided, and with it, our anger. All of our clothing had been soaked completely, but as it dried it turned to cardboard from being saturated with salt. We then began the difficult task of cleaning the ship and everyone aboard.

With the calming of the Mediterranean the fifth day of our operation began. The sun, which had finally shown her face, had never looked more beautiful. We were sure that the baked potatoes had saved us from seasickness. We were even more determined, at that point, to prove that just as those potatoes had saved us, we were going to save our nation, and that we were not the rootless hot potatoes that we had been accused of being.

Dealings With The French

Espahbod, along with many other naval officers, believed that the storm of the previous night had been one of the most powerful storms that they had ever seen. No one had slept. Each member of our crew had his or her hands full: whether technical – keeping our ship afloat, emotional – making sure that everyone is well, or medical – taking care of the crew that could not handle the rough storm.

Some of the people tried to remain in bed from sheer exhaustion, while others took stock of the shape our ship, making sure that no critical systems had been damaged. The chef was busy preparing breakfast and the day was looking bright.

After several hours we approached the French national waters. As we approached the French border we made radio contact with the French authorities at the Toulon Naval Base. Our crew was very optimistic about our approaching land again. We were all hopeful that negotiations would go better with the French than the negotiations with the Moroccans had gone. If we were able to survive that storm, then we could overcome anything.

We announced to the prisoners our new plan and they reacted similarly to the previous time. Some of our prisoners complained, but nothing out of the ordinary. Many were optimistic, while others were anxious about the prospect of becoming political prisoners in France.

The commanders of our crew were not as hopeful as the rest of the crew. We had made up the strongest arm of the Opposition of the Shiite-Islamic Republic of Iran in France right up until we left for this mission. We were not sure if the French authorities would cooperate with us, or arrest us.

In preparation for the next docking we all arranged our belongings and cleaned ourselves up. Clean laundry was hanging from every available spot. Our prisoners agreed to join us for a group photograph; we had been together, so far, for five days. A lot can happen over the course of five days, and we had become quite close.

As we drew closer to Toulon communication between the commander's room and the naval base continued. At first they would not believe us who we claimed to be. But since our story, of the pirates, had been all over the media, after some time and much questioning they allowed us to approach the port. There were many questions: Who were we? Why we wanted to come to France? What did we want?

The negotiations began with the naval base, but it did not take long for negotiations to begin with the French government itself. We needed three things: First, to hand over our prisoners to be deported to Iran. Second, we needed fuel and supplies. We had sufficient funds to pay for them, but we needed the government to supply us with what we needed.

Third, we needed cooperation, for the government to allow the opposition leaders to board our ship so that we would be able to establish our new government aboard.

We were not sure how the government would react. A year and a half prior to our operation the French government had fully supported Khomeini and had helped him enter into power. So we were fearful that the government would not help us, or worse, attack us. On the other hand, we knew that some time before to our operation the French ambassador to Lebanon had been assassinated in Beirut. The media was blaming Khomeini and we had heard that, as a result, cooperation between the two countries had fallen apart. We hoped to take advantage of this fallout to bring a successful end to our operation.

Negotiations take hours. We were authorized to come closer to the border, but were assigned coordinates outside of the border to drop our anchor. We were the hot potato of the mass media, the government had to allow time for policy-makers to decide whether they would get involved, and how. As our ship sat at the given coordinates, we could see bathers swimming on the shore of the country from which we had recently come. It seemed a lifetime ago that we had left France.

We Will Return

ON THE ONE HAND we were enjoying the sun. After six days of high tension we were finally able to relax, even if only a little. Several members of our crew jumped into the water for a swim. On the other hand, the tensions with our prisoners were high. They knew that we were negotiating again, and were worried. There were arguments over why we had chosen the French. But all in all things were going well.

In the distance, a half-mile in each direction, we saw French naval ships. We wondered why they did not come closer. After a while a helicopter flew over us. We heard over the radio that they wanted to see with their own eyes our situation. While negotiations with the French were under way the Admiral tried to make contact with our contacts in France, General Aryana, the head of the Iranian National Liberation Army based in Paris. The general's son, along with two other members had been our contacts up until we left. He did not know that these contacts had been arrested and he was not able to make contact with the General.

The helicopter presented itself as the representative of the French navy. It went on to inquire about our business, and affairs – what we were doing and why, why France, what had happened – along with many other questions. They inquired as well about each of our backgrounds: our French IDs, which universities we had come from, and where were our residences. As our negotiations continued it became clear that the only way the French would help us at all was if we sent over our prisoners.

The helicopter informed us that one of the ships surrounding us would send us several Geminis, inflatable motorboat used often in the navy. We were told that we should send over our prisoners on them. We were promised that they would send them back to Iran.

A small motorboat came from the ship to our left, which was anchored between the sea and us. To our right was the shore. We could not see the shore with our own eyes, only with binoculars, since we were several miles away. The motorboat came towing six Geminis and left them along side our boat and left. We then removed the handcuffs from our prisoners and brought them up to the deck and from there down into the small boats. There was a two-meter difference in height between our deck and the Geminis so we had to use rope ladders. Once they were all in the boats they went to the ship from which the Geminis had come.

Before we took them on deck the Admiral came down to our makeshift "prison" to speak with our captives. He thanked them for their cooperation; he told them that he was looking forward to seeing them again in Iran; and he asked that they bring our message of peace and nationalism back with them. There were captives that were warm and accepted our message, although, many were against us. They said that we were the ones who should be leaving. It is a big deal to send a sailor from his boat. It is like sending a man from his home.

We brought the more cooperative captives up first, removed their handcuffs, and sent them on their way. The two most argumentative captives were the young officer and the big man in the one-piece suit. As they shoved off in their Gemini, the latter shouted back at us: "We will return." I saw a strong sense of nationalism in him and hoped that one day he would feel as strongly about his true heritage.

We watched them go over to the ship to our left. Once they were safely aboard we turned our focus to the next tasks ahead of us: Preparing Tabarzin for the next step of our operation.

Companions Standing Alone

SHORTLY AFTER THE PRISONERS left we saw that we were being attacked. Helicopters flew by; boats came closer and began to surround us. The media had been made aware of our situation and now they were converging upon us. They wanted pictures and interviews. We had wanted three things from the French and had only received the first so far. We were anxious to buy supplies for the rest of our mission and bring the opposition leaders on board to join us.

The Admiral made it clear to me that I not give any interviews and I not allow anyone to come closer than ten meters from our boat. We contacted the officials demanding an explanation. We were completely surrounded by press. The questions that they were asking were based on information that they could only have received from the authorities. What was happening?

The Admiral made me aware of the dangers that the press could raise for us. If the press were allowed too close to us, terrorists could easily be among them. It would only take one diver with a bomb and we, along with all of the press, would be blown out of the water. I made it clear over our loudspeaker that no one would be granted an interview and that no one would be allowed to come closer than ten meters to our boat.

Despite our efforts, pieces of our story leaked out and our story was broadcasted over the news stations and was printed in the papers. When we each had left home we did not tell our loved-ones where we were going; each person had his own story. But now it became clear to everyone what we were doing. The left labeled us as pirates, the right, as patriots.

Many photos were taken of us then. There is one where I am standing on the deck with an Uzi in my right hand, a colt in my belt and I was making a victory symbol with my left hand. This picture became well known and won awards. It was nominated the best photo of a sailor in 1981. I remember a giant 10-meter copy of that photo was placed in Chalet Les Halles, a Parisian cultural center, for the duration of that year.

We had only one engine working at that time. We needed it to keep the electricity running and water clean. The Admiral continued to negotiate, but it was slow going. Sometimes we would not receive any reply, other times it would take hours before we got a response. We were much more relaxed now. No prisoners to take care of and we felt that we were finally moving forward with our plan.

Our rest did not last long. We received word from the French

On the deck of the Tabarzin.

authorities that they would not comply with our second and third requests. They gave us one option: we would surrender the gunboat and in return, they would grant us political asylum. The French President, Francois Mitterrand's personal representative negotiated directly with the Admiral. Since we were the world's hot potatoes, he wanted the story to end peacefully.

Their offer sparked a heated debate among us, and split our crew. There were those who felt that it would be fine to give in at this point. We had made our statement and that was a success. I, along with ten of my men, felt that it would not be right to quit yet. We had come so far. Our goal was to establish the new government and bring down the Shiite-Islamic Republic. We could not quit!

Those who were not happy to continue our operation said: "We have no food, water, or fuel left. The statement we have made is huge and hopefully will spark more uprisings like ours." I replied: "No! Our homeland is at stake. As long as we have air in our lungs, we cannot surrender." The Admiral, along with the six people from the original crew of Tabarzin was not on either side of the debate. They only watched our debate, assessing both sides.

While the debate continued, I went down to the barracks and brought up one of the gas revolvers with which we had captured the gunboat. I went over to the Admiral and, in front of everyone, I shot myself in my chest with the gun.

The sound of the revolver sounds exactly like a real gun. It took a while for anyone to realize what I had shot myself with. A cloud of gas engulfed us and everyone began coughing.

I shouted: "We captured this boat with this stupid gun! That is a huge accomplishment and now you want to give that away?! If you are hungry, we have fish surrounding us!" I did this to shock everyone. And it did. We were all coughing for several hours after the fact. I myself was injured from shrapnel from the explosion. I was cut all over, but nothing serious.

The debate continued, but many were not happy. Finally we went down to the dining room, and the chef prepared for us something to eat and drink. The side, which was insisting on surrendering, backed down. But even though, it was clear that we had no way to continue. In the middle of the dining room I spoke up again. I said how I felt again, but I said that in the end we have to give the decision to the Admiral and Espahbod. The Admiral is our leader, our father. And Espahbod is the Captain of Tabarzin. We can fight forever, but it should really be their decision.

The debate continued but the Admiral and Espahbod decided to try to renegotiate with the French authorities one last time.

THE OPINION OF THE mass media was split between the communists and the pro-Muslims – slandering us as pirates or terrorists. Only a few presented our acts as heroic and patriotic. Those who did favor our actions and wanted to portray our operation in a positive light compared it with Entebbe and Cherbourg.

Those journalists who compared our Tabarzin operation with Entebbe and Cherbourg completely ignored the fact that while experts in the field had executed those operations, Tabarzin had been captured by a group of University students. Despite this, I, Abayef, am proud to have been compared to these legends, Netanyahu and Rimon, with whom I now share a heritage.

A short year and a half after the elevation of a terrorist organization into power over my homeland, we were able to send a message to the world. We were able to do this with only one minor injury. I am proud that we were able to send that message that we were a peaceful, yet serious, opponent.

The End of Tabarzin

IT IS NOT EASY to express our feelings of patriotism, nationalism and our burning desire for national liberty. But we fully identified with the feelings of King Cyrus and Artimus, who was a 30-year-old woman who had been the commander of the Iranian navy. She led one million soldiers to victory in Greece in the Gogmel and Granicus wars, 2,300 years ago. These legends were symbols and an inspiration to us – King Cyrus, for is peaceful acts, and Artimus, for her heroism and leadership.

Our crew was split between those who felt that we could not continue any more and those who did not want to give up until we had no more options. We had placed the decision into the hands of our Admiral. After long discussions between the Admiral and the French authorities the Admiral said that we had no choice; we had to deal with the French authorities. We had no line of communication with any of our supporters and to go out again would not be possible with no support or supplies. The French were insisting that we end our operation here, peacefully, now, and in return they would offer us political asylum.

It was half past five in the afternoon on the sixth day of our operation when we began to prepare ourselves for our departure from our Tabarzin. Many of us wrote notes and messages and hid them throughout the boat. We hoped that our messages would be found and plant a spark in the reader's heart – a spark of true national pride. The Admiral ordered that we remove the plaque with our gunboat's name, Tabarzin, to bring as a gift for the Iranian National Liberation Army.

The Admiral, along with the six officers of Tabarzin, changed into civilian clothing. It surprised me how this simple act transformed them from being officers, leaders and a symbol of power for us all into plain civilians. The rest of the crew remained in our uniforms. Everyone packed up his or her belongings and we cleaned every corner of the boat.

A group of French officers arrived on a gunboat, which pulled up along side Tabarzin. We transferred all of our ammunition and weapons to the armory on the boat and the French officers checked Tabarzin over. They had the original checklist from Cherbourg of everything that was supposed to be on the boat before it would be delivered to the Shiite-Islamic Republic. Everything was there and in perfect order.

At the back of Tabarzin we had placed an Iranian national flag. Before we left the boat each of us went down one knee, before the flag, kissed it, and then left to board the French gunboat. I believe that everyone was filled with a deep feeling of sadness, that we were deliberately abandoning our home and our dream.

I, as the first person who had come aboard Tabarzin, had the right to be the last to leave her. As I was kneeling before my flag I began to cry. I am told that while I was there the rest of the crew lined up along the side of the French gunboat and began to sing the Iranian national anthem. As the French boat left Tabarzin we all looked back at her and we each swore in our hearts: "One day we will return and rebuild our country."

After Tabarzin

WITHIN 20 MINUTES WE were in the French naval base in Toulon. The French police collected all of our things. Our gas pistols, any military objects that we had, including my dagger. We were each interrogated briefly and then we were transferred, via helicopter, to a French police base in Paris. We were there for a day while the interrogations continued. We did not know that tens of thousands of Iranians had been waiting for us in Toulon. They all had come to welcome us there, but the French authorities had brought us away too quickly to receive the heroic welcome that they were waiting to give us.

During the interrogations the French police asked us what our next plans were. We had not known that we would be going to capture a gunboat in the first place and we had originally thought that we were going to Kurdistan to join Azadegan and the Iranian National Liberation Army. But over 90 percent of our Javan members, independently, had answered that we will continue to bigger and greater operations until we bring the downfall of the Shiite-Islamic Republic.

Our lawyers came to negotiate our release. Before we left the police warned us that we would have to be careful from now on. We would be targets of any supporter of the current government in Iran. For several weeks we lived out of our Javan headquarters in the country and our office in Paris. We realized that it would be dangerous to go straight to our families.

Checko, Shirmard, and I were invited to visit Princess Ashraf, the sister of the Shah, who at that time was living in Nice, in the south of France. Checko and Shirmard had been my two hands throughout the entire operation. She wanted us to tell her all about our Tabarzin. We went on our journey there with Princess Azadeh, her daughter. While we were visiting Nice we met many people and operation leaders.

On our final day visiting, the youngest son of the Shah asked me why we hadn't thrown our captives in the water when we had captured the gunboat. I was horrified and I could not answer him. This man is the son of our symbol, the Shah; how could he say such a thing? That is not what we stood for. I felt disheartened and betrayed. Those people, even though they are on the wrong side, were still our Iranian brethren. At that time I did not now that I was Abayef. God has his ways of guiding our paths.

The Next Battle

THE OPERATION OF TABARZIN gave our group a very good reputation. We were interviewed by the media and developed connections within the opposition in Iran and we were planning to do higher profile operations. We got involved with various groups, one of them was Kurdish and with them we pulled off another operation in Turkey.

Some of the people involved quit university in order to work with Javan full time. In September of 1980 I received my Diplome D'etudes Approfondies (DEA), a well-respected degree that is considered higher than a masters degree. In 1984, I finished my doctorate in constitutional comparative law at Paris University. I did this while I was still involved with Javan. Because of my experiences back in Iran, completing my degree while working with the police and competing in various sport competitions, I had no trouble keeping up with my studies while being involved with these political activities.

I had additional motivation as well, since I strongly believed in the importance of continuing education and wanted to set a good example to the other Javan members. But I did not always succeed in passing over this message. A few of the members, as a result from being involved in our paramilitary operations, got distracted from their previous goals. Some were even good students, but they got involved in drugs. Two close friends of mine, Kurosh and Reza, not only began dealing drugs but also started taking them as well. I tried to get involved and pull them out of the pit they had gotten themselves into, but in the end they both died from overdosing.

I remember several times when different CIA members were interested in finding out more about our Javan. Once I was even invited to the US. There, I met the Senator of Texas. Over the course of these meetings I proposed, as I had to General Oveissi, that our group could penetrate into Iran from one of the remote provinces and, from there, continue. However they only wanted to buy me out, make me their agent, and keep me in their pocket for their needs. I pointed out that I could be useful to them since we both, by that time, had a common enemy. But I refused to be swayed from my agenda, and they would not work with me unless I could be bought out.

In the summer of 1982, again, I was approached by a governmental agency. However, this time it was Iraq that wanted to work with us. It was in the middle of the Iran-Iraq eight-years war. They said that they were from the embassy and invited me to go to Baghdad for negotiations. I was in Baghdad for the course of a week and they were very hospitable. They reserved a room for me in the Cabaret Hotel. My room had a beautiful view of the Euphrates River. But with all of these luxuries I could not shake the feelings of guilt. These two Islamic peoples were fighting, Saddam and Khomeini, but it was my people who were being bombed and were suffering as a result of this war.

After a week of negotiations they advised me that they had decided to support our operations and us completely, however, on one condition. We had to prove ourselves first. The mission they gave us to do was to kill Tabatabai, the son-in-law of Khomeini who was a weapons dealer for the Islamic republic. At that time Tabatabai was in the city of Bochum, Germany. I returned to Paris and discussed their offer with the other leaders of our group but in the end we decided to opt out.

Nouf Le Châteaux

Due to the 37 times I had been interrogated by the French police and French Intelligence Agency I had developed a special relationship with them. To a certain extent, we had similar goals. While the French leftists were against us and the Muslims of France were our complete enemy, the political right identified with our goals. The police understood that it would be dangerous to the French culture and society give free reign to Khomeini's supporters. However, they couldn't support any para-military group, such as ours, even if they did agree with the many of the ideals of our group.

Thirty-seven times I was arrested in France and in other European countries; many members of Javan were arrested as well. A number of times I spent time in jail, but never more than a week. Several of our members were from the upper class of society, millionaires' and top generals' sons. It was shocking for these young men to be thrown in jail, coming from the strata from which they were accustomed. The police, in these situations, did not always treat us well. Sometimes they withheld food and water, other times we were beaten. However, I used these opportunities to strengthen my men's morale. I told them about the important roles, which they were filling. "This discomfort is temporary and when we are successful with what we have accomplished, we will go down in history books as heroes."

1981-Daniel presenting the para-military activities of Javan in Frankfurt to Prince Gholareza, brother of the Shah.

I was open with the police about the political goals of Javan, excluding our para-military operations, of course. However, since during our operations, on principle, we never took lives, and they saw that I had western values, similar to theirs, the police, more or less, left us alone. It did help that we had some very talented lawyers supporting us.

The police tried to keep on top of what we were doing at all times. They would ask that I inform them of our plans. I would always agree, but I never did. Always after the fact they would ask: "Why didn't you tell us what you were planning?" And of course we would deny ever being involved with what they were trying to pin on us.

That year I attended a public meeting; participating were a few hundred Iranian opposition leaders, many of them quite wealthy. I told these leaders that the members of Javan, now that they had truly experienced what it was to pull off a true operation, they couldn't go back to their normal lives and real jobs. My men have to be trained properly. Put to real work. We have to send our people to be trained to become more professional, in Israel or elsewhere, so that they can go back to Iran and make a real difference. The real battlefield has to be in Iran and not in Europe, and the people fighting have to be volunteers. I asked for their support for this cause. The opposition did not accept my pleas. They claimed that I had become too extreme and they did not want to support such extremism. I had heard this from Princess Ashraf herself; she explained that I was running so fast with my ideas that they could not keep up with me.

Later that year, during autumn of 1982, Colonel H. V. approached me. He was one of the well-known imperial guards of the Shah. Colonel H. V. asked me why Javan had stopped its activities. I repeated to him what I had said at that meeting earlier. He told me that the Queen wanted to fully support our efforts and provide whatever financial assistance we needed to continue our operations.

The new Shiite regime in Iran wanted, in honor of their third-year anniversary of power, to build a mosque in Nouf Le Châteaux, where Khomeini had lived before his rise into power. They wanted to make it the largest mosque in the greater Paris area. Because of Colonel H.V.'s military position, he was very careful and secretive, and was afraid of the current regime. I disagreed with him. As the opposition, we would have to be bold, out in the open. The French police knew us for who we were. But Javan's approach stressed Colonel H.V. greatly.

Dr. Ali Noini had originally been against the Shah. He had studied medicine in Lebanon for many years and during that period he studied guerrilla warfare there. Some time after my meetings with Colonel H.V., Dr. Noini approached me to work with us. I negotiated with him to help our operation.

The price we came to was $100,000. For this sum, Dr. Noini would provide us explosives and two Falange officers to train my men in how to use them. Several days before the operation was to take place, I contacted Colonel H.V. to make sure that everything was in order for us to go ahead with the operation. He informed me that there was no money left and all he could pay was 40,000 Toman, the equivalent of 7,000 Franks, instead of the 100,000 Dollars originally promised.

Despite this setback we discovered an alternative way to pull off the operation without the help of Dr. Noini. Forty-eight hours before the operation was supposed to take place I contacted Dr. K. Vadaii, who was the teacher of the young Shah and an old acquaintance. I asked that he tell the Queen that we were planning to implement the operation despite her inability to support us.

The Nouf Le Châteaux was blown up on the 22nd of Bahman, the 14th of April in 1983 at 4 a.m. At 5 a.m., Dr. Vadaii called to tell me that the Queen was crying with happiness.

So that I could deny my involvement in that operation, I went to England for the duration of the operation. I stayed with Captain Bizhan Azarbaijani, who was one of the leaders of the Iranian opposition in

England. Captain Azarbaijani had arranged a meeting with the members of the opposition in England so that I could speak with them. We met in Hyde Park on the morning that the operation was to take place. I was so enthusiastic that during my speech they were excited and focused on me. At approximately 11:30, we saw a man running towards us. He shouted: "Khomeini's castle has been blown up in Nouf Le Châteaux. His government will fall!" Everyone was excited. Captain Azarbaijani knew, however, what really had happened. We were all excited. Later we discussed the next operation, in Iran. But that operation was never to succeed. We suffered greatly from empty promises.

Part Three
Downfall

A Deadly Accident

SOME OF THE ORIGINAL supporters of the revolution were not actually for an Islamic revolution at all. Their plan was to bring down the Shah with the Islamic revolution and then overthrow the government and bring in communism. Dr. Ali Noini was one of those people; Admiral Ahmad Madani was well. Admiral Madani was the first Defense Minister of Khomeini and a number of weeks after the revolution he became the governor of Khuzestan, the sixth province, and the oil-heart of Iran. Roughly a year and a half after the revolution they saw that they would not be able to overthrow Khomeini. At that point both Dr. Noini and Admiral Madani left the Shiite regime.

I met Dr. Noini at a political meeting in Paris in 1982. Over the course of that year we negotiated the future of Javan. He thought that we should work out of France, create a stronghold in Europe and from there we could go back to Iran. I believed we should work out of Israel or Lebanon.

During those days I had negotiations with Miki Don, an Israeli diplomat in Paris. These negotiations took place in secret. I thought that since the Shiite-Islamic Revolution was a direct threat to Israel it would be an ideal place to work from, however Miki Don did not take me seriously.

Dr. Noini was a very faithful friend. In the spring 1984, he bought property in the village of Shovrue, which was eighty kilometers from Paris. The property housed a small hotel called Au Feu de Bois, meaning: "In the fires of the jungle." It was a rundown hotel and took us several weeks of hard work to get the property into shape. However, it was perfect for what we needed. It had many rooms, a garden in the back and even a cellar under the garden. We used these facilities for our training.

We kept the hotel active. People came to stay with us; we had a working restaurant and bar. We had cleaning services. Our "front" was a hotel. At night and over the weekends, we trained.

I graduated and received my PhD in September of 1984. My family was proud on that very special day. On the 24th of September, one week later, I was driving in my Volkswagen from our hotel towards the main road. This road went along the ridge of a hilltop and on both sides of this narrow road there were steep declines. In those days we had a watch on the top of the hotel. They told me that they had seen an Austin car driving back and forth on the main road a number of times that day. As I was driving I saw that it was following me. The Austin drove up right next to my car and tried to push me off the road. I tried to push it back, but when I turned my wheel towards it, we went off the side of the road. My very close friend was killed instantly and another close friend, a French woman, was paralyzed. I ended up in the hospital for six months. Later we found out that the Shiite agents had sent this car, and during that period they had assassinated many people who were working against them.

I had a very difficult time supporting my family during those six months, while I was in the hospital. While I was there I realized that I had to change my political direction. I was extremely sad about my two close friends. My wife, rightfully so, was very upset with me and told me that I had to take proper care of my family and worry about my children as well. I realized that there was truth in her words and when finally, after being in the hospital for several months, I was able to move again I started to apply for jobs in various universities and organizations.

A Final Solution

DURING THESE YEARS I was working as a translator and legal advisor for Iranians in Paris. I did not have regular work and it was difficult for me to support my family on this income. After I was discharged from the hospital I got a job as a salesman in a company called Daniel Corot.

Despite these insecure situations in Paris, I found a way to leave France and move to Italy. At night I worked in discothèques as a bodyguard; by day I started studying Italian. During that time my brother called me to tell me that our father had passed away. I was shocked. I was sorry that I hadn't been able to see him before he died. I was so upset that I could not cry. My father had been very healthy and he was not old. He died from stress as a result of the current political situation. I remember that when the Shah died, I closed the door of my room and cried for two days. But when my father died, I felt helpless. I could do nothing.

My father had been illiterate when he was young. After he got a job in the national railway, he started studying at nights and eventually finished high school. His greatest dream was that at least one of his children would receive a university degree. It was some solace to me that before he passed away he had the privilege of seeing all six of his children finish university. His other wish was that all of his children would live close together. Unfortunately, as a result of the Shiite-Islamic Revolution, that was impossible.

Emotionally, I was suffering that I had so much trouble finding a job, despite having one of the top degrees in law. Because I was from Iran and in the western countries, in those days, Iran had a very negative reputation and I could not find work in academia. But that was not the only area of my life that was difficult in those days. I had just lost a very close friend and had lost six months of my life in recovery. I saw that despite all of my efforts in the political spectrum, I was not getting anywhere.

Because I was so focused on my political activities during my free time I had next to no social life. My wife constantly criticized me that I should give up my political activities. I was always away at meetings, sometimes for a week or more. She just wanted a normal life. This activity brought me a very negative reputation amongst our contemporaries. While she saw now that the Shiite-Islamic Revolution had been very bad in the end, she was afraid for my life. Opposition leaders were being assassinated left and right and Khomeini's power was growing day by day. She had good reason to fear for me. Finally, as a result of my political involvement, I was not able to properly support us. That only added pressure.

Due to all of these pressures, the political situation, my financial situation, the pressures coming from my family, having a good degree yet only having poor job options, and watching the opposition fall apart, I felt completely helpless and emotionally I was falling apart at the seams. As a result of the terrible state that I was in, the only way out I could see was suicide.

I preoccupied my time trying to decide how I wanted to go. Whether by jumping off of our apartment building, from the 25th floor, or jumping in front of a train. Did I want to poison myself? Or perhaps it would be better to electrify myself? That was where these pressures had led me. I suffered from nightmares and horrible dreams. During one of those dreams I decided that it was better to submit myself to the enemy. Being a soldier, I understood that execution from the hands of my enemy was the most honorable way to go.

In March of 1986 I went to the Shiite-Islamic Republic's embassy in Paris to hand myself over. They did not believe me that I truly wanted to surrender myself. They questioned me for hours to make sure that I really didn't mean to just blow myself up. After their interrogation they advised me that the French police would probably not allow me to fly directly to Teheran and I would be better off traveling via Germany. When I was in the embassy, they called one of the students who been an agent of the Shiite-Islamic Republic in order to identify me positively as the leader of Javan. He identified me positively, but I saw that he was gloating. His eyes were clearly saying: "See, this is where you have come to, in the end you are broken and have lost everything."

It was during the Iranian new year, around March 20th, that I wrote a letter to my wife and children. It was sad for me to contemplate ending my life. I was interrogated again in the Shiite-Islamic embassy in Frankfurt. I was asked to write a letter confessing what I had told them, and as I did in Paris; I wrote a confession there as well. I wrote that I was a broken man; that I was totally against everything that they stood for. But instead of jumping off of a building on foreign soil I wanted to be executed, as a soldier for my country, and return to join my homeland's soil. I had to negotiate with them for a ticket and a *laiseer passer* because I had no money left.

It is impossible to express this horrible feeling that I was feeling, to choose to end my life. While I was still alive, I had lost the battle. I was sure that as soon as I set foot in Teheran the officials would rush me off to be executed instantly. In the embassy they insisted that their Islam is a religion of forgiveness, and because I had come with my own two legs, I would be given a chance to live my life out in Iran as a good citizen. I believed that these were only empty words.

Approximately for the seven hours that I was flying from the Frankfurt airport to Mehrabad in Teheran I was imagining what it would feel like, during instant of execution, where would I receive the bullet? What would death taste like? I thought about the path, which brought me to here. I had mixed feelings. On the one hand I was fulfilling my dream to be a faithful soldier to my nation, on the other hand I was filled with apprehension towards death. Thinking back on that moment these 22 years later, I can identify that my feelings of pride overwhelmed my feelings of sadness for my family and my fear of death. My feelings of joy were stronger than the sadness I felt.

Despite all that, I was one hundred percent sure that I would be executed. From experience I saw that the current regime would execute a "traitor" even if he had a single paper in his file, which implied his treachery. Here, I, who had been fighting for years already, openly against them, would surely be executed. However, despite all this, I did have one gleam of hope for two reasons:

First, while I was being interrogated in the embassies I sensed in the diplomats and agents a jealousy and respect, that a man, such as myself, was giving himself over willingly. Second, one of these diplomats gave me a telephone number to use in Teheran if I came by any trouble while

I was there.

My plane landed a little after eight in the evening. You can imagine that I was not excited to be returning despite not being in Iran in over nine years. I did not run to get off the plane, as the other passengers did. I was expecting officials to come and take me away immediately. I was the last in the queue for passport control. Everyone else was jumping, excited and happy to be back home. You can imagine how my feelings were far from that. However, I was deep in contemplation, how my life was coming to an end.

I had no baggage, only a small handbag with a few books and papers. When I got to passport control they asked me a few questions about my laiseer passer and a few basic questions about when I had been in Iran last, where had I been and did I know anyone in Iran. After a few minutes he rang a buzzer by his desk to call for security. The security guards brought me to a small room. The room had a few metal chairs a simple table, a portrait of Khomeini on the wall; a simple room. We waited there for roughly half an hour.

The guards were clearly Hezbollah agents; I could tell this by their attire, head coverings and style of facial hair. Finally, more officials came into the room and began interrogating me. They went over all of the same questions that I had been asked in France and Germany. Mainly, why had I come back?

I was expecting that they would arrest me immediately, to be blindfolded and sent to execution. I expected that they would treat me horribly; I expected to be beaten and humiliated. But that could not have been farther from the truth. These Hezbollah agents were extremely respectful and they welcomed me. They were excited to ask me when I had first decided to make this decision to come back home, what were my feelings to be here, who had I spoken to about my decision to return home, how was I treated in the other embassies. A word was not spoken about my past para-military activities.

I tried to convince them from the bottom of my heart that this was for the sake of suicide. I had not come for the sake of coming home, as a regular citizen. Their reaction was only one of respect. It was not their decision to make, the courts would decide. They told me that they did not think that even the courts would hold me guilty for my political crimes since I had come out and confessed by my own free will.

These interrogations lasted until 5:30 the following morning. During that time there were three sets of intelligence agents who came to interrogate me, each was just as respectful as the previous. When they were done, they searched my person and belongings.

Finally the chief investigator asked me to call a friend to be a guarantor for me, in case they needed to get in touch with me. And then I was free to go. I was shocked. Free to go? I said: "Listen, for close to ten years I out of the country and I do not have any contact information for any of the people that I once had known. Aside from that, none of my friends and family know that I am here, they all know that I am one of the leaders of the opposition so, they would be crazy to believe such a story, even if I could contact anyone." Finally, I told them that I appreciated their treating me so well, but I had come here to hand over my life. There is no way I would involve any of my friends and family, even if they would come.

In the end the agent asked me to give him a document as collateral that I would come back to this office in another eight days to receive. I opened up my suitcase and said: "This is what I have, take your pick." He took a motorcycle license from 15 years ago, one with a picture of myself in my police uniform, and told me that I was free to go. It was ridiculous, in my mind, that I was leaving on my own two feet. I looked back over my shoulder as I left that room. I expected that one of the guards would shoot me in the back, or come at me with a knife and I was sick to my stomach with this fear.

I had been through this airport hundreds of times with tour groups and I knew it very well. I kept expecting guards to come at me from any of the many dark corners. When I left the building I thought that maybe they had set up an "accident" to happen to me. How could it be that I was leaving this airport?!

THERE IS AN OLD Jewish story, which comes to mind at this point. In Judaism, before one fulfills one of the commandments, one is required to make a blessing. For the commandments which one does not make a blessing before, there are discourses about why. For instance, before one gives charity, which is a greatly revered commandment, one does not make a blessing. Why is this so?

The reason is that it is difficult to define the act of charity, at what point is one supposed make the blessing? And what if it really is not an act of charity? It is considered a terrible thing to make a blessing in vain, since one uses God's name to make a blessing, it would be using God's name in vain to make a blessing in vain. So because of the vagueness of the commandment of giving charity, one does not make a blessing before the act.

A similar question is asked about the commandment of dying to sanctify God's name. In Judaism it is a terrible thing to end one's life willingly; life is a gift from God. Who are we to decide when it should end? However, if one is being persecuted, the highest form of death is to have given it for the sake of God; to be killed because one is God-fearing.

The question is asked, If one is in the position that he knows his life is about to be taken in the name of God, should he make a blessing beforehand? A similar answer is given. It is said that if a sword is placed upon your neck you should still not give up hope because God is always with you and might still save you.

There is a famous Jewish fable about an old Rabbi in Europe during the Crusades. It is told that a group of marauders were attacking this Rabbi's village. They were doing as many of the marauders would do in those days: burn anything that would burn, steal whatever could be stolen, and rape any woman who could be raped and kill whoever could be killed.

This Rabbi was hiding in one of the houses when a marauder smashed through the door. The Rabbi, at this point saw that it was his end. He told himself that there was no way out. At that point the question of whether to make a blessing for dying for the sake of God came to his mind. He told himself that there was NO way he would NOT be killed at this point, by this marauder. So the Rabbi stood up and as the marauder lifted his sword to strike him down, the Rabbi blessed with great fervor: "Blessed are You, oh Lord, King of the universe, that You have blessed us with Your commandments and have commanded us to die for the sanctity of Your name." The marauder was so taken aback by the fervor and holiness of this Rabbi's blessing that he decided not to kill him.

In Judaism, as I said, it is a terrible thing to make a blessing in vain. Aside from that, it is considered a nullification of the blessing if one is distracted and one talks in between the time that one makes the blessing and one performs the commandment. Or if one allows too much time to pass between when one makes the blessing and when one has a chance to fulfill it. So when the old Rabbi saw that the marauder wasn't going to kill him, he couldn't talk, for he might nullify his blessing and say the Lord's name in vain. The story is told that he ran up to the marauder making the sound "eh eh", so as not to say any words, and motioned for the marauder to kill him. This is how I felt leaving the airport on that day.

Back Home

WHEN I LEFT THE airport all I had in my pockets was 20 Marks. I went to the queues of taxis and asked one of the drivers if he could take me for the amount of 20 Marks to Khosh Street, in the middle of Teheran. I was in such a daze at that point that I did not realize that it was more than double the fare. My cousin, Ali, lived on Khosh Street. He had always looked up to me, respected me and we shared many of the same views. I thought that going to him would be the safest route, for both myself and for him.

It was a day before Now-Rooz, the Iranian new year. Ali lived in a three-story building on Khosh Street, which he owned. Aside from himself and his family living there, our uncle, Khalu-Muossa and his parents lived there as well. I figured that they would still be there since they owned the building. It was not even six in the morning when I rang the doorbell. I waited for a minute and rang again. I heard footsteps on the stairs and I heard my cousin's voice call out: "Who's there?" I answered: "It's me!" He opened the door and was in such complete and total shock that he could not control his bladder and he wet himself.

Ali cared for me very much; growing up I was a role model for him. He used to speak to everyone so highly of my accomplishments: the army, police, and my degrees in university. I loved him as well. In fact I felt closer to him and his family than to my own siblings and it was because of this relationship that I decided to go to them instead of my own siblings.

I saw that Ali was in such shock at my arrival that he could not say anything. There was no way in anyone's mind that I could be in Teheran. He looked around to see if there were any guards escorting me. I saw that he was trying to talk, but he couldn't, out of shock. I told him to calm down, that everything is okay, that he shouldn't worry and that yes, it really is me.

He introduced his wife and children to me. His parents came down to see me, and after a few minutes, Khalu-Muossa came down as well. Everyone was so happy to see me. There were sounds of laughter and joy filling the room. They all wanted to know why I had come back. I told them that it was for another discussion and would tell them later, but, yes, I was home again.

After settling down I asked Khalu-Muossa if he could take me to the cemetery to visit my father. Aside from wanting to visit my father I also wanted the opportunity to speak with my uncle, and mentor, in confidence. It would be an hour's ride there and an hour back, so that meant that I would have at least two hours with him alone. I felt that, out of everyone there, I could really only tell him the real reasons why I had returned and what I had really been up to over the past ten years since I had left Iran. He would truly understand the dangers involved and would be able to advise me intelligently.

My uncle was happy to oblige. During the ride he asked me why I had come back home, how could I be there? I asked him: "How much do you know about my life? How much do you know about what I have been up to over the past ten years?" His answer was: "I know everything, from A-Z."

Since the Shiite-Islamic Revolution in Iran, a week did not go by without an article in the press mentioning my activities. I was not looking for popularity and fame; rather, it was my burning desire to help my people, which had pushed me into the limelight. I had been interviewed numerous times on news shows about my beliefs and activities. I had become quite a celebrity. So when my uncle said that he knew everything I knew that he had been following me in the press.

I told my uncle in short what had happened to me, what my feelings had been, what had, eventually, pushed me to come on this suicide mission. He had nothing to say. He was in complete shock. He advised me that I not to talk about this with anyone. He said that it was a very different atmosphere today than when I had left Iran ten years earlier.

Khalu-Muossa was my mother's brother. My father's brother was in the Imperial Guard and a very accomplished soldier. Khalu-Muossa advised me that I speak with him about how to deal with the government. He also reminded me of the first article, which had been written about me, when I had been sixteen: "Self-made Champion." The article was about how I had become a sports champion in my high school. He reminded me that back then he told me that I had a long way to go to become a "self made man" and that now I had surpassed even that.

We discussed my father, how he died, and the cause. He told me about the service, which I was anxious to hear about. We entered the cemetery and found his grave. When we got there my uncle recited a traditional prayer, but I was too broken up to say anything. While standing at his grave all of my memories of my father passed before my eyes. When I was five how he taught me to write and read, when I was six and was in school how he asked me to write something every day. But two memories came to my mind specifically, tangible, as if they had happened just then. The first memory was when I had received a letter from my father during the final days of the Shah. This was the letter, which had been titled "Vive Shah, Vive Iran".

The second memory was when I was fifteen. I had lead an acrobatic troupe of students in the city of Khoramshahr. There was no circus in Iran in those days and I decided to establish an acrobatic troupe. We toured through different schools and performed at various events. Sometimes we got money for our performances. With this money we would buy uniforms and various supplies for our performance.

My father was very much against these performances. He would tell me that it was only getting in the way of my becoming a doctor and I was not only destroying my own life, but also the futures of my two brothers, who were performing with me, and the other children in the neighborhood.

One day my father took all of our supplies into the front yard, poured gasoline on them and set them on fire. He did this in the front yard so that not only would my brothers and I would get the message that it was over, but also, so that all of the other children in the neighborhood would see as well.

When they saw what my father was doing, they all came running, crying, "what shall we do now?" I knew that my father wanted me to cry as well, but I did not. He turned to me and asked: "What do you think now?" I turned to him and said: "I'm thinking that I have to start all over again." That is exactly what we did. My father had wanted to stop us but instead he ended up pushing us even farther. We worked harder and became even more famous.

In the car ride home we reminisced about the old days. We shared with each other our memories of my father. It was a very moving experience for me. This was my uncle, who I hadn't seen in years and this was the same uncle, who had been my role model and spiritual influence.

IN JUNE OF 2007 I flew to America for my brother's wedding. He had been going out with the same woman for 15 years and we were all extremely happy for him that he was finally tying the knot. Everyone in my extended family who could, came.

While I was there I met my cousin, Khalu-Muossa's daughter and she told me the following story. She told me that several months earlier, that April, she went to visit her father who was very ill, in a hospital in Teheran. On his deathbed he asked her: "Why have you become Christian?" She answered that they had spoken about it many times over the past 25 years since she had been baptized in the Roman Catholic Church in Rome. She explained to him that she hated the Shiite-Islamic way and didn't want to be a Shiite Muslim anymore and that was why she had converted.

At that point her father told her that their family had come from Azerbaijan when he was eight. His younger sister, my mother, was three at the time. He told my cousin that several years after the Red Revolution, their family left for Iran to escape communism. When they reached the immigration office the officials there asked them what their name was. My uncle told his daughter that their name had been Abayef, a Jewish name, and that they in fact were Jewish. The immigration officials told them that it would be difficult to be Jewish in Iran so they advised that they take on a different name.

Khalu-Muossa told his daughter that his father had been well respected in the Jewish community and in the last job, which he held before they left, he had been the Russian-Persian translator in the Iranian Consulate in Baku, the capital city of the state of Azerbaijan in the Soviet Union. Because of his status, the people of the community would call him "Dana" wise. So they chose the name "Danandeh" the Persian form of the word "Dana" and when they entered the community, no one there knew they were Jewish.

After hearing this story from my cousin, I remembered that when I had been very young I learned that my great grandmother's family had originally lived in the city of Mashhad. In 1836, there was a pogrom in the city. I knew that it was around that time that my great grandmother's family had left to move to the city of Eshghabad, the capital of Turkmenistan, as thousands of other Jews had at that time.

In the early 20th century my grandmother's family moved from there to Bukhara, where Khalu-Muossa was born and from there to Samarghand and Tashkand where my other uncles and aunts were born. Finally my grandmother's family came to Baku, where my mother was born. It was from Baku that her family returned to Iran via the Caspian Sea. I am sure that even today I have relatives living in Mashhad who are really Jewish but are not aware of it since, their ancestors converted back in the time of that pogrom of 1836.

On the ID card of my mother, before the Islamic revolution, was written "Ministry of Foreign Affairs" under place of birth. It was shameful to speak about these things back then so the topic did not come up often. One of the few gifts that the Shiite-Islamic Revolution in Iran gave many people was their identity, since it changed that protocol and from then on a person's place of birth was written on his ID card.

Surviving In The Heart Of The Furnace

MY FIRST FEW WEEKS back in Iran were extremely stressful for me. I could not sleep. I was sure that there were officials following me at every turn. I was sure that every person I would pass on the street was an agent checking up on me. Meanwhile, all of my friends and family came to visit; everyone wanted to take me out, to catch up with me. This month was the Now-Rooz, the new-year, and traditionally there were celebrations for two weeks in its honor.

Four days after I left France, on the second day of Now-Rooz I went to visit my in-laws. While I was there I called home to France to speak with my wife, their daughter. She was shocked and did not believe me that I had flown back to Iran. I put her parents on the phone and they confirmed my story. She was very upset and wouldn't speak with me immediately. After a while she called back, she was angry that I had left her. She understood, with the current political situation, that it was a suicide mission. But I told her what had happened and that if nothing happens to me over the next month or so she and the kids can move back to Iran as well to be with me.

Eight days after I had come to the country I went back to the office, which I had been interrogated in at the airport. Again, they were very respectful and welcoming. They asked me to fill out a form and provide them with some contact information. When I finished they gave me back my old motorcycle license and I was off. I was in and out in less than ten minutes.

By the end of the celebrations I had calmed down quite a bit. My anxiety levels had lessened significantly and I was able to begin searching for a job. I contacted the Iranian Bar Association. They informed me that since the government had changed, the legal system was different as well and I would have to do half a year of legal clerkship. Since that does not pay well, while I was doing my clerkship I found a job with a construction company, Kish-Iran, which had contracts in several Franco-African companies. I acted as their legal advisor and translator.

When I had been in the Islamic-Republic embassy in Frankfurt one of the investigators gave me a name and phone number to call if I had any trouble in Iran. I did not forget this gesture, however I did not need to call the number, everything seemed to be going fine.

Twenty-eight days after landing in Teheran I received a call. I was told that the man, whom I was supposed to contact if I had any trouble in Teheran, would like to meet with me. They said that I should be at a specific place at a specific time and a white Renault would pick me up.

When I got into the car I saw that there were three other people in the car with me, two in the front and another in the back. We drove around for two and a half hours and they, very respectfully, interrogated me again. They asked me about what I had done over the past ten years, why I had come back, what had led me to this decision, all the same questions that I had answered in previous interrogations.

At the end of this session they informed me that they would like to meet with me every few weeks in a similar fashion to how we had now. They also requested that I write down for them, in my own writing and my own words, everything which I had done over the past ten years.

I had expected such a request. I was not afraid to confess. That had been the whole reason why I had come back. Thinking back, it was because I was so open and honest with them, because I was willing to give up everything, that they did not give me any trouble and I was granted my life.

When I had lived in Teheran previously I had bought a beautiful apartment. Before I left I had rented it out to the East German Embassy in Teheran. On my return I informed them that I would appreciate if they could leave the apartment as soon as possible. A month and a half later I was able to move back into my old apartment. After the six months I was obligated to do of clerkship, I received, in a special ceremony from the Bar Association, my certificate. Once I was able to work as a lawyer and not only as a legal advisor, I set up an office in my apartment.

I told the intelligence agents, with whom I met regularly, that they could come meet me at my office instead of driving around for hours. They were fine with the new arrangements on the condition that I send everyone out of my office for the duration of our meetings. I was not allowed any other lawyers or even secretaries on premise. That was fine since the car rides had become quite tedious.

For the first few months the agents did their best to make sure that I had told everything. They saw that I was not holding anything back from them and after a while they ceased with their inquiries into my history. From that point on their efforts changed from information-gathering purposes to reprogramming.

The agents never tried to forcefully brainwash me; they were very open with me about their intentions. They insisted that I be completely honest with them about my views and feelings. We discussed the philosophy of the Shiite-Islamic Republic of Iran. I told them how I had not been comfortable with religion ever since I had been fifteen. I told them that I could not accept their views. I could see that they greatly appreciated my honesty.

I was known to be one of the heads of the opposition so it was difficult for the agents to believe that I had any criticism. So I told them how I was very upset with the opposition. I felt that they were not doing their job. I felt that the members of the opposition were more worried about safeguarding their millions of assets than act in opposition to the government. Even so, I could never, honestly, accept the coalition.

The agents asked me if I would mind interviewing with them for television broadcast about my views and why I had come back. I happily obliged. I understood that they wanted me to talk about how now I supported the Shiite-Islamic Republic in Iran. But they told me that I should be completely honest. So I was. I could not, on live television, announce that I now supported them. I did, however, speak out strongly against the opposition.

Several months after that interview, I was asked for more interviews. And again, I knew that they genuinely wanted me to speak in support of the current government. But again, I could not.

For the first few months back in Iran, I had a very interesting relationship with my family members. My uncles: Ali, my father's brother, and Khalu-Muossa my mother's brother, impressed upon me how important it was for me to be extremely cautious. The relationships I had with other family members oscillated between their being extremely happy and excited that I had returned, to being cautious of me because I might be dangerous to know, and then back to being friendly again.

A few weeks after I had come back to Iran my sister contacted me and asked me if I could help her friend Fereshteh, "Angela" in English. Angela was a political prisoner and had been in jail for two years out of her ten-year sentence. Her husband had been a colonel in the navy before the revolution. After the revolution he fled to Turkey. Angela had been arrested after returning home from visiting her husband. The revolutionary court accused her of treason; that her trips had not only been to see her husband but that there were more devious intentions involved.

I was happy to help my sister and her friend and because of my connections with the Iranian intelligence service I was able to arrange for her release from prison.

After the revolution a law was passed that political prisoners cannot leave the country for ten years after their release from prison. Since Angela had been a political prisoner the government would not reissue her passport, however Angela's children were in Australia and it was her dream that she be able to visit them. She knew that the government would not allow her to visit her children since she had been a political prisoner and she had only just gotten out of jail. Again I used my connections and was able to arrange for her to receive a passport.

Once Angela got out of jail she was in the need of a job. Before the revolution she had been a high school teacher. I hired her to be a secretary in my law office and we became close friends. After we had worked together for a while, our relationship began to develop into something more.

In Shiite law, one is not allowed to be seen in public with someone of the opposite gender, except if they are your spouse, sibling or parent. Twice we were stopped and brought into the police station for questioning because we had been caught late at night walking in the street. Both times I was driving her home from the office. I tried to explain that her being my secretary the outing had been completely innocent and I was only making sure that she got home safely; however, my insistence was to no avail. The police did not forgive the deed and I was forced to pay a fine.

Since I had returned to Iran, my wife had filed for divorce. However, at that point, the papers had not gone through the system yet. Angela and I could not get married because of my pending status. In order to simplify the logistics of our relationship we arranged to have a temporary marriage. In Shiite law one can set a marriage for a temporary period of time. We arranged for a six-month marriage and then we were free to be seen in public together without being harassed by the police.

It is not respectful in society to have a temporary marriage, so we did not announce to the world that we had gotten married. We only introduced ourselves as friends; the marriage was on paper only. Angela was a wonderful companion but she was also a very capable secretary. I was always thankful for the way she ran my office so competently. Her father was a military judge and she already had basic knowledge of law and was able to keep my office running, even in my absence.

TWICE A WEEK, FOR my health, I went mountain climbing at 4:30 in the morning. After several months, once I was sure that the government was not going to execute me, I started thinking about my future and my health again. I saw this mountain climbing as a minimum amount of exercise that I would need to maintain my health.

Once, while climbing on the mountain, I met an old friend, Joseph. I first met him in Paris at the university. He had been a boxing champion and I recruited him into Javan. Joseph quickly became one of the most active members of Javan so I was very surprised to see him back in Iran.

When we met on that mountain, we were very happy to see each other. I was curious, though, how he had been allowed back into the country. He told me that once I had left for Iran and had not been executed, the other members of Javan understood that the doors were open to them as well. The Intelligence had told Joseph that if anyone who had been part of Javan wanted to return as I had, they were welcome. They told him that the intelligence agency saw me as Ali.

It is part of the Shiite tradition that Ali, the son-in-law of Mohammad, the fourth Caliph and founder of Islam was revered as one of the bravest men of Islam. It is said that he killed over 700 Jews, prisoners in Medina, in a single day. Another story tells how Mohammad did not like dogs. When Mohammad first came to Medina, he asked Ali to kill all of the dogs. Ali received the reputation of being a killer of dogs and Jews. The Intelligence Service told Joseph that they saw my act of turning myself in as a great act of bravery, worthy of Ali.

Later on, as I met more and more with the Intelligence agents, I understood that not all of the agents in the Intelligence saw me as Ali. Some did not trust me. They thought that I had only turned myself in so that I would be able to poison them from the inside. Just as one had to make sure to cover one's boots at night so that a scorpion would not climb inside and poison you in the morning when you would put on your boot, so too they saw me as a scorpion, looking to poison them, now that they had let me back inside.

Why I Had Been Spared

AHMAD MUSSAVI WAS ONE of the student leaders of Hezbollah. Our paths had crossed back in Paris many times, usually with much friction; often our disagreements would turn violent. One day walking along the street in Teheran, I ran into Ahmad! I saw on his face that he was surprised to see me. He came over to me with a big smile on his face and gave me a big hug. I was bewildered. How had my worst enemy, back in Paris, become so open and friendly?

It turned out that Ahmad, after the revolution, had come back to Iran. Many members in his family were Ayatollah and well connected. Now he was running 17 different companies. He had told me that he had heard that I had come back and that he was very happy to see me again. He gave me his number and insisted that we keep in touch. I kept my promise and contacted him; eventually I became his personal legal consultant.

There were periods when I worked with him for ten hours a day; over time we became very close. I understood that aside from being involved in business that he was also an intelligence agent. He never told me outright but I understood, based upon the information that he would share with me, that he could only know such things if he were directly involved in my case.

Many times I had seen him escorted by official guards of the Shiite-Islamic Revolution. Via the connection that I had with him, I understood from what I was able to piece together, that there were intelligence agents who were not happy that I had not been executed. These agents did not believe that my intentions were as I said; given my background they did not trust me.

From what I pieced together, I understood that there were five major benefits, which the Intelligence agents received from not executing me:

First, as a well-known former member of the opposition, a man who should have been executed by law, by not killing me the government could show Amnesty International and Human Rights Watch that they were tolerant towards their opposition. This was a smart maneuver and they took advantage of it as well.

Second, by one of the opposition leaders surrendering, they were minimizing their opposition and had less fronts to manage.

Third, they believed that by treating me well they would be able to get a lot of information from me about the opposition and penetrate into their system outside of Iran.

Fourth, by treating me well, they were able to show others in the opposition that if they choose, the path is open to them as well, and thus minimizing the opposition more. In fact, many people from the opposition came back to Iran after I had.

One example is man named Mohssan Pozeshgpoor, the chairman of the Pan-Iranian party. Another is Manoochehr Kalali, the leader of the Mardom party. They both returned to Iran after I had and they too were welcomed with open arms, even though they had been very high up in their parties.

Dr. Ali Noini, with whom I had collaborated when planning the Chovrou operation, also wanted to come back. I had been told by my intelligence connection that he had become part of the Israeli Mossad and even though he was trying to return, he was still involved with them. Later, his car was blown up.

Captain Yadollah Noori had been a police officer in Iran before the revolution. We had known each other well and he ran the German chapter of Javan. I had heard that he had tried to come to Iran via the underground in order to facilitate an operation; however, he had been caught and executed.

Lieutenant Hussein Heydari was also a police officer before the revolution and he was one of our activists in Javan, but I had not known that he had also been a member of Mujahidin, a terrorist organization. He also tried to return via the underground, but he too had been caught and executed as well.

These people had been my friends. It was wonderful to hear about the ones who were doing well and it was difficult to hear about the ones who had been caught. I made a point of contacting the families of the ones who were gone and tried to console them the best way I could. They had been soldiers and died trying to fight for the good of the generations to come.

The last benefit that the regime received beyond the apparent good will gesture, was that they understood that they had destroyed my reputation in the opposition. Because I had come by my own free will and obviously collaborated with them, there was no way I could ever resume my previous ways and fight against them.

On the 20th of March 1986, until the 19th of December 1989, for three and a half years I lived in Iran. During that period I left Iran, with the passport of the Shiite-Islamic Republic, three times.

The first time was in 1988. After many months of negotiations, I was sent indirectly by the Shiite-Islamic Republic to Europe in order to assess the best way to bring down Yasser Arafat and Massoud Rajavi, the head of Mujahidin. While I was on that operation I went to Istanbul to go to the German embassy in order to ask for a visa to go to Germany. They obliged my request and I received the visa.

Back when I had been living in Paris I met, on several occasions, with a number of American intelligence agents. When I reached Istanbul, I met agents from the American diplomatic corps in Istanbul. I knew that there were Iranian supporters all over and that I had to be very careful, at the same time I didn't know anyone in the embassy and did not know with whom I could safely talk. But, because of my security situation, I could not contact them by phone.

The way in which I arranged the meeting was I went up to the passport desk and inside my passport I placed a note saying that I wanted to speak with someone in private. When I handed the clerk my passport he opened it up, saw the note, and asked me to wait for a moment. A few minutes later I was escorted to the back of the embassy and was able to meet with their agents.

After a long introduction, I told them that I wanted to do something in support for the Iranian opposition from the inside. I met with them for several hours; however, they would not believe my story to be authentic. How could a leader of the opposition turn himself in to the Islamic Republic authority, not get executed, and then come back to Europe without having turned? As much as I negotiated I could not convince them that my intentions were honest and genuine. It would appear that the Islamic Republic authorities had gotten their way and successfully cut me off from the opposition.

I had been worried that when I went to the American Embassy that I would be followed by Shiite-Islamic agents and later questioned about my visit. In order to avoid their suspicion, I brought my mother with me on my trip to Europe. I had two siblings living in the United States so I would be able to tell the suspicious Intelligence agents that I was simply asking for a visa for my mother so that she would be able to visit her children.

Why had I wanted to go to Germany? I had a client in Germany. One day, when I was in my law office in Teheran, a man entered and requested that I take the case of his friend in Germany. His friend, Vahab-Zadeh, was a multi-billionaire Iranian living in Germany. He wanted me to manage one of his properties, worth over five million dollars, back in Iran.

From Istanbul I went to Frankfurt to have Mr. Vahab-Zadeh sign a power of attorney so that I could arrange for his case in the national court in Teheran. When I was in Frankfurt I contacted the US Embassy there as well. I came to the passport desk, as I had in Istanbul, with a note in my passport. Again I met with agents but they would not believe my story either. They, as had the agents back in Istanbul, thought that I was doing this so that they would give my mother a visa. I told them that they could do whatever they wanted to in regard to my mother. I had come in order to talk with them and needed a cover. But they would not believe me. I only wanted to do something positive for my nation. They knew the real opposition and I wanted to be useful for the real opposition and negotiate towards this goal.

Once I knew that I was going to be in Germany, I called my wife and arranged for her and our children to come to Frankfurt so that we would be able to see each other. I had not seen them for over two years and it was very moving for everyone, especially for my children. My son had grown to be three centimeters taller than myself!

For years and years, when I was still in Paris with my family, I had promised my son that I would take him to Disneyland. As each year went by, and my son grew older I saw my chances to take him slipping through my fingers. Seeing them again, seeing how my son had grown, I remembered that conversation and was sorry that I could not be a good father and fill that basic wish of my son. I had sacrificed my personal life for an ideal that I believed in, but I saw that I hadn't been a good soldier either.

It was a great feeling to see my children after so long. They were upset that I had left them and I tried to explain to them how life can be complicated and how I had to go to Iran. I did my best not to mention the tensions, which had been between their mother and myself. Those tensions had been one of the stronger elements of why I had been pushed to go.

In the end of this trip to Germany, when I returned to Iran, the people who had sent me to Europe to assess the best way to bring down Arafat and Rajavi were not satisfied with the results of my report. I imagined that this mission, in fact, had been arranged so that they could check the validity of one of the pieces of information, which I had supplied them with about my past.

An Endless Challenge

ON THE SIXTH OF January 1979, at Guadeloupe, by the invitation of Valery Giscard d'Estaing, the leaders of the four great Western Powers assembled to discuss the crisis in Iran. On that day, Jimmy Carter, Helmut Schmidt, James Callaghan and the French president, Giscard d'Estaing, sealed the fate of Iran. Those four men destroyed Iran.

In 1982, I was very close with the Shah's niece, Azadeh. In those days we had worked many hours a day together planning various operations.

After Tabarzin and Nouf Le Châteaux I wanted to execute an even bigger operation. I wanted to arrange an operation that would show the world how wrong they had been.

Several key members of Javan had come up with the idea of capturing the nuclear power plant in Strasburg, on the French-German border and then threaten that if our demands were not met we would blow it up. What we wanted to arrange was for the four leaders who had been at that summit, Giscard d'Estaing, Carter, Schmidt and Callaghan, to come for a live interview to be broadcasted around the world. What had been their motivation to destroy a nation? We wanted to show our nation that these people did the worst thing they could have for our nation. We weren't against the western civilization; but we wanted to show our people how wrong they had been.

If those four leaders would not come for this interview we would blow up the nuclear power plant. We calculated that this could be potentially damaging to 200 million people. We worked very hard to minimize the potential direct casualties, direct loss of human lives; however, we believed that authorities would not allow for this to happen. Despite that, we felt that we were fighting for the basic human right – freedom of choice – and we planned to hand ourselves over for prosecution after we succeeded with our interview.

We had consulted with Yugoslavian, Russian and French experts on how to technically enter into the facility, the technicalities of exploding the plant and how to bypass the security. We had everything ready, except for the money that we would need to fund this operation.

We needed half a million dollars in order to pull of the operation. I asked Azadeh to arrange a private meeting with her mother, Princess Ashraf. Princess Ashraf was known as a very strong, passionate woman. The opposition called her "Iron Woman." Her father, Reza Shah, was known for his strength as well. Princess Ashraf was very fond of me and was happy to meet with me. I asked her: "Prove to me that you are the Iron Woman which, they say you are, your father's daughter. If you cannot I will never bother you again."

When Princess Ashraf heard my plan she began to shake. She looked around the room with suspicion, fearful that someone might be listening. She told me that she could not help me. Until this day I have never seen her again, despite many messages she has sent to me.

I assumed that when the Iranian Intelligence Agency allowed me to go to Istanbul and then to Germany for my business, what they were really interested in was to feel out the connections, which I had used to plan the Strasburg operation. They wanted to see if I could get in touch with my connections for the benefit of the Republic. When I returned with my report I do not think that they were happy with it since they did not follow up with my assessment.

Once I found myself in Iran again and once I felt secure with my new life there, I got back in touch with some of my old friends. I started thinking about gathering together these friends and plant the seeds of a true opposition from within the country. I accidentally found one friend, Shahrokh. We discussed establishing an underground system of resistance.

For a long time we were discussing this plan. Shahrokh was a custom's officer. Our friendship went back to years before the rise of the Republic. He had followed my life back in Europe and I trusted him. After many discussions we understood that we would have to gather people together to build this opposition.

We arranged small intimate parties, gathering people from every aspect of our lives. I met many people as a lawyer, and I met many students as a teacher. Shahrokh had many friends and family as well. At these parties we discussed the political situation, our ideologies, our visions. It was exciting for them to find out about my background and for me to hear fresh ideas.

Shahrokh had a friend, Soroushian, a travel agent. We arranged a weekend where we rented a bus and went away as a group to the beach. It was exciting for the group to sing national hymns and have more serious discussions. We felt safer on these busses than at our parties.

These trips were family trips. Men, women and children came along. For two whole days we gathered together and exchanged ideas. Angela, as always, was a faithful secretary and cooperator.

We assumed that it was safe to gather together since I was still meeting with the intelligence agents every few weeks. I told them that we arranged family get-togethers. If I failed to mention that what we were discussing was against the law and considered treason, well I can't be expected to remember everything.

During these trips I told about the history of Iranian nationalism. How our culture had been destroyed 14 centuries ago. How our main religion is not Shiite; rather, Shiite had been the result of the Iranian nationalism after the Arab invasion in 638. The people who had survived the invasion created their own sect of Islam. They had hoped that if they create a separate sect of Islam that they would be able to break free of Islam altogether. This sect was called Shiite Islam. I explained about the value of democracy and why it would be beneficial to achieve it.

One story in particular, which I told, touched the heart of many people. It was retold many times, and became a symbol of our nationalism. This story was the story of a man whose story had been told by so many people that he had different names in the different countries in which his story is told. His name was Piruz, Vakhshuran, Maya, Naja and many other names as well. He had one other name, which every Muslim knows. The name, which Muhammad, Prophet of Islam, gave him, was Salman Farsi.

Just as every state in the US has a governor, in the seventh century Iran also had governors for each of its provinces, called the Satrap. The people of their province chose these Satraps. They chose them based upon the personal leadership skills, military skills and wisdom of the candidate. Every seven years in a special assembly, the Mahestan, the Satraps chose one to be the King of Kings over all of the provinces. This was the political system of the Sassanid Dynasty. It was set up in the third century and was brought down with the Shiite-Islamic invasion. Maya was the son of the Satrap of the Pars province in which was the state Persepolis.

Six to seven decades before the Arab invasion there was a new prophet in Iran under the name of Mazdak. He abused this democratic system to create a divide in Zoroastrianism and establish a new branch. This new branch had many aspects of what is today known as socialist-communism, the same ideologies which Marx and Lenin applied in the 20th century.

It was during this period in time that there was great freedom of religion and choice in Iran. It is well known that the Yeshivot, Jewish study houses, called "Sura" and "Pompadita" thrived during this period. In each yeshiva there were an excess of ten thousand students. Throughout history there has never been a rival to such numbers in any yeshiva as there had been in those yeshivot in Iran.

In the book of Matthew, three Magi, Zoroastrian leaders, came to Bethlehem to visit the newborn Jesus. In the book of Acts the Iranian presence is clear as well. It is also known that the first Christian missionaries to China were Iranian. To this day those churches are called "Persian temples." We can see that for all faiths, in those days, there was freedom to practice openly in Iran.

Because of the conflict between the Zoroastrian leaders and Mazdak, the kingship stopped what was going on. Maya grew angry and became the leader of the opposition and left the country. When Maya left Iran he was approximately 28 years of age. Maya was physically a superman and he was wise beyond his years.

Maya went from Iran to Damascus, which in those days was predominately Christian. In Damascus he studied to become a minister. While he had become a minister of a church, his motivation had never changed. He wanted to influence the representatives of the Roman Empire in Damascus to attack Iran and usurp the system, which had thrown him out for being a follower of Mazdak. Iran and Rome, in those days, had a very tense relationship, much like the US and the Soviet Union during the cold war.

Because he did not receive a positive answer from Rome, he realized that he would have to try from another angle. From Damascus, Maya moved to Jerusalem. There he converted, married a Jewish woman and became a gabbi, an assistant to the Rabbi. Maya became a very well-known member of the Jewish community of Jerusalem. From there he tried to influence the Jewish faction of Rome with hope that he would be able to convince that community that it was imperative to attack Iran.

After two decades when Maya saw that he was not getting anywhere with the Jewish community he left that community as well and went to what is now Saudi Arabia. In those days the area of land, which today is Saudi Arabia, consisted of three wildernesses: Najad, Nfood, and Rabolkhali. Maya had heard that in those areas there was a strong religious awakening and there were many prophets, each one attempting to father his own religion.

It was in the area of Najad in a city called Mecca that Maya met a man named Muhammad the son of Abdullah. It was there that Muhammad gave Maya the name of Salman Farsi.

During the seventh century the city of Mecca was the center of Arabian Idols. In that culture there were 365 gods, each god representing one day of the year. Muhammad's father was a cleric for the biggest idol, Allah. The name Abdullah means the servant of Allah. Muhammad's new religion stated that it was that God that was the only true God.

Until he met Maya, though, he had not been very successful in convincing others of his faith. In those first ten years, in fact, he had only managed to convince ten people to follow him. Among them was his wife Khadijeh, who was fifteen years his elder and a successful merchant, and his nephew Ali. Maya found Muhammad and saw in him much potential and decided to use him for his own purposes.

Maya convinced Muhammad that he needed to try from another angle and they left Mecca for the city of Medina. In Medina Maya told Muhammad to kill all of the Jews and take their money so that he would have a strong financial base to begin with. With Maya's diverse ideological background he was able to help Muhammad develop his own ideology.

Maya tried to convince his "puppet" to insert into his faith the elements of the Judeo-Christian God. In Arabia, during that time, the people were not familiar with the concept of a monotheistic God. Maya taught Muhammad to use a symbol, which they understood as a God, Allah, to impress the concepts of a Judeo-Christian God, and it was through that Godhead that he could bring in these monotheistic concepts.

After collecting funds, via the murdering of all of the Jews in Medina, Muhammad was able to hire an army. Muhammad fought three battles with his army; in Badr, Ohod and Khandagh. After he met Maya, Muhammad became very charismatic and he convinced his warriors that if they die, they would get paradise in the next world, and if they lived he promised them that they would get the women and possessions of the people they killed. It became a win-win situation for his warriors and they fought bravely because they had nothing to lose.

It was reported in many historical sources that Maya had brilliant tactical abilities and many times he saved Mohammad's army during battle. For instance, Maya taught Mohammad how to use catapults. Or, during the Khandagh war Mohammad's army was situated in Medina. The army of Mecca was ten times Mohammad's army's size and they didn't have much of a chance against it. Maya suggested that they dig ditches around the city of Medina and fill them with water.

When the army of Mecca got to Medina they could not reach the city and archers from Mohammad's army picked off soldiers from the army of Mecca. After several weeks, when the army of Mecca decided to give up and go home, Maya suggested that Mohammad send his army after them and attack them from behind. It was in this fashion that Mohammad overcame the army of Mecca.

During the many journeys, which my friends and I went on, I told them about different historical events from our heritage. I told them about the successors of Mohammad: Abu-Bakr, who was the Caliph for two years and after him Omar. It was under his reign that in July of 638 that the Arab-Muslim invasion of Iran took place. Consequently, the chief of staff of Omar's army was Maya. Maya had two commanders under him: Ebn-Vaghass and Khaled-Ebn-Valid.

The Islamic army was supported by the Roman Empire. The Arabian warriors were the guerrilla fighters who came before the Roman army in the conquest. Finally Maya was able to convince the Romans that it would be worth their while to support his invasion of Iran. Once Maya had been so successful in conquering the Arabian Peninsula, Rome saw that these warriors were of a different breed: strong, brave and fearless. Finally, Maya was able to rally Rome's support.

Arab historians tend to ignore Maya's role in this invasion. They do not want to admit that a Persian was responsible for the downfall of Iran. There are, however, many other sources which support Maya's role as the chief of staff of Omar's army in the invasion of Iran.

Iran had two capital cities, one for the winter months: Persipolis, with a castle called Passargad. The other capital, for the summer months was called Tissfun. Its castle was known as Kakh-e-Sephid or in English, "White House." Maya conquered Tissfun, massacred everyone who lived there, and for the last two years of his life he was the governor of Tissfun. He finally reached the position, which he had coveted and sought after all of his life.

During these journeys I tried to expose my friends to the idea that the foundations of our sufferings were a direct result of the Shiite-Islamic invasion. I drew the parallel between the current Shiite-Islamic revolution and the previous one in 638. I shared with them our mutual history from pre-Islamic time, from the ethical philosophies of King Cyrus to the greatness of King Akhashverosh. I told them of Daniel, the finance minister of King Darioush and how there had been great religious tolerance in Iran, once upon a time.

From time to time friends would ask me for the sources of my ideas. The books that I relied upon were from the first two centuries after the Islamic invasion of Iran in 638. These books are written in Arabic and, because of their revealing content, have not been translated as of yet. As a result, these books are usually overlooked in academic studies. I would lend these books to my friends and had many wonderful discussions as a result.

Many nights, after work, I was invited out to many people's houses and communities. I would talk about many positive things; how our future can be better. I wanted to give hope to my nation, my people and help them persevere during this very difficult time.

FIRE WAS THE FIRST invention of man. As many discoveries, the first time it was discovered was quite by accident. It was revolutionary and was to change the course of humanity forever. It was fire that allowed man to cook his food, defend himself against wild animals, and it was fire that allowed further invention. But after that first flame went out man had to discover how to re-create this miracle. It probably took years, perhaps more, and when man finally created fire again his holiest men, the clergy, guarded it. Since that time fire has been a central theme of all religions, whether as sacrifices in temples, or expressed in the centrality of candles in religion.

Iran, being the father of civilization and Zoroastrianism, originally its official religion, holds fire in the highest regard. Fire is celebrated especially on the Wednesday before the Now Rooz.

One night, after work, it was the last Wednesday before the Now Rooz. There was a tradition that teenagers and children would go around with metal bowls banging. These kids would go from door to door and people would give them a small gift or candy. This tradition, Chaharshabeh-Soori, has been celebrated by children for many thousands of years. On that evening I was in my office along with Angela and another colleague of mine, Massoud Ghodss.

Massoud and I had been close friends for over fifteen years, from even before the Shiite-Islamic Revolution. He had been a technical officer in the Iranian national air force before the revolution. While he had cooperated with the revolution at the time, now he was against the Shiite-Islamic Republic and was very active amongst our new group of revolutionaries.

This had been during the Iran-Iraq war. Because of the situation the government did not allow us to use power. Because of this, all of the lights were out in my office and the curtains were drawn. I remember that the three of us were sitting in my office around a small candle and we were sharing a bottle of Persian wine.

I was talking to them about Tozih-ol-Massael, the most popular book written by Ayatollah Khomeini. Every Ayatollah before he graduates must write a Ressaleh, a thesis. The Ressaleh of Khomeini was called Tozih-ol-Massael, and on that evening I was discussing this book with Angela and Massoud. I tried to express to them two points from this four hundred and fifty page book. I asked them: "How can a man who can make these statements be a good spiritual leader?" I would like to share with you, my readers, these two points and I ask you for your judgment.

I have thousands of similar ideas I could share with you.

Ayatollah Khomeini explained in his book that a person, man or woman, after he relieves himself should make sure to clean his bottom properly. After he washes himself he should insert his index finger, up to his first knuckle, into his rear in order make sure that he is properly clean. Then he must clean himself again. Can a man who believes such truly be a healthy and well-balanced human?

The other idea, which I presented of what Khomeini proposed was the following question: A man is sleeping on the second floor of a building. If an earthquake takes place and the man who is sleeping on the second floor falls to the first floor onto the bed where his aunt, mother-in-law, sister-in-law or other family member is sleeping, and he then has intercourse with that family member, and a child comes out of this relationship, What is the legal status of this child? What sort of sick individual thinks of such a horrible circumstance?

We were discussing these horrible issues and Angela and Massoud were completely involved in with our discussion. I showed them the passages in the book. While we were involved in our discourse, we heard a group of approximately 15 to 20 people singing traditional Persian carols outside our front door, and banging spoons against metal bowls. I was extremely excited since this is the traditional way in which people celebrate Chaharshabeh-Soori. Since it was part of our pre-Islamic heritage, I thought that these people were nationalists as myself.

Overwhelmed with a great sense of comradeship I opened up the window and began to sing along with them, however I did not sing the words that they sung. Instead I sang, in a very loud voice, in the same tune as their song: "Death to Khomeini." I sang this three times. Once they heard what I was singing, there was complete silence. After a few moments they turned on us and began trying to break down the front door.

You may ask: Why had I done such a thing? I had been fighting and debating for the sake of the Iranian purity and nationalism my entire life. To hear these people singing, out in public, their carols awoke in me strong overwhelming pro-Nationalist and anti-Islamic sentiment. Inside me these feelings were connected and I was sure that there was no way that these people could be pro-Khomeini.

In the Shiite-Islamic Republic of Iran, if a person writes anti-Islamic sentiments on a small piece of paper, he can be punished with death and if a person were to call out into a public street those same sentiments, all the more so. When Angela and Massoud heard what I was saying, they broke down with fright. Angela lost consciousness and could not contain her fear, and Massoud turned absolutely white. I realized, at that point, how incredibly irresponsible my actions had been and quickly closed the window and blew out the candle.

The concierge of the building was a sweet older man named Baba-Ali. He and I had a close relationship and always had kind words for each other. Baba-Ali came to the front door, but he refused to open it up for the mob. He called to them through the door and said that this is a professional place of work, there are no residential flats here and no one, beside himself, is in the building.

The mob was not satisfied with his answer and went in search of the police. Shortly after, they returned with several officers. Baba-Ali allowed for them to come in and we heard him repeat his previous response. Several long minutes later we heard a knock at the door of our office. We, of course, were silent and the officers eventually left.

We stayed in my office the entire night. Our nerves were so on edge that every sound we heard made us jump. Angela and Massoud were fearful that the mob would return, and I was upset with myself for putting them in this position. Finally the morning came and we were able to leave. We left separately.

As I was leaving Baba-Ali pulled me aside. He told me that he too had heard my calling. He told me, as a father would a son he cared for, that there is a need for young intelligent lawyers in Iran and that I should take care of myself.

Rotten To The Core

IN JUNE OF 1986, Ahmad Moussavi, the wealthy client I had mentioned before who had ties with Hezbollah, handed me a check for 175 million Toman. One dollar was worth then, 100 Iranian Toman, so that was worth roughly 1.75 million dollars. This check had been made out to him by a woman named Robabeh Aminian, but the check had not cleared. Moussavi asked that I pursue this woman in court in order to claim the money he was rightfully owed.

I discovered that Robabeh had private bodyguards who were connected with the Iraqi community living in Iran. This Iraqi community was in competition with the current Iranian leadership. This was an extremely exciting case for me. It brought me a lot of fame and eventually led to the development of one of the most famous court cases in Iran. As this case developed I realized that Moussavi was utilizing my legal prowess, while at the same time he was using his connections, working behind the scene, to attack Robabeh as well.

I discovered that this woman was supported by Zahra Rahnavard, the wife of the Prime Minister, Hussein Moussavian. She was also supported by Hadi Ghaffari, a member of the Parliament and the head of the military faction of the Parliament. She was also close with the family of Ayatollah Mehdi Karrubi, the head of the Parliament.

I was able to attain a special warrant from the court to capture Robabeh and detain her. It was very difficult to get a hold of her because powerful connections and her private bodyguards. I convinced the judge that if we do not detain her, she could leave the country owing hundreds of millions of dollars and that that is unacceptable. We received the warrant for her arrest.

Because of Moussavi's connections I was able to arrange to be in charge of the operation and I was supported by the police and Moussavi's personal bodyguards. It was exciting for me to be back involved again with an operation of this sort. We broke into her home at 4:30 in the morning and brought her directly to court where the judge ordered for her detention until her trial.

Once word got out to the mass media of her detention I was approached by everyone else who had been owed money by Robabeh. Before the case was out, I was heading a class-action suit representing 1,278 clients against Robabeh for over $370 million.

One of my clients was a company by the name of Owj LTD. This client consisted of over 1,200 officers of the Iranian marine corps and air force. The seven officers who were the top executives of the company researched my background and were very excited to be in contact with me. Not only because of my legal abilities, but also because they discovered that I had had military experience. They were also excited when they became aware of my political leanings.

These officers requested to meet with me in private. They told me that they would support me in any way I may need support, to get their money from Robabeh. This was during the Iran-Iraq war and they told me that, as a last resort, they were even willing to bomb Jamaran, where Khomeini was staying, on their way to bomb Baghdad.

A day before, one of the open hearings of the case that was to take place in criminal court number 137, I met with the judge of the court,

Moussa Nowroozi. I had found out then that Robabeh, as I mentioned before, was supported by the wife of the Prime Minister, a member of the Parliament who was the head of the military faction of the Parliament and close with the head of the Parliament himself. I spoke with the judge and told him of my findings.

Judge Nowroozi told me to leave it alone. He told me that I was young, I didn't understand how these things worked, and if I wanted to remain a lawyer, and remain alive, I would find a way to convict Robabeh of the charges, without trying to pull down the whole government along with her.

The next day, in front of the mass media, in front of many of my 1278 clients and the people of the court, I came out with my allegations against these powerful people. The case was immediately put on hold, in order to investigate these charges. However, the damage was done.

In December of 1989, two days after this public court assessment, I left Iran to go to a conference in London. I had been invited by the international bar association, since the conference was about the policy of the European currency and its effect on the Middle Eastern and Persian Gulf currencies.

I was in London for eight days and while there I received many calls from Angela. She told me that I should not come back to Iran. She said that I had received many anonymous death-threats and she was worried for my life. I did not think that it was so bad; however, when I returned I saw that it was serious. I could not contact my friends in the intelligence agency to see whether I should take these threats seriously or not. So eight days after I came back from London, on December 19, 1989, I left Iran for the last time for Bombay. I stayed in Bombay for two weeks, where Angela met me, and on January 4, 1990, we arrived in Australia.

I left Iran under the guise of business. I had a client in Bombay, a petroleum company, and I arranged to meet with them there. Once I was out of the country, I was safe, and I was able to make further arrangements.

The event that took place, which finally pushed me to leave the country, happened during the eight days after I came back from London. A man named Ahmad Amin came to visit me. He told me that the government had unofficially decided to kill me. He spat on the floor of my office and told me that I must leave Iran before that spit has a chance to dry, otherwise I will be killed.

Who was Ahmad Amin? During the time that I was studying for the

Iranian bar exam, for the second time, after I had first come back to Iran, I placed an advertisement in the paper offering to teach French and the French culture. One day, I received a call from Ahmad Amin, asking that I teach him, his wife, and his two children. The only problem was that the only time he had available was from four to six in the morning and that I had to come to him.

Ahmad told me that since he wanted me to come to his house, which was difficult to get to, and since the hour was so irregular, he was willing to pay me whatever price I requested. In those days, I normally charged 50 Toman for an hour of tutoring and I requested payment for 20 lessons in advance. I asked for double what I normally charged, expecting to receive 75 percent of my asking price. However without flinching, he accepted and wrote out a check to me for 100 lessons in advance: 100,000 Toman. I was shocked, but since my financial situation was so difficult at that time, I was happy to take them on.

Ahmad and his family were a very nice. I thought that he might be a clergyman but there were no outward signs confirming my suspicion. He was excited when he found out about my education and he was impressed with my skills in the French language, along with my abilities to teach.

We became very close. He was very impressed with my work ethic and me in general. He asked me if I would be interested in receiving an official government position. He felt that the government was wasting a potential asset by not utilizing my skills. He consulted, on my behalf, with one of his friends in the government and several days later he offered me a position as governor of the province of Boyr-Ahmad-e Bakhtiary, a relatively small province. When he offered me this position he asked me if this province was too small for me.

I was touched by the very suggestion that I should be working in an official position. While I was opposed to the current government I still had a strong desire to help my countrymen. When he first suggested that I take on this role, I wasn't sure. However, I felt that through this capacity I would be able to help my people, even if I would be a part of the terrible machine, which I so opposed. When he offered me the governorship of Boyr-Ahmad, I asked him if I could take a few days to think it over. On our next meeting I told him that I would accept.

Following this proposal, Ahmad arranged that I meet with the Minister of Interior Affairs, Ali Akbar Mohtashami. Mohtashami was a very powerful clergyman and in the 1980s he had been the founder of Hezbollah in Lebanon. In his current role as Minister of Interior, he was an international activist of Shiite Islam.

I arrived along with Ahmad to Mohtashami's office. As soon as we sat down, in his large, top floor, corner office the first question I was asked was whether I prayed five times a day. I froze; I did not know what to say. Ahmad knew that I was not religious. I imagine that Mohtashami knew as well. I could not lie; on the other hand I understood at that point that the job's fate hinged upon this point. I stumbled over the most diplomatic answer I could come up with on the spot, "I believe prayer is a very positive thing..." But the conversation ended there. Mohtashami said: "Thank you very much, we will consider Mr. Amin's proposal." I knew that I would never work for this government.

When we left the office Ahmad tried to console me: "What an idiot!" he exclaimed. "How could they squander such an opportunity?!" But we both knew that they were not interested in my credentials, the only thing that was of importance was my "faith."

Ahmad did not give up hope, though. He offered me a position as the legal advisor of the President of the Republic, Hojjatoislam Rafssanjani. However I did not receive that job as well, over the same prejudice. I must say that Ahmad's faith in me was touching.

One day Ahmad came to me with a file. He told me that this was an official bulletin of the government only meant for its top members. I did not ask him how he got this file. He gave it to me and told me that he thought I should know what is really going on in the country. This file contained information that would not make it to the mass media, only certain members of the government had access to this type of information. He told me that it is very important hat I keep it under lock-and-key when I am not reading it and insisted that I return these papers to him by a certain time.

I was afraid that this was an attempt, by the Intelligence, to trap me, to test me and to see how faithful I am. I thought that Ahmad was collaborating with the intelligence agents to see where my fidelity laid. At my next meeting with the intelligence agents, I told them about the file I received and gave them a copy. They were very excited that I came to them with this information and were very pleased with me. I assumed that I had guessed right, based upon their reactions.

It was around that time that I had been teaching Ahmad and his family for five to six months. He told me that he was leaving for France and we finished our lessons together. Until this day I do not know if he ever actually went to France. Three years after he had said goodbye, he showed up in my office. He had only been there once before. I had just come back from my trip to London and had received several death-threats on my return. It was Ahmad who finally convinced me that I should leave Iran.

When he entered my office he told me what had happened to him. He scolded me, telling me that he had just finished a two-year jail sentence because of a mistake I had made. He said that it was for good reason that he had wanted me to keep the file that he had given me under lock-and-key. He said that someone had broken into my office and had taken it. As a result, he had been sent to jail.

Ironically, it would seem that it was the intelligence agents who saved my life on that day. They had not told Ahmad how they had gotten hold of the file, which he had given me. If he had known, I am not sure that he would have come to my office on that day. When he came in, after telling me where he had been, he told me that the threats were real. Some people in the government wanted my head and I had to leave the country as soon as possible, leaving everything behind.

At that time I was the representative for an Indian petroleum company based in Bombay. I visited that company on a regular basis. After Ahmad's visit, I arranged to go to Bombay on business and had Angela come several days later. From Bombay we went to Australia. As I had promised Angela, I had helped her to go and see her children again. They were happy to see us and welcomed us with open arms. There, we started a new life together in Melbourne.

Part Four
Redemption

Australia

FOR THE FIRST FEW days in Australia, after getting acquainted with Angela's children and son-in-law, I attempted to communicate with some of my colleagues in Europe and the US in order to find out what was happening in the opposition. I was convinced that this was it and that I had no chance to return to Iran. After two weeks, I went to Canberra and spoke with Aalamol-hoda, the right-hand-man of the Shiite-Islamic Ambassador in Australia.

I wanted to assess my position for one last time. How dangerous it would be for me to return? He was very nice, and welcoming. After speaking with him for over two and a half hours he told me that he would get in touch with me. After several weeks I did not receive an answer from Aalamol-hoda and I tried to contact him again.

Once I saw that I could not get any straight answer from him I understood that there was no chance for my return. I applied for political refugee status in Australia, this was my second time requesting this status, and three and a half years later I was granted the status. Today, writing this, sitting in my office in Jerusalem, I am a political refugee for a third time, but I am getting ahead of myself, and I'll get to that later.

I had been officially divorced, by that time, for two years. But I saw that as only a formality. I did not want to cause further damage to my family and the entire time away I sent my ex-wife and children whatever financial aid I could and many presents. I understood that the divorce, officiated by the French legal system, had happened as a result of my being in Iran, so when I got to Australia I contacted my family and asked if they would join me there. I was still involved, at that time, with Angela, however we both considered it as a social arrangement; my original family came first. However, they preferred to remain in France.

After I settled into Australia I began a three-month English language course at TAFE College. I wanted to begin working as a lawyer as soon as possible so I contacted the Australia Bar Association to find out what the requirements for acceptance were. They told me that before taking the Bar examination there is a requirement to attend 10 University courses on various topics relating to Australia law. I discovered, to my dismay, that these courses would cost $18,000. I was not sure what to do; I needed to pass the Bar in order to work as a lawyer, however I had just left all of my assets behind in Teheran.

One of my Iranian friends told me that one could earn quite decently, in Melbourne, as a taxi driver. So I got the taxi-driver's license, so that I could save up the money I would need to take the courses, so that I would be allowed to register to take the bar exam.

While I was studying in the course, "English for Professionals" at T.A.F.E., one day the teacher of the course asked a question about the Koran. There were several Muslims in the class with me, myself included. One of them, a Jordanian, was dressed in traditional garb and had a big black beard, as is customary of the devotee. He spoke up and gave an answer to the teacher's question.

Listening to his answer I understood that he was answering with propaganda and it was completely misrepresenting the topic. Hearing this, I spoke up as well and told the class where I thought where he was mistaken. The rest of the class was interested in the differences. How could two Muslims have such a diverse understanding of their book, which is the foundation of their religion? My classmate became angry that I was contradicting him. The atmosphere of the classroom usually was very open, welcoming, non-confrontational, however, that quickly changed.

Angrily, my classmate began to yell insults towards me; how could I say such things about Islam? Personally, I thought that I had been quite fair in my presentation. Feeling threatened, I yelled similar insults back, but you can imagine that that did not help the situation. My teacher, who had a gentle soul and was not used to these confrontations, implored us that we sit, calm down and stop fighting. But the argument escalated to the point where my opponent physically attacked him.

With my police and military background, being attacked was no big deal for me. I countered his attack, grabbed him by his shoulders and sat him down. I exclaimed to the class: "This is what terrorist Islam is! If you oppose them, they attack you!" Thinking back now, I am ashamed of my response. I turned to the man who had attacked me and declared angrily: "I will take you and flush you down the toilet, leave now and don't come back!"

He got up and left with several other students, who had supported him, however before he left he threatened: "If I ever find you again, I will kill you!" I was not too worried; this was not the first time that my life had been threatened. Still, I was always aware, when walking down the street that some unexpected passerby might attack me.

This event brought me a negative reputation with the Iranian community of Melbourne. I was very involved with that community, however I did not understand them. They were in Australia as political refugees, as I was, trying to escape the current Shiite regime. Even so, they still held onto their Shiite faith. How could this be?

Being involved with the community I had an interesting relationship with its leader, H. Khanbashi. We spoke at length many times. I saw that he felt conflicted by my ideas. On the one hand, he was drawn to what I had to say, on the other, though, he was afraid of the conclusions which had to be drawn from them.

One day Khanbashi invited me to come and meet with him. He wanted me to come with him to a religious meeting that he had heard about. He told me that they preach peaceful ideas and he thought that I would like to come. When we arrived at the place of meeting I saw that they were in the traditional white garb that people of the Zoroastrian faith wear, as a symbol of purity, during their liturgical services.

I was excited by this idea; there are many beautiful ideas in the Zoroastrian religion and truly, the leader of the group, Ghandchi, preached peaceful ideas. However, at the end of his sermon the group began swaying and chanting: "Ali, Ali, Ali" and I understood then that this was only another Shiite sect, one of the 178 sects of Shiite Islam. I became very angry. Ali, the father of Shiite Islam, was a violent man who massacred thousands of Jews, Christians and Zoroastrians. How could these people preach peaceful ideas in his name?!

I turned to Khanbashi and asked that we leave at once. He asked that we remain to the end. I was very uncomfortable and needed all of my self-control to contain my frustration with them. But I remained. At the end of the service I got up to leave and asked Khanbashi to come as well; however, Ghandchi turned to me. He said that he saw that I had something to say. I told him that it was okay and I preferred to keep my thoughts to myself. I did not want to cause another ruckus. But Ghandchi insisted. So I told him that I was extremely angry with him for deceiving these people who had come to him for messages of peace.

He replied that he did not know what I was talking about and wanted me to elaborate. He was forceful, but very friendly and understanding, so I did. I explained to the group how primitive tribes conquered Iran, forcefully, and how Ali, one of their leaders, was a murderer. The service we had attended lasted for an hour and a half. I spoke afterwards with them for two and a half hours. During this discussion I asked them the following question: "You consider yourselves followers of the Persian culture, do you not?" They all answered in the affirmative. I continued, "I disagree." I had had this conversation many times before, with many people. I explained how after the Islamic invasion the conquerors would not allow the people of Iran to speak in the language of their mother tongue. Because the invaders could not speak the local language, and wanted to be able to communicate, for the first two hundred years anyone who would speak Persian would have his or her tongue cut out. It was only 83 years after the Islamic invasion of Iran, between 721-725, that Sibovich, a Persian, wrote a comprehensive study, for the first time, of the grammar of the Arab language so that the people of Iran would be able to keep their tongues.

I focused on the well-known, 40 protocols of Omar. These protocols were set out dictating how the people conquering should treat the people they conquer. These were the same protocols used when Jerusalem was conquered. Here are several examples of these laws set out: On rainy days non-Muslims may not go outside. What is the reason for this? Non-Muslims are spiritually unclean and rainy weather makes this un-cleanliness more easily transferable.

Any non-Muslim who wants to build a house must build it one meter shorter than Muslim houses so that the un-cleanliness of their house will not fall onto the clean houses of their Muslim neighbors.

Every non-Muslim must leave his door always open so that any Muslim walking by may enter as he pleases. The owner of the house has an obligation to be hospitable.

Non-Muslims do not have the right to ride a horse or wear a sword even though the Iranians were the best horse-riders and sword-makers of that time.

If a Muslim is walking in one direction without any form of travel and coming opposite him is a non-Muslim with a donkey or cart, by law, he must give his donkey to the Muslim.

Every non-Muslim, no matter what position he held, may not wear fancy clothes and must always wear a badge on his clothing stating his religion: Jew, Christian, or Zoroastrian.

The Muslims also added a poll tax, jazieh, for non-Muslims who wanted to keep their religion. They claimed that the natives were the minority, even though they, the foreigners, were.

Non-Muslims were not allowed to build a new temple, synagogue or church. They had to receive special permission and pay an extra tax for doing so.

Women completely lost their status as well. Despite the fact that the Iranian heritage held women in high esteem, polygamy was instated.

Zoroastrians were originally monogamists. Several of the national heroes were women: Artimus, a woman general, who brought one million soldiers to attack Athens. There were two Queens, Iran-Dokht and Puran-Dokht, who were considered amongst the greatest leaders ever to reign. Despite these examples, polygamy destroyed the woman's status. Men were allowed as many concubines as they wanted.

There were many other articles like these. I explained that it was for this reason that the Iranian leaders created Shiite Islam, in order to separate themselves from the original conquerors, with the hope that in a generation or two their successors would be able to break free and return to their original faiths.

Many of the people in the group were not happy with what I had been talking about. I saw them struggling. However, several people were very receptive and contacted me subsequently. I helped these people learn more about their heritage, even today I am still in contact with several of these people.

Born Again

FROM THE AGE OF fifteen, when I lost my grandmother, until late in the year of 1990, I gradually became an atheist; I was quite antagonistic towards religion. My political activities, since the rise of Khomeini in 1978, pushed me even farther away from Shiite Islam and religion. I was full of belief that it was man who had created God, and not God who had created man. I was convinced that it is only through the power of man alone that dreams come true. A strong heart, mind and body can get you far. In short, I did not believe in any supernatural powers.

One day, when I was in Melbourne University studying Australian Administration Law for the bar exam, I met a man named Bruce Thomson. He talked to me about Jesus Christ; it was only for a few minutes, though. I was shocked, a man in university proselytizing! But he was a nice man and I thanked him. He gave me his card in case I wanted to hear more.

I soon forgot this conversation. However, several weeks later I had a very powerful and vivid dream. This dream turned my life, my perspective, and my views upside down. I cannot claim that the few minutes' talk with Bruce could have changed anything, however, this dream had changed everything.

Several years later I wrote my testimony: "Walk to the Heights" for my conversion to Christianity. Little did I know that it was the bridge I needed to build, which would take me to my true heritage, Abayef.

On the 14th of July 1990, I had a vision-dream. This dream penetrated into my soul. All of the walls which I had built fortifying against religion came crashing down. Since I had been a boy of 15, I had not felt or thought ideas and feelings of this nature. It washed over me, awakening my inner being and notions of the Divine.

When I was 15 my grandmother, who had been my spiritual guide, passed away. From that point I grew away from her faith. I had had questions that developed in my mind and no one could answer these questions. By the time I reached university my religious beliefs could be summarized with the statement that man had created God. However, this dream awakened doubt in that belief. I could not shake the idea that perhaps there is a God.

During my entire life I had never been in any church in Iran. While I worked as an international tour guide I visited many churches in the west, but only as a tourist. Never before had I felt any connection to Christianity.

When you see God in a dream, when you do not have any doubt that it is God you are seeing; you cannot ignore this. It did not matter that in the waking world I was a card-carrying atheist, having been one for over 30 years. When you dream, you are in a different state of mind. And when you see God in your dream, it can shake the very foundations of your being. I had come from a very different background, religiously. What I saw was a very different God from what I had been raised to believe.

I saw God's kind eyes; He beckoned me to come to Him. God told me that He would teach me how to lead my people. In one moment I went from being sure that the concept of God was a figment of man's collective awareness, to knowing that I was face to face with God. God was there, right before me, and I knew this with a greater awareness than I had ever felt in my entire life before.

I awoke with a start. I was covered with sweat and my heart was racing. I took a shower and left my home. It was 4:30 in the morning, but, with how I was feeling at that moment, I could not be confined to my small, dark home.

I lived, then, in a suburb of Coularoo, Melbourne, Australia. I walked for five hours, not completely sure where I was going. All I knew was that I had to get out. My mind was a mess. My entire world-view had been turned on its head, like a glass of Turkish coffee being stirred, all of the sediment, which had set peacefully at the bottom of the glass, mixed up into the coffee of my mind clouding it with grits.

At 9:30 that morning I found myself in the heart of the city of Melbourne, standing in front of the non-denominational Melbourne Church of Christ. I went inside, I felt, for the first time. I had been in churches many times before, as I had mentioned, as a tour guide. This time I was entering as a man searching to understand his encounter with God.

Several years later I found myself standing in front of five Rabbis, all members of the Rabbinical Council of America. I was standing there in order to re-discover myself in Judaism. When they asked me how I got to be standing there in front of them, I told them how I began as a Muslim, how I converted to Christianity and was on my way to becoming a priest. Then I had discovered that Jewish blood was running through my veins and I decided that I should return to the home of my parents before me.

While standing there I could not ignore how I had gotten there. I was thankful to Christianity for bringing me out of the darkness of atheism that I had fallen into. I was thankful to Christianity for teaching me about a different God than the God that Shiite Islam had taught. Because I could not completely reject this, I had to return to this tribunal of Rabbis three times before they saw that I was truly committed to Judaism.

When I entered the church I was welcomed with warm, open arms, by several young members of the church. This was strange for me. I had been the leader of the opposition to the Shiite-Islamic Republic of Iran. I had founded a para-military group and led several operations. Who were these people asking about who I was? On the other hand, I had come into their church. I was weighted down by my dream and I felt extremely raw inside, like the skin underneath a bandage being exposed to the world for the first time. I did not know how to react.

I eventually became friends with these people. I read the Bible and as I was drawn deeper into my studies I learned about miracles and how the world was full with them and I was baptized. My English was not great but I found that the Anglican Church in Melbourne had a Persian translation and I became affiliated with them. It was there where I had a ceremony of reconfirmation to the Anglican Church. I was affiliated with both churches and was very active in both communities. As I studied more I saw the ideas of Christianity filtering into my daily life. I saw more and more the hand of God in the world and came to love this view of the world.

I came closer to the Aplington Anglican Church of Melbourne and its minister, Reverend Khalil Razmara. Reverend Razmara saw that I was becoming more and more involved and encouraged me to accept Christ fully. Eventually I agreed and I began my studies in Ridley College of Melbourne University, the Center of Theological Studies of the university, affiliated with the Anglican Church.

For poor Angela this was not the first time that she had come in contact with Christianity. Her ex-husband had been a Christian back in Iran. He had converted several years before their marriage, at the age of nineteen. This was unheard of in Iran, even then, during the reign of the Shah. He had been completely rejected by his family. So Angela knew what it meant to be Christian. As a result she knew that it was important for her not to reject my views; however, she did have problems with my new direction, and rightfully so. I am a radical person by nature and with every spare moment I had I began working for the Church, for free. Angela confronted me: "You have a PhD and are a lawyer. Why are you working for them for free? You need to support yourself!" But I was too excited with my newfound faith.

I was invited to share my testimony with many churches across Australia and I became well known within the community. I was given the opportunity to translate several books to Persian as a result of my fame as well. The first book I translated was "Islamic Invasion" by Dr. Robert Murray. This was a small work comparing Christianity and Islam and was very popular in the Christian community. It was suggested to me that this book could help my people understand more about their situation, coming from an Islamic regime.

The second book I started to translate was "The Satanic Verses" by Salman Rushdie. In this book I found a harsh criticism by Salman Rushdie of Islam. I had learned that Rushdie had converted back and forth several times between Islam and Christianity and this intrigued me. I had heard that he had received several awards by the Islamic Republic for his research and now, because of his new book, had a death warrant on his head, put out by the Shiite leaders of the Islamic Republic.

Rushdie's book interested me, but my English was not on a level that I could understand his message. With the help of several friends I fought my way through his book. When I finished, I decided that I wanted to translate the book.

"The Satanic Verses" is a novel with fictitious names. Salman Rushdie was trying to introduce to his readers, using this venue, the life and background of the prophet of Islam. He did not change any of the facts. His aim was simply to present what the religion of Islam is founded upon. The story, I found, was not anything I hadn't heard before, growing up Muslim; however, this was the first time that it had been presented in such a mocking manner. I believe that it was for that reason, seeing their prophet portrayed such, that Rushdie had a price on his head.

It is unclear in the Koran, who it was that gave the Prophet of Islam his message. In some places it mentions the angel Gabriel, in other places it says a strange creature gave him his message. There are many references in Islam about how the prophet came to Abu-Bakr, his father-in-law and one of the first Arabs to convert to Islam, requesting that he write the message down.

Once, he came to Abu-Bakr and told him that in the previous night Satan came to him in a dream. Abu-Bakr told him that it is important that he include it in the Koran. Othman, the third Caliph of Islam, collected all of the parts of the Koran, which had been written down and put them, for the first time, into a book. This is the book that we have today. When doing so, Othman decided not to include these satanic verses into the final edition.

There were several editions of the Koran which did have these three verses included. Salman Rushdie, in his book, claims that these three verses are not the only satanic verses; rather, the entire Koran is compiled with satanic verses. He claims that if you study the life and behavior of the prophet, than you cannot hold otherwise.

The prophet had 26 wives, who used to compete with each other, outside of the house, for his sexual favors. The prophet's last wife, Ayesheh, the daughter of Abu-Bakr, was only six when she was taken to be his wife. How can the leader of any sane society think it is humane to marry a girl of six? Also, when the prophet would capture and kill the leader of a tribe, on that same night, the prophet would take the leader's daughter to be his wife. There were no other societies then which did that. Rushdie also brought the following story: At the very beginning of Islam a man, Abu-Ssarah, was one of the scribes of the prophet. He told him that, grammatically, several verses should be written differently. The prophet said that that sounded like a good idea. This happened several times. Eventually Abu-Ssarah decided that if he was willing to change his prophecy on account of his own suggestion then he cannot really be a prophet and thus Abu-Ssarah left Islam. On the prophet's return to

Mecca from Medina, several years later, Abu-Ssarah was the first person he killed when capturing the city.

I felt that it was extremely important to translate this book. There were millions of Iranians who did not understand English. I knew that the story of Rushdie's condemnation was widespread and that there must be a great readership interested in reading why. I worked night and day, translating this book.

Persona Non-Grata

ONE DAY, WHILE I was studying Christianity at Ridley College of Melbourne University, one of my colleagues approached me. He had arranged to interview an Imam of a local Mosque and he wanted me, a former Muslim, to work with him on this project.

There were three of us who came on this interview: a cameraman – also a student, my colleague and I. They both knew that I was antagonistic of the Shiite ideology. Not wanting to cause problems, so I agreed to be quiet during the interview, unless he did not understand something. We entered the mosque and began to look for the Imam.

As we looked around, we came across my former classmate from the English class at TAFE College. This was the person with whom I had had an argument and fought with about the nature of Islam. It seemed that he was one of the clergymen of this mosque.

The moment he saw me his face went white and he started yelling. When we had previously met, I had told him that I would flush him along with one billion Muslims down the toilet. He was afraid that we were there to do just that. We calmly showed him the letter agreeing for the interview, but we could not console him. The police came. Someone had called in a terrorist threat, and we were escorted out.

As we left my colleagues turned to me and asked: "Didn't we tell you not to incite them?!" I answered that he was angry over an incident that had happened over year prior. From then on I was somewhat of a celebrity at Ridley. I was asked to retell my story several times. My colleague who had wanted to interview the Imam ended up interviewing me instead.

During January of 1991, I was invited to teach a course in Political Science in the New South Wales University of Sydney. The course focused on diplomacy training for countries of the Pacific Ocean. The man who invited me, because of my expertise in Iranian law, was Jose

Ramos-Horta, the coordinator of the course. We became close friends, for we had similar backgrounds.

Jose was a freedom fighter, like myself. He had been fighting for the freedom of his country East Timor from Indonesia. In 1996, he received the Nobel Peace Prize. The Nobel Committee chose to honor him and his colleague, Bishop Carlos Filipe Ximenes Belo, for their "sustained efforts to hinder the oppression of a small people," hoping that "this award will spur efforts to find a diplomatic solution to the conflict of East Timor based on the people's right to self-determination."

After East Timor achieved independence in 2002, Ramos-Horta was appointed as the country's first Foreign Minister. Several years later he became its Prime Minister. Today, Ramos-Horta is the President of East Timor.

I was one of the top students of the course and he and I became close friends, sharing our stories, dreams and hopes. We promised each other that when one of us reaches his goal he would help the other. Today he is the President of East Timor; unfortunately, he could not help me with my cause.

During this course I was representing Iran. I gave a very strong presentation against the current Shiite government of Iran. This happened at the very beginning of the first Gulf War. I wrote a scathing article about the political situation in the Middle East and my article became a hot potato amongst my fellow students.

While I was back in Ridley College, I conducted approximately one hundred and fifty video interviews of religious people from many different faiths. My interviews were for the research of my comparative religion studies. I wanted to try to prove that Shiite Islam is not really a religion, rather, a political movement. I went to many churches, mosques, synagogues and even Baha'i communities. I met with people in my home, and theirs. I even interviewed someone in a barbershop.

I told my interviewee that I was doing a study on the idea of freedom of religion in Shiite Islam, for the purpose of my comparative religions studies. I would ask about the person's own beliefs and then what they knew of Shiite Islam. Many people were happy to be interviewed. However, when I interviewed Shiite Muslims, most of my interviews ended in the same way. Once I was able to show the interviewee how they were not really supporters of the concept of freedom of religion, they would get very uncomfortable and request to end the interview at once.

Before the Shiite-Islamic Revolution, Angela had been a high school teacher. One day in Australia she ran into one of her former students, M. Husseini. She had remembered him fondly and they got reacquainted. Husseini invited us over several times and we became friends. Husseini was a member of the Mujahidin, a communist, Shiite-Islamic, organization, which had been established ten years before the Shiite-Islamic Revolution.

Mujahidin had strong religious and communist ties and originally were one of the strongest supporters of the revolution. After the Shiite-Islamic Revolution they broke away from the coalition because of various differences. They were a terrorist organization and before the revolution, they organized an attack against the American military attaché along with several diplomats in Iran. In each attack many people were killed.

Husseini introduced me to his friends and I spoke at length about my previous political activities. They became very excited. Several weeks later I saw in the media that Mujahidin had attacked the Islamic Republic Embassy and Consulate in Cambera. The scenes on the television were terrible; they caused much damage.

Several days later I was invited by the Iranian community of Melbourne to speak at a public meeting about current affairs in the Iranian community. I spoke out strongly against the attack. "If we are really looking for freedom in our country, we cannot do so without a Shiite reformation." I claimed, "We need to incorporate the positive aspects of democracy and true pluralism." I tried to express who are the true opponents of the Shiite-Islamic Republic. I presented several member organizations of the opposition, analyzed their beliefs, and tried to show who would be a "strong horse to back" if we were to create a true revolution.

During my lecture I showed how Mujahidin was really the same wolf as the Republic, just in different clothing. Because they held onto their Shiite beliefs they would only continue the same bloodshed what Khomeini had brought, just under a different cause. Proof of that was the attack that they had arranged days before. I drew a parallel between them and Pol Pot, of Cambodia. I explained that he too was a strong Communist supporter and when he came into power he killed over a million people. So too, I believed, Mujahidin, would do the same.

I did not know that there were many members of Mujahidin in the audience and my speech caused an outrage. I was thrown out of the lecture hall. I truly believed what I had said at that lecture. I did not care that I might insult someone in the audience.

Mujahidin, I felt, would be worse than Pol Pot. They present themselves as the civilized opposition to the Islamic Republic, however the communist and Islamic ideals, which they hold onto so strongly, terribly contradict Western views. Mujahidin originally was working hand in hand with the current Shiite-Islamic Republic. Whatever disputes they have, I see them only as family quarrels; they are from the same mold.

Andrew Young was the UN representative at the time of the Shiite-Islamic Revolution; he called Khomeini "Holy." William H. Sullivan, the US ambassador to Iran in 1979, declared that Khomeini was another Gandhi. Jimmy Carter made a terrible mistake for supporting Khomeini. Today's horrible result is a regime that supports terror all over the world, including the attacks of September 11th, and is defying the world with its insistence to continue developing atomic weapons. Subsequently, the US apologized at least three times for putting Khomeini into power; twice, Jimmy Carter himself, and another time I heard Madeline Albright apologize as well. The entire time Abayef was calling out against them, however, no one would hear his voice.

There is a current trend between European and US leaders today to support Mujahidin. Mujahidin presents itself as a modern organization with western values. However, until they reform their ideological platform they can never be any better than the current regime in power. In my opinion they will be much worse.

OVER THE YEARS I had many opportunities to share and write about the ideology of Mujahidin. Pure Iranian culture is based upon Zoroastrianism, good thought, good actions and good speech. King Cyrus is a symbol of this culture. Mujahidin stands for the complete opposite.

> *My eye is full of compassion for my friend.*
> *I am joyous with this feeling because my friend is always in my eyes.*
> *I cannot separate the value of my eye from the value of my friend.*
> *Either he is in my eye or the power of my eye is he.*
> Saiid Abu Kheyr 11c

The pre-Islamic society was a culture that the value of friendship was highly regarded, and sexual relationships were respected; a society based upon monogamy. This culture was replaced with polygamy. One Shiite sect would offer their wives and daughters to the leaders, Abbass Eghbal Ashtiani, a well-known Islamic historian, explains. Mujahidin adopted this practice awakening it from a century of disuse. The second in command, Hussein Abrishamchi, divorced his wife, Maryam Azadanlu, so that the leader, Massoud Rajavi could take her as his wife. How could this organization claim to represent the true Iranian culture?

Mujahidin claims that over one hundred thousand young Iranians were killed for the support of Mujahidin. They have to stand up in international tribunals to answer for this atrocity. The majority of Iranians hate them. They understand that Mujahidin was responsible for rise of Khomeini into power. Mujahidin has already prepared a flag for when they rise into power. On the top of the flag there is a red communist star and several sentences in Arabic: "We will triumph with the support of Allah." Many people are not happy with their behavior.

Over a million people died in the Iran-Iraq war. There were over five million casualties and the war cost over one trillion dollars. The Iran-Iraq war was essentially a war between Khomeini and Saddam representing their sects: Shiite and Sunni Islam. It had nothing to do with the nation of Iran. The Iranian people were angry. However, more than that, during this war Mujahidin set up a military base in Iraq, Ashraf, near Bagdad and their militia fought against the Iranians and were responsible for many deaths.

Mujahidin was responsible for leaking the nuclear activity of the regime. It would appear that they have several powerful people placed in the hierarchy and cooperate with the regime. It is a result of this leak that economic sanctions were recently placed against Iran, destroying the economy.

For the sake of our next generation we have to let everyone know the destructive power of Mujahidin. Mujahidin has many ties with the West and is negotiating for help to overthrow the current regime. We cannot let this happen and that is why I was so outspoken at that meeting and seemed to have caught the attention of the Australian intelligence service.

Hundreds of faithful people who had been supporters of this organization, once they discovered how destructive the organization they worked for was, left. These people wrote many articles and reports against Mujahidin in the media. One is a close friend of the Peace and Love International Movement (PLIM), Jamshid Tafreshi. He left Iraq several years ago and came to Europe. We have had a very close relationship for many years and he is a well-known community leader. Jamshid reported that many members of Mujahidin who dissent are tortured and incarcerated. Since he began working with PLIM he has become interested in Israel, the Hebrew language and Judaism.

Angela's brother, M. Aminian, was one of the leaders of Mujahidin in the US for many years. His father had been the top colonel for the Shah. However the poison that Mujahidin injected into the society was so potent that they were able to corrupt the mind of Angela's brother to work against his own father.

I admire Angela. She is a very sweet woman. She lived a difficult life. Her husband had been a political activist in Turkey working against the Shiite-Islamic Republic. During the reign of the Shah he had been a navy Colonel. Angela had gone to visit him and on her return she had been arrested. While she was in jail her husband sent her divorce papers. They mutually felt that since he was wanted by the current regime that she would have a better chance to get out of jail if they were not married anymore.

One day in jail, Angela recalled to me, that the head of her division, a clergyman, gathered all of the prisoners together. He commanded: "all the supporters of the left go to the left side of the room" and several hundred women went off to the left. He continued: "all the supporters of Mujahidin go to the right" and several more hundred prisoners went off to the right. Angela was left all alone in the middle of the room. The clergyman barked at her: "Who are you?" She answered meekly: "I support the Shah." Angela told me that at that point everyone in the room jeered and mocked her. She explained that those few minutes had been her most difficult experience in jail. Even more difficult than receiving her husbands divorce papers.

When women in prison wash their clothing they have to hang them up to dry on a rope outside of cell's window. One day after washing her clothing, the women of her cell, Mujahidin followers, approached Angela: "Oh it is terrible, we are so sorry, but you are going to have to wash your clothing again." Angela did not understand. Her cellmates explained: "The rope on which you hung your clothing is the rope on which the Baha'i hang their clothing. They are unclean. You will have to re-wash all of your clothes and take another shower before you can live with us." The Mujahidin were responsible for making her sentence difficult, even more than the prison guards had.

Even today, thinking about her, I can imagine her sad green eyes, and how simply terrible it must have been for her. Angela's brother was always filled with hatred. Her brother's activities tore her family apart. Her father had been killed in the Iran-Iraq war and her husband was forced to divorce her. The rise of the Shiite-Islamic Regime destroyed millions of families; hers was only one of many. I myself felt a victim to the same destruction. My wife and I separated over similar issues. Her family supported the new regime completely; her cousin, Dr. Ibrahim Yazdi, was the first foreign minister of the regime. I was against the revolution and we could not reconcile our views.

Exile

As a result of these incidents, which happened while I was in Australia I am sure that there were several complaints filed against me. One day I received word from the Australian Intelligence Service. They requested to meet with me and told me when and where they wanted to meet. We had a very pleasant and respectful meeting. They asked me about my background, my life story and I happily told them everything they wanted to know. At the end of the meeting they told me that they highly recommended that I cease translating "The Satanic Verses."

I was surprised that they even knew about this project. I had not mentioned it to anyone. The agents told me that four translators of the book had been murdered already: the Swedish, Japanese, Turkish and Italian translators had all been assassinated. They did not want the same thing to happen to me. I told them that this is a democratic country and that it was their job to protect me as a political prisoner. There were no laws against translating a book; nevertheless, they insisted.

I continued with my work translating Rushdie's book. After several more weeks I received word from the intelligence agents that they would like to meet with me. They advised me that I cease with my project, again and instead that I apply to Hobart University in Tasmania for a second Doctorate in International Private law. They told me that if I go there I would be able to take the course for the bar exam free of cost.

I hadn't finished yet studying for the bar in Australia and with the financial difficulties I was having, since I could not yet work as a lawyer, this was a very tempting offer. In Tasmania I worked on a comparative study on Australian Westminster Common Law, Shiite-Islamic Law and International Private Law (Personal Law). I was living close to the university.

I truly believe that Tasmania is the paradise of the world. I think fondly of my time there and Angela was very happy there as well. I was working five nights a week as a taxi driver. During the day I continued my research.

I was also working on a Masters degree in Comparative Religion at T.A.F.E. college of Tasmania and I was continuing my studies to be ordained as a priest. I was planning to do the course for the Bar the following year, since my religious studies and research was a higher priority for me.

While I was in Tasmania I became very close with the Baha'i community there. I had been exposed before to Baha'i. Between the ages of 10 and 12, my parents became involved in the Baha'i community of Iran. At that time I was a devotee Shiite Muslim and was not interested with what my parents were involved in religiously, my grandmother was my guide. My parents were intrigued; however, they did not become Baha'i in the end. I understood, even then, that they were lovely people, but mainstream Shiite Islam saw it as unclean.

IN THE 10TH CENTURY the Islamic sect of Shiite Islam became very powerful. The 11th Imam of Shiite Islam was named Hassan Asgari. Imam Hassan could not have children, he was infertile, the word Asgar means without seed. Some scholars say that his wife had a child who had been lost; others say that he had never had a child. Shiite Islam, from that time, developed a messianic philosophy. They believed that Mehdi, the son of Hassan, would come one day as the messiah. Sunni Islam completely rejects this idea since it contradicts the Koran and much of Islamic theology. The legend says that when Medhi comes he will kill everyone who stands against him, everywhere he goes and there will be blood up to the knees of his horse, all around the world. They also believe that Judaic and Christian Messiahs will follow him.

There are 178 sects of the Shiite sect of Islam. Baha'i is the most recent. The people of the Baha'i faith claim that they are not part of Islam, however. Originally, Baha'i came out of a sect of Shiite Islam called Sheykheyeh over 168 years ago. Mirza Ali Mohammad Shirazi, from the city of Shiraz, was a young clergyman and called himself "Bab." Bab in Islam means a "gate." Mirza claimed: "I am the gate of the coming Mehdi," just as John the Baptist prophesized the coming of Jesus. Mirza was a young man, but very charismatic and very nice. However, Shiite Clergy leaders influenced the local government to execute him for provoking the masses.

At his execution, the rope from which he was being hung, broke. According to Shiite law if this happens, the man being executed is considered free of the charge and is free to go; however, they did not let him go. They recaptured him and sent him to a firing squad. The historical accounts write that he was shot with 750 bullets.

His successor Bahalleh, his cousin, was an extremely intelligent man. He claimed that it is a new religion but at the same time, a sect of Shiite Islam. Bahalleh preached love and unity and peace for the whole world. He said that man, all, are searching for one God. He proposed a universal language, law and religion; everyone is a child of God, we must all work together to create harmony. His and his cousin's ideas can be found in their three holy books: Agdass, Ighan and Kalemat-e Maknooneh. Many people came to follow him, including clergymen. The government became uneasy again with this upstart religion and exiled Bahalleh to Iraq.

In Iraq, Bahalleh collected many more followers and eventually the Iraqis asked their rulers to send him to Acre, which was considered the most devastated region of the Ottoman Empire. Bahalleh stayed there until the end of his life. Once he settled, he arranged for the body of Bab to be brought and buried in Acre. Later on this leader received permission to buy property in Haifa and was buried there at the end of his life. Today, one can see his garden from most of Haifa. This beautiful garden cost billions of dollars to build and its design was based upon Persian traditions.

The Baha'i faith accepts all religions and believes that all religions, one day, will cooperate under the ideology of Baha'i. I think that the Baha'i community is wonderful and I have had many opportunities to study their beliefs. While I think that the world is a much better place as a result of their existence, I have two major critiques of their ideology:

First, I believe, based upon my studies of his works, that Mirza was not trying to create a separate religion; rather, he was trying to create a social revolution. From my studies of his teachings I believe that his claim: "I am Bab" was an attempt to put an end to the ugly face of Shiite Islam. He realized that he could not separate between the religion and the social ideas so he chose the messiah concept in order to infuse his peaceful beliefs into society. Thus he planned to minimize the Shiite dictatorship in Iran and maximize the rationalistic ideas he was presenting.

Second, I do not think that it is correct for Baha'i to preach that it is a separate religion. Baha'i came out of Shiite Islam from the Sheykheyeh sect. While the Baha'i claim that they are not Muslim, they have adopted, almost completely, the Shiite ideology and practice. They have softened it, replacing the violence inherent within with western socialistic values; still, it is misleading to ignore this fact.

I have a wonderful relationship with the Baha'i. Even since I arrived to Israel I have contacted their community and have been in touch with them ever since.

FOR CLOSE TO FIVE years I lived in Australia. For that time I had a close relationship with Angela and her children. I received an offer from Hobart University for a scholarship to conduct research for the Sir Henry Baker Research Institute for the duration of two months at the Hebrew University of Jerusalem. I received a visa from the Israeli Embassy in Cambera and travel documents from the Australian Immigration and Ethnic Affairs Ministry for my trip.

Angela was concerned, because of my political and religious background, that I might have problems traveling to the Middle East. I calmed her down. I assured her that I would only be in Israel for eight weeks. I planned to travel to Europe for a week to see my family and on my way back to Australia I planned to stop off in the US for a week. Ten weeks total and I would be back home.

On the 22nd of November 1994, I left for Israel. When I was in the Melbourne International Airport the customs officer told me that the office, which had given me travel documents, neglected to give me a return visa. The officer told me that I would have to go back to the Ministry of Immigration and Ethnic Affairs to receive this document.

I had a dilemma. I would not be able to return if I got on this flight, but on the other hand, I paid over $2,500 for my ticket. I told the officer my problem and he assured me that I would be able to receive the missing document from the Tel Aviv embassy.

Israel

MY FLIGHT STOPPED OVER in Rome and on the 24th of November. I arrived in Israel for the first time. The Hobart Anglican Church set me up to stay in St. George's Cathedral to conduct my research. For the first few days I did not have anyone to show me around. I thought that the Old City of Jerusalem was the entirety of Jerusalem, when in fact Jerusalem encompasses a much greater area. I had heard that Israel was technologically advanced so I was surprised to see the state in which the residents of the Old City lived.

The day after I arrived in Israel I had a meeting with Professor Lifshitz, the head of the faculty of Law at the Hebrew University of Jerusalem. It was a very fruitful meeting. Professor Lifshitz introduced me to someone who would be able to help me with the Law Library at the University. He also gave me a list of experts in International Law in Tel Aviv, Haifa and Bar Ilan Universities. He also introduced me to Professor Menasheri, the head of Persian studies at the Moshe Dayan Research Institute at Tel Aviv University. Along with many other experts in Islamic studies, including Professor Moshe Maoz, the head of the Truman Institute in Jerusalem and Professor Amnon Netzer the head of Indian, Armenian and Persian studies at the Hebrew University of Jerusalem.

After discussing business for over an hour Professor Lifshitz then asked me about my personal understanding of Israel, from the eyes of a non-Jewish Iranian, and why I had accepted the scholarship to conduct research here. My answer was full of warm feelings and sentiment to Israel; I expressed my love for Israel including the connection between our two nations from 2,500 years ago. He advised me to meet with MK Yossi Beilin, then, the Minister of Foreign Affairs. In January, I had a similar meeting with Professor Maoz about my feelings and beliefs about Israel. It was also a fruitful meeting and he too introduced me to several of his friends.

When I went to meet Professor Lifshitz, we had arranged to meet at 9 a.m. however when I arrived his secretary informed me that he would only be available at 10:30 a.m. I took this time to explore the university. During my explorations I discovered a barber and decided to get my hair cut. My barber was a lovely French woman and we conversed. During our discussion I asked her if there were any Iranians living in Israel. She exclaimed: "Of course there are!" In fact the florist one floor below the barber was Iranian. Mrs. Nassir, that florist, was the first Iranian woman I met from the Israeli-Iranian community.

Mrs. Nassir was very sympathetic to my situation and invited me for a Shabbat dinner. At that time I had never heard of Shabbat and was not familiar with Jewish customs. But Mrs. Nassir was patient and explained to me all about it. At her home I met Dr. Rahamani and his family. This was my initiation into the Iranian community of Israel. My contacts, through them, continued to grow on a daily and weekly basis.

I met at that meal a well-known Iranian poet, Homayoun Amiri. His views were far to the left and he always criticized Israel. He always tried to convince me that I was naïve, in a few weeks I would understand what he meant. Fourteen years later I still have very warm feelings towards Israel and I still must say that he is wrong. Several years ago Homayoun passed away, suffering for many years from multiple sclerosis.

Several weeks after my first Shabbat meal the Nassirs invited me over again to introduce me to more of their friends. At that meal I was encouraged to contact the Persian department of the Israel National Radio Authority. I quickly became one of their top activists.

National Security Risk

During my eight weeks of research I made many friends and had a wonderful time in Israel. At the end of my research I had to arrange for a return visa so that I could go back to Australia. I also needed a visa to visit my family in Europe and to visit the US. I needed a re-entry visa in order to receive visas from the US and French consulates. So I went to the Australian consulate in Tel Aviv.

At the consulate the clerk asked me for my travel documents and my certificate of refugee status. I handed them over to him and he gave me a receipt in return. The clerk asked that I return a week later. I was not sure why, the customs official at the airport assured me that the procedure would only take ten minutes; however, I had no choice so I set to return on the following week.

This happened five times. Five times I went back to the Australian consulate and five times I was sent away. During my eleventh week in Israel I returned to the consulate for the fifth time and I would not let the clerk send me away without an answer.

I told the clerk at the consulate that when I had been in the airport the official there had said that arranging a re-entry visa would take only ten minutes, what was taking three weeks? He answered me that he does not have permission to issue the visa. At that point I got angry and I told them to contact Australian Security Intelligence Organization (ASIO). How could they reject me after granting me refugee status? I had no money, I had a family in Australia; my life was there. The clerk told me to return in a few days and told me that someone else would talk with me.

When I returned I met with Mr. Callonen, the head of Australian Immigration and Ethnic affairs in the Middle East. He told me that he had come from Athens to give me a letter. In the letter it said that they could not give me a re-entry visa because the ASIO decided that I was a threat to national security.

I was fuming. This was against my rights. No intelligence agency was authorized to make such decisions. Only a court could. When I told Mr. Callonen this he answered that I could appeal to the government, but he could not do more for me. How could they split up a family like that? All of my possessions were there; my work and my life was there. I found myself a political refugee again, for the third time.

Angela and our friends submitted several appeals to the government. After several weeks she informed me that ASIO was afraid that I would hijack the Quantass airplane, Australia's Airline. Thinking back to my flight from Melbourne, I remember that the two men sitting next to me were of a special quality.

Receipt from the Australian Embassy to reissue travel documents as required for political refugees.

Our discussion, over the course of the 20-hour flight, was not the average conversation that one has on an airplane. At the last minute of the flight one of the men turned to me and told me that he was acquainted with Mr. Cook. Mr. Cook was the first intelligence agent who interviewed me in Australia. I understood at that point who they were, and when Angela told me their fears I understood why they sat next to me.

I sent out thousands of letters to various people, organizations, and Parliament Members, the Bar Association and Church ministers. I argued: "How can you treat me this way? How can you split up my family? According to the Geneva Convention I cannot be declared a threat without a trial. You accepted me as a political refugee, today you are throwing me out to the wolves." Despite my letters I received no positive response. It is better for everyone, they claimed, if I just stay in Israel.

The head of the Aplington Church, Khalil Razm-Ara was my first supporter when I first entered the Church. He was an ex-Muslim who had converted to Christianity over forty years ago. When I contacted him he told me that I should leave it and not challenge the Australian government. When I asked "Why?" he answered: "Don't ask why, just accept what they say." When I contacted Archbishop Kait Rainer, the head of the Anglican Church in Australia, he answered similarly.

The Minister of the Hobart Anglican Church was also a Major in the Australian navy and a chaplain. When I contacted him he accused me: "The whole time you were in my church you never mentioned to me that you had hijacked a gunboat." I answered that this had been public information, had he asked me I would have happily shared with him my past. I continued, my past political activities had been the very reason why the government had accepted me as a political refugee. I had told the Intelligence everything when I first met with them.

In 1992, during the time of the Oslo agreement, I wrote a ten-page letter in order to share with the world my feelings as an ex-Muslim and citizen of the world.

In 1992 and 1993, I sent a letter to Archbishop Kafity, the Archbishop of Jerusalem. I sent my feelings, as a new Christian and former Muslim, of what my thoughts were on the Israeli-Palestinian peace process, taking place in Oslo. I wrote that I feared that it could be very dangerous and that they should be careful. In 1995, when I found out about my rejection from Australia I met with Archbishop Kafity. I wanted to ask him to pray for a positive outcome from my situation and perhaps that he could use his political connections to help me. He respectfully declined to help me. I mentioned, at that point, my letter I had written to him previously and he replied in a very cynical tone: "Yes, I remember."

I had the opportunity, last year, to meet with Dr. Khuri, a minister in a church in Bethlehem. I met with him about arranging a conference for the Peace and Love International Movement. He told me, at that meeting, that he knows some members of the Anglican clergy who are strongly pro-Palestinian. In fact, he mentioned, that these clergymen do not read the Old Testament, claiming that it is a forgery and simply a history of the Zionists.

During the period that I was living in St. George's Cathedral I was involved with a non-denominational Christian-Arab Church in the Old City. One member of the church was a well-known Palestinian journalist. He informed me that the Foreign Minister of Australia, Gareth Evans, was meeting the next morning in the King David Hotel in Jerusalem with the Jerusalem Mayor, Mr. Ehud Olmert.

AUSTRALIAN EMBASSY, TEL AVIV

19 January 1995

Mr Jam Shid Hassani
St George's Guesthouse
20 Nablus Road
East Jerusalem

Dear Mr Hassani

This letter is to confirm the advice I gave to you over the telephone yesterday concerning your request to return to Australia.

As you left Australia without first obtaining a re-entry visa – I understand, in spite of advice from the Department that you required one – there is now no provision in the Migration Regulations to grant you a visa on the basis of your previous Class 784 temporary entry permit.

If you wish to return to Australia to reside permanently you would need to make an application for migration and meet the legal criteria relevant to the class of visa, including public interest criteria. However, I must tell you again that in respect of public interest criterion 4002 of the Migration Regulations I have received advice that the competent Australian authorities have assessed you to be a direct risk to Australian national security. As a result, any application which you might make for a visa would be refused on this basis.

Yours sincerely

Christopher Callanan
First Secretary (Immigration)
Australian Embassy, Athens

Letter from the Australian Embassy in Tel Aviv informing Hassani (Daniel) that the Australian authorities considered him to be a direct risk to Australian national security.

UNITED NATIONS		NATIONS UNIES
HIGH COMMISSIONER FOR REFUGEES	האומות המאוחדות	HAUT COMMISSARIAT POUR LES RÉFUGIÉS
Correspondent for Israel	הנציב העליון לפליטים	*Le Correspondant pour Israël*
	משרד הקורספונדנט בישראל	

Telephone: 557111
Telex: 2 62 12 JOINT IL
Fax: 661244

P.O. Box 3489
91034 JERUSALEM

Jerusalem, 16 August 1995

Dr. Jamshid Hassani
c/o Christian Embassy
P.O. Box 1192
Jerusalem 91010

Dear Dr. Hassani:

I regret to inform you that I have just received a fax from Geneva stating that despite the fact that you were permitted to remain in Australia initially, the implication being that you were a refugee, does not alter their position that you cannot be considered a refugee under the Mandate of the UNHCR. I quote:

" WE CONFIRM THAT HEADQUARTERS CONSIDERS UNHCR NOT BOUND BY HIS CONVENTION STATUS IN AUSTRALIA AND HAS EXAMINED THE CASE AFRESH... AS INDICATED IN OUR PREVIOUS CABLE ....AND FOLLOWING CLOSE EXAMINATION OF ALL INFORMATION PROVIDED BY HIM TO UNHCR. IT IS HENCE OUR ASSESSMENT THAT HIS CLAIM IS NOT CREDIBLE AND THEREFORE SHOULD BE REJECTED. "

Hoping that you will find a solution to your problems in a country that will be pleased to grant you entry and reunification with your wife.

With kind regards.

Yours sincerely,

Zena Harman
Honorary Correspondent

Letter from the UN office in Israel indicating that Hassani (Daniel) cannot be considered a refugee under the Mandate of the UNHCR.

I knew that if I approached him directly, from the crowd, that he would probably dismiss me immediately. However, I had had much experience meeting with distinguished people and I set out the next morning to arrange a meeting with him. I was dressed formally, in my suit, and as the entourage rounded a corner in the lobby, I sidestepped security and stepped in line with them. Each group assumed that I was part of the other group. When we entered the meeting room I approached the Minister and he asked me: "Aren't you from their group?" I answered that I wasn't and that I come to meet with him.

He was taken aback but friendly and we conversed for several minutes. I took that opportunity to tell him my story. At the end he took my contact information and asked that I write him a formal letter. Unfortunately he could not help me in the end either.

Being from an Islamic Iranian family, once I saw that I would not get anywhere with the Australian government, I became fearful of what Israel would do with me. While many times before I had spoken very positively about Israel I could not deny where I had come from. So I decided to apply for political refugee with the United Nations and I arranged a meeting with Mrs. Zena Herman, the Chief Commissioner of the UN in Israel for assessing political refugee cases.

Mrs. Herman was very sympathetic to my story and was surprised how the Australian government had dealt with me. Her first action was to contact the Australian government to confirm my story and see what she could do about perhaps regaining their trust in me. I kept in touch with her over the next few weeks and eventually she realized that there was no way to convince the Australian government to accept me back.

Mrs. Herman asked me if there was any specific country I would like to move to. I answered her that I had lived in Europe for several years and that I had family in the US and Canada. After several more tense weeks of waiting she informed me that no one would accept me as a refugee because of Australia's extreme reaction. I felt terrible. No one on this planet would accept me.

At that time I had many financial troubles; I had to leave St. George's Cathedral because it was too expensive. I borrowed money from my brother in the United States and my sister in Germany just to stay afloat. Australia left me without any form of ID and I had no access to any of my funds back in Australia. I asked Mrs. Herman to help me find a job and a place to live.

After several weeks, Mrs. Herman introduced me to the International Christian Embassy and Reverend Jan Williem von der Houven. Reverend von der Houven's father had been a close friend to the Queen of Netherlands and a chaplain of her court. It was hopeless. I called the Embassy every few days and it took several weeks to arrange an appointment with him.

I met with Reverend von der Houven in his beautiful office in Jerusalem. I had a wonderful conversation with him. He had founded the embassy and it is one of the most Zionist Christian organizations and supporters of Israel. When I told him of my background he became overjoyed. He was convinced that God had arranged for me to go through what I had gone through, being stranded in Israel, so that I could work with him. He told me that he had been looking for someone with my background, a Christian who had formerly been a Muslim, for years to do research in comparative religions.

I worked with him and his staff for over five years. Our research focused on the differences between Shiite Islam and Judeo-Christianity. The major point on which I was concentrating on during those years was actually Iran.

In Isaiah, chapter 45 speaks of King Cyrus. In fact, this is the only mention of a non-Jew as the Messiah. I researched what had happened that instigated this drastic change in relationships between these two sister countries of Israel and Iran.

Studying this history I discovered volumes. In 1879, a cylinder was discovered from the year 558 BCE. This cylinder, known as the Cyrus Cylinder, is considered the world's first known charter for human rights. There are passages in the text on the cylinder that have been interpreted as expressing Cyrus' respect for humanity. It promotes a form of religious tolerance and freedom, and the abolishment of slavery. He allowed his subjects to continue worshipping their gods, despite his own religious beliefs.

Roughly 55 years before King Cyrus reigned, Nebuchadnezzar, the Assyrian Emperor, conquered Babylon and with it Israel. When doing so he destroyed Jerusalem including the great Temple and exiled all of the inhabitants to Babylon. Fifty-five years later Cyrus recaptured Babylon and allowed the Jewish people to return to Israel and bring with them the vessels that had been captured with the destruction of their Temple.

Also in the books of Esther and Daniel, Ezra and Nehemiah as well as many other sources I found a profound connection between the Zoroastrian and the Jewish nations. In 333 BCE, after Alexander invaded Jerusalem, the Iranian nationalists, partisans, worked hand in hand with the Jewish Maccabees to overthrow the oppressive Greek culture.

In the 4th century BCE, the Northern-Central province of Iran was known as "Part," named after the builder of the Parthian Dynasty, also sometimes known as "Ashk" or "Ashkanian." These people were very patriotic and fought against the Greek invaders. Their heroism and patriotism became legendary. The term "partisan" is named after these people's actions.

There is a well-known French expression: "Uous n'est pas assez fort qu'un Parti, quil emporter l'arow de la Civilization a' d'autre Cote' de leue." This phrase means: "You are not strong enough as a Parti-man who brought the arrow of civilization to the other part of the ocean." This phrase goes back to the time of Alexander. After he conquered Iran, he brought back, as Xenophon describes, 80,000 volumes of Persian literature to Greece.

Farhad V was one of the kings of the Parthian dynasty. During his dynasty three Magi came to Jerusalem to bring the prophesy of the coming Christ, as described in Matthew. A magus is a Zoroastrian high priest. This shows the religious openness and acceptance of Zoroastrianism and the Iranian empire, as was expressed in the Cyrus Cylinder. This was the same tolerance that allowed the Jewish community to compile one of its greatest works, the Mishna.

The second dynasty after the Parthian/Ashkanian was the Sassanid Dynasty. They ruled for centuries and it was during their reign that the great Roman/Persian wars took place. It was during this dynasty, in the light of the same Zoroastrian religious freedom given, that some of the greatest Jewish Yeshivot, study-houses, existed in the cities of Sura and Pompadita, each Yeshiva with an excess of 10,000 students. It was in these Yeshivot that the Talmud was complied.

There are in fact two Talmuds: the Jerusalem Talmud and the Babylonian Talmud. The Babylonian Talmud is much greater in size and depth than the Jerusalem Talmud. This is because they had much more religious freedom than their brethren in Jerusalem. This is yet another expression of the religious tolerance given by the Iranian empire of that time.

The lifestyle of the Jewish community in those days is comparable with the current status of the Jewish people in America today. For example, some of the largest Yeshivot are in the US, just as they were in Iran.

If we were to make a survey of the history of civilizations on earth, compared with the barbaric practices of 1700 years ago, Zoroastrianism's tolerance would come out on top. My main research at the International Christian Embassy of Jerusalem (ICEJ) focused on comparing pre-Islamic

Iran with post the Islamic Invasion; how Zoroastrianism was tolerant and Shiite Islam was not.

During my meeting with Reverend von der Houven my financial situation came up. I told him about my problems and he was able to help me. He gave me the key to a beautiful apartment in the center of Jerusalem, close to the Prime Minister's house. He also handed me $1,000 to help me with the debts, which I had incurred as a result of my situation. Throughout my entire five years working with Reverend von der Houven I could not have asked for a better employer. Even today we are great friends.

After several months I became convinced that I had no hope in returning to my refuge in Australia. I had sent many letters and appealed several times to the rejections I received. However, once I realized that my efforts were in vain, I set out to study Hebrew, the language of my new home.

I registered to study in Ulpan "Bet Am" in Jerusalem. It was during my first three months there, sometime during June of 1995, where I met Marina. And six months later we were married in Uruguay.

Marina

WHEN WE FIRST MET, our relationship was complicated. I was known in Israel as a married man. On top of that I was a pillar in my Christian community. Extra-marital relationships in Christianity are strictly forbidden.

When we first started going out I told Marina about Angela and the nature of what our relationship had been. She was shocked, for many reasons. First of all because of the difference in cultures: how could someone have a temporary marriage? Also, my background is incredulous. It was hard for her to believe my story: an ex-Muslim, one of the former heads of the Iranian opposition, with no citizenship in any country of the world and now in Israel. I had been a spy. I had only come for eight weeks for a research project. What was I still doing here? I know that my story did not make sense.

Marina told me later that during our first few months together in class, before we came together, she had already been trying to get my attention. She said that when we first met she knew that we were meant for each other. The evening after she had first seen me, when she went home she

2009-Marina and Daniel in front of the Great Synagogue of Rome.

told Dina, her daughter, her feelings and that she had thought that she had met me before. However, how could she have? Our paths could not have ever crossed before then. Eventually, Marina realized how she had recognized me.

Several months after her divorce from her first husband, Dina, who was 12 at that time, drew a painting. She showed this painting to her mother and said: "This man will be your future." After we had been going out for a while Marina realized that that painting was an exact replica of me. She called a family member back in Russia and requested that they find that painting and send it to her. When she received it, she saw that the man in the painting was, in fact, me.

Over the course of this entire period I was in contact with Angela daily. Once I saw that I would be staying in Israel I invited her to join me here but she declined. Just as I had feared, the Australian government tore my family apart. I believe that there are three main reasons why she would not come.

First, and foremost, her children were there. She did not want to leave them. Second, her brother was one of the leaders of the Mujahidin organization in the US. After several weeks he contacted me and asked me: "Why Israel?" I answered him that I had not chosen Israel. I had come for a research project and was stranded. Mujahidin could not hate any

2005-Marina and Daniel at the Dead Sea. Marina is a supporter and symbol of Zionism for Daniel.

country more than they hate Israel. I imagine that he had a strong influence on Angela.

The final reason, I believe, was the Australian Intelligence Agency. After several meetings, I believe that they were able to persuade Angela that I really was not trustworthy.

And so, I had not only been rejected by the world, but by my love as well. I cannot blame Angela. She was always as supportive as she could be. She did her best to help me return home; she contacted numerous human-rights organizations including Amnesty International and Human Rights Watch. Also, after I had been here for a while, Angela had all of my books from Australia sent to me. One day I opened the door and there were two, meter square boxes filled with books. I have the greatest respect for that woman.

Once I had been going out with Marina for a while I needed proof that I was not married. Angela could easily have caused me many problems. But she did not. Angela went to a lawyer and wrote a letter confirming that we had had only a temporary marriage and had the letter notarized. It was because of that letter that I was able to marry Marina.

At the same time I contacted my ex-wife and children in Paris. I let them know that I was in Israel and that they would be welcome to visit me here and I would love to be their host. However, they declined as well, each for their own reason.

After three years in Israel I finally received travel documents and I decided to go and visit my family in Paris. While I was there we had a lovely meeting for the duration of two hours. I tried to convince them to come and visit me in Israel again however they would not. Before I left my son, Payman, told me that he was about to begin his year as an intern in medical school. I was so proud of him. He continued to tell me that he was struggling financially and asked if I could help him. Even though I had little resources myself, when I got home I took out a loan from the First International Bank for 25,000 Shekels and sent the money to him. Because of my financial issues, that loan turned into 56,000 Shekels. It took me 11 years to pay it off. These are the things we do for love.

Despite that, I did not succeed in bringing my children to Israel, even for a visit. I was very proud of my children. Payman finished top of his class and now is an expert in his field and Bahareh received her PhD. from Paris University in International Private Law. They both have done very well for themselves.

My relationship with Marina was growing day-by-day. Her honesty, beauty, intelligence and determination were overwhelming me. Despite having two advanced degrees in Architecture and Construction Engineering and despite her having experience working for the Moscow Municipality, in Israel she worked cleaning houses and babysitting so that she could support her parents and her daughter.

Her father had been a member of the Orthodox Russian Church in Moscow but her mother was Jewish and her family was very Zionist and supporters of Israel. She came for the first time in 1993 on a visit and immediately fell in love with the country. Her love for Israel caused her to extend her trip and eventually Marina applied for citizenship. She convinced her parents and her daughter to come to Israel as well.

Marina's daughter, Dina, was in her first year of law school at Moscow University. Dina left to come live with her mother and had to start her degree from the beginning at Hebrew University. She graduated with a degree in Japanese literature and received a Masters Degree from Kyoto University in Japan. Today Dina is a well-known Russian/Hebrew/English/Japanese translator and is very successful, working for Yad Vashem.

Their faith and love for Israel has always been a light for me. They were well-known professionals in Moscow and they left everything to come live in Israel. Marina and her family have planted in me a deep love for Israel and Judaism. Today, when I introduce Marina at parties or to my colleagues I introduce her as my muse.

Once Marina and I decided to get married the first hurdle was to prove that I was not already married. Angela was very helpful there. However, that was only the first of many hurdles. I was a Christian and wanted to marry a Jew in Israel. That is impossible. It happens all of the time; yet, those couples usually fly to Cyprus for a weekend and register there. Israel will recognize a legal marriage from other countries, but will not facilitate them.

The problem with going to Cyprus was that I did not have, at that time, travel documents. I had no citizenship in any country. We arranged with a lawyer, who had a colleague in Uruguay, to have us legally married there, without having to leave the country. And that is how we were married in Uruguay.

Marina has always been supportive and loving, through thick and thin, through financial woes and through problems with the Interior Ministry.

In Israel, if one is married to a resident, one is eligible to receive citizenship after four years; it took me thirteen. The Chief Rabbinate did not want to accept my application for conversion until the Interior Ministry would accept me as a citizen. The Interior Ministry would not accept me as a citizen until the Chief Rabbinate would accept my application for conversion. Marina could not have been more supportive or loving throughout.

From the first days before marriage many friends advised Marina to break off our relationship because of my background. Several very close friends rebuked her for staying with me. She has been one hundred percent faithful to her decision and fourteen years together has shown that she had been right.

Marina's mother was a complete angel. She sacrificed herself for her family. After Marina and I were married for several years we were setting up an office in the Bet Hakerem neighborhood of Jerusalem. I would practice law there and Marina could run her architecture firm there as well.

Marina's mother was helping us set up this office and one day she caught a cold. We did not think much of it initially, however it progressed and her left leg became paralyzed and we had to hospitalize her. No one knew exactly what had caused the paralysis. The doctors said that it was because of a virus.

Less than two months later I received a phone call from Marina: "My mother is dead." I did not believe her. How could this be? I thought that she was exaggerating. But I rushed immediately to the hospital. On my arrival I found out that yes indeed she had passed away as a result of a mistake in her medication.

Marina is a very strong woman and I can never remember her crying, except for once. At the funeral of her mother, the Hevra Kadisha, the members of the Jewish burial committee, had just placed her body into the grave. Marina was on the side and noticed flies flying around the dust near the grave. She bent down to brush them away and I remember seeing tears in her eyes. I will always remember the feeling that that sight left in me.

Marina's father was one of the well-known colonels of the Engineers' corps of the Red Army. After his retirement, Marina convinced him to come with her mother to Israel. Several weeks after his wife's passing, he became very sick and his left hand became paralyzed. While the Israeli medical insurance agency provided a caretaker for him, Marina, at his wishes, came twice a week to take care of him. Marina did this task with much compassion and love despite her having many criticisms of the way he had treated her and her mother at times.

One day we received a message from his caretaker that he had fallen down in the bathroom and had been knocked unconscious. Marina anxiously left her job to check on her father. She called me and I met her at his apartment. When I arrived, I saw her father lying in the middle of the bathroom and there were medics in the room. It seemed that he hit his head very hard when he fell. The medics were trying to revive him, however they were unable and he passed away.

Marina's grandfather had been a member of the Russian Orthodox Church, but her father, who had been in the Red Army all his life, was not religious. Despite not being religious, he still wore his cross wherever he went.

When the medics were wrapping her father up, Marina knew that there was going to be a problem with the Hevra Kadisha because her father was not Jewish, so she removed the cross from around his neck.

It is against Jewish law for a non-Jew to be buried in a Jewish cemetery. However, it had always been Marina's father's wish to be buried next to his wife.

In order for the Hevra Kadisha to allow for his wishes to be fulfilled, by law he had to be circumcised. This was a very difficult time for us and it was beyond our contemplation that this was the law, but we went ahead with the circumcision so that he could have his final wishes fulfilled.

MARINA IS MY MUSE; she was the best child that she could be for her parents; she is the best mother and best wife. She is a faithful Zionist. She is always in my heart as a symbol of a faith in the Holy Land. But most of all she is the best human being I have every known and my best friend.

For the first few years that we knew each other Marina's friends did their best to discourage her from pursuing a relationship with me. I was born a Muslim and had been studying to become an Anglican priest. I had fled Iran and was sent away from Australia. My background was not the most stable one could wish for in a partner. But Marina stood by me.

When I first arrived in Israel I was so unsure of who I could trust I did not share my real name with anyone. I was known by all of my friends, even Marina, as "Danny." I did not know if the Shiite-Islamic Republic was still looking for me, or who from my past might be trying to track me down.

From the time that Marina and I got married, it took me more than 10 years to receive any official paperwork from the Israeli government: I had no ID, visa nor even simple travel documents. Each month, for the course of 10 years we went to the Interior Ministry for more appeals and interviews. They asked both of us very personal questions about our married life, private and public. And more often than not Marina would leave the interview room in tears. The interviewers would reproach her for marrying me. "Aren't there so many other Jews around? Why did you marry him?" they would say. But throughout all of this, Marina stood with me.

There were times that I got so fed up with the entire process that I was ready to leave Israel, find my way to Europe and buy identification documents off the black market. But Marina's strength kept me here; and our connection only grew stronger. When I say that Marina is my muse I do not only mean that she inspires me to create, but also she inspires me to live.

Marina is a caring and supportive mother as well. When her father passed away she inherited a small property in Moscow. Marina sold that property and gave that money to her daughter so that she would be able to continue her studies in Japan. Her daughter had received a degree in Japanese literature at the Hebrew University of Jerusalem. She wanted to continue her degree in Kyoto University in Japan, but the cost of living in Japan is very high.

Marina truly deserves to be called my muse. And everywhere I go, at every meeting, every chance I can, I introduce Marina as my muse and love.

The Israeli Bar Association

Despite how this marriage supported me socially, I still had much anxiety as a result of my professional and financial issues. I had many difficulties finding a job for two reasons: first of all, because of my lack of proficiency in the Hebrew language; secondly, because of my age.

1984-The graduation ceremony at Paris University where Daniel received his Ph.D in Constitutional Law.

For my first five years living in Israel I had been working with Reverend von der Houven; however, he split from the International Christian Embassy and created a new organization: the International Zionist Christian Center. I was faithful to Reverend von der Houven and as a result I had to leave as well.

While I was working with the International Christian Embassy, during my first five years in Israel, I studied in order to join the Israeli Bar Association. I did the obligatory law internship in a wonderful law firm in Jerusalem with Zale Yaffe. Zale is a wonderful man and an excellent lawyer. He was very supportive and helped me acclimate as much as he could into society and the Israeli law arena. We became friends and I have spent many shabbatot with him and his family since then.

This was to be the fifth time that I would study to join a Bar Association. Twice I studied in Teheran to become an attorney of law, once before the Revolution and once after. I also joined the Bar Associations of France and Australia, where I worked on behalf of Iranian refugees in those countries as a legal advisor. In each Bar association there are two types of certifications that one can receive. One is as an attorney of law. This means that one can represent clients in court. The other certification is as a legal advisor. The examinations to become an advisor cover less material and are therefore easier to pass. In Israel I wanted to become an attorney.

I was not familiar with the legal and educational system in Israel.

Redemption | 189

2005-Daniel, with his colleague, Michael Hanaii, representing a client at the Labor Court in Tel Aviv.

For foreign lawyers to be accepted to work in Israel there is a five-year minimum of work experience and a committee has to assess the lawyer's professional background. His educational background is assessed as well. Then there is a requirement to work for a year as an intern with a local law firm. Finally he must pass an exam in Hebrew legal terminology as well as the bar examination itself. The Bar exam covers eight separate topics including constitutional law, civil law, penal law, administrational law, civil and penal procedure, contracts, obligations and family law.

I have heard that there are American and European Jewish lawyers who come for several weeks and take the tests very quickly. They have a strong background in law, Hebrew, English and Judaism. So while this feat is exceptional it is possible. It took me, though, three and a half years. English was not my mother tongue nor was Hebrew. Israeli law has its foundations in the British Mandate law from pre-state times. However it has a strong spirit rooted in Jewish law as well. I had no background in that area. Many members of the bar association tried to convince me to stop and continue with business, I persevered and, after three and a half years, I did pass.

All Israeli lawyers, when they finish all of their requirements to join the Bar Association, have a graduation ceremony. At my ceremony the head of the Israeli Bar Association, Dr. Moses Cohen, approached me and told me that Israel has many Iranian lawyers, however, I was the first to have graduated from Teheran University. He expressed that he hoped that this could act as a beginning of a positive relationship between Israel and Iran.

During this conversation, I told Dr. Cohen that I believed, given my background, that I could be helpful with negotiating for the safe return of Ron Arad. Lieutenant Colonel Arad was an F-4 Phantom WSO. On a mission to attack PLO targets near Sidon, in Lebanon, on October 16, 1986, it is believed that a bomb that was dropped by the jet exploded prematurely in the air causing damage to the aircraft and forced Arad and the pilot to eject. The pilot was rescued a few hours later, but Arad had been captured by the Lebanese Shiite militia Amal.

I also spoke with Dr. Cohen about the Israeli consulate in Teheran. When the Shiite-Islamic Regime took over the government in 1979, a Palestinian group took over the Israeli consulate in Teheran. I explained to Dr. Cohen what would have to be done legally in order to recapture the consulate and claim for damages, which was estimated to be worth $70 million in reparations.

Dr. Cohen became very excited about the consulate and he advised that I begin negotiating with the Ministry of Foreign Affairs. As for negotiations for the return of Rod Arad, nothing came of it in the end. I campaigned via the mass media in order to rally support for these negotiations yet my efforts were in vain.

The Iranian Community In Israel

THE STATISTICS OF THE Israeli Ministry of Interior states that there are approximately 300,000 Iranians living in Israel. As I mentioned previously, from my first days in Israel I was already building ties in Israel's Iranian community and these ties grew daily.

Before I had come to Israel, both before and after the Shiite-Islamic Revolution, I had experienced living outside of Iran for more than 20 years, in several places including, France, Australia, Italy, Germany and England. My connections with the Iranian communities in these countries, throughout that time, had always been based upon my political affiliations and activities, rarely were my interactions purely social. During those 20 years I had never felt a part of any of those communities. However, when I got to Israel those feelings changed and for the first time I found myself a member of a community.

The feelings that gave me a sense of affiliation to the community here were surreal and it almost a supernatural experience. Throughout my life I had never felt that I could trust anyone.

When I first had come to Israel I had not felt safe. I did not know if anyone was pursuing me and I did not know whom I could trust. But I also felt a strong sense of belonging, acceptance and love from all of my new friends. As my connections with the Iranian community grew my feelings of insecurity lessened and I felt more and more a part of the Israeli society. The support of my new friends along with the support and faith in me from my wonderful Marina gave me a strong sense of belonging.

One of the first people I met from the Iranian community was a man named Baback Itzchaki. After discussing with him some of my political ideas and a little about my past, he became very excited and invited me to speak in his community synagogue, Bet Knesset Halleli Dakah of Holon. My talk was organized by Shahyad, the only Persian language magazine in Israel. After introducing myself, I recited a poem that I had composed based upon the story of David and Goliath, in Persian. In my translation I used the same poetic style and meter as Fredossi, one of the most celebrated Iranian poets. I also included in my poem aspects of current political issues of today.

My speech took place two years after I first came to Israel and it was my first time speaking here. My poem moved everyone in the audience. People came over to me with tears in their eyes expressing how they felt. The Rabbi's assistant gave me a big hug and stated that there was no way that I was not of Jewish decent. Professor Ze'ev Magen, the head of the Persian department of Bar Ilan University told me that I could be a valuable asset to the Persian community here in Israel and I must continue with this work. Since then I have written more than 150 articles and poems including the stories of Esther and Mordechai, Samson and Delilah amongst others. In fact, I have created and presented poetry based upon most of the Tanach.

I have spoken many times in public all over Israel. I have been interviewed many times by the media. Each time I spoke I presented the same message:

Up until the Shiite-Islamic Revolution in Iran, as a result of the political leftist orientation of the universities, students in Iran saw Israel as an imperialistic society and evil. But after the revolution, as much as the Shiite-Islamic regime would preach against Israel, the student community grew to be more and more supportive of Israel. Since the liberal academic society is so against their government, as the government preached of the evils of Israel, the students finally began to see that Israel is their only ally in the Middle East; the only democracy in the region.

The other message I wanted to present was how rich the Iranian culture had been. I spoke about how Iran was the home of the first civilization of man. I spoke of Kings Cyrus, Darius and Achashveirosh and their connection and support of the Israeli people. I spoke about Daniel, Ezra and Nehemiah and all of the common Biblical elements between Israel and Iran. During the Greek and Roman invasions of the Middle East, Iranian soldiers always cooperated with the Israeli military factions: the Maccabees and the Hasmoneans. And I spoke about how these twin-sister nations had always had, until 30 years ago, a strong and healthy connection.

I still had many contacts amongst the Iranian opposition leaders throughout the world. I sent them many articles with these ideas. I added that if they were serious about rebuilding Iran to the true glory that she had been, then they should use Israel as their inspiration. In a short period of time Israel, surrounded by her enemies, had build a beautiful country from a desert and the only democracy in the region.

I invited many Iranian leaders, of the opposition, of culture and other activists to come to Israel in order to see the true, beautiful, Israel. Not only through my articles but also through my invitations I sent out my message of peace and love. Despite the extremely negative propaganda against Israel, many of these leaders came and their visit transformed them. Whether they were politically left or right, they finally saw the true Israel, and that it was not what they were being told it was. When each one left I sent them as an emissary with the message of peace and love.

The Peace and Love International Movement, via this pro-Israel activity, has been able to influence many Christians, Muslims and Zoroastrians from all over the world, to come and visit Israel. Now, many of these people are studying Hebrew abroad in hopes of coming closer to the Jewish people and their homeland.

I have been invited to many conferences. I used this opportunity to introduce the Biblical connections between Israel and Iran. But I did not leave the parallels to the Bible. I translated selections from the Israeli left-wing author Amos Oz and the right-wing author Shai Agnon. I compared their works with Iranian left and right-wing literature and tried to show how similar we all are.

If I could condense my cultural activity over the past 14 years in Israel into a few words I would say that I have positioned myself as a bridge. For the Israeli-Iranian community I have arranged hundreds of meetings with the objective of introducing Iranian culture and literature to the community here. My hopes are that via this cultivation of knowledge and heritage it will inspire them to continue as peacemakers themselves and overwhelm the poison being spread by the current Shiite regime in Iran.

I have also written hundreds of articles for the non-Jewish Iranians around the world and I have spoken with hundreds of people and been interviewed countless times. My objective has always been to present the rich historical connections between Israel and Iran with the hope that it will undermine the destructive message currently being presented about the evils of Israel.

My Jewish Blood

During my first five years in Israel I continued my research in comparative religions at the International Christian Embassy of Jerusalem. After those first five years my employer, Reverend Jan William von der Houven, for various reasons separated from the embassy. I was very close with the Reverend and felt that it necessary to leave as well. As a result, though, my financial problems began again.

I applied at different law firms for a job. I interviewed and applied for several positions at many different places. For six months I was out of a job. There were three major reasons why I could not find a work, despite my vast experience: my age, my religion and my nationality. I was much older, by that time, than most lawyers applying to firms. I was not Jewish, in a Jewish state. I was an anomaly; most of the non-Jews are not integrated into society. And I am Iranian – the tensions between modern Israel and Iran were never strong, even more so after the Shiite-Islamic revolution.

My connections in the Iranian community here helped me. Through my connections I found work translating to Persian from English and

French and I edited previously translated works. I translated Naguib Mahfouz's, the 1988 Nobel Laureate, edition of *Arabian Nights* for a French-Persian-Israeli film company. I also edited the memoirs of Meir Ezri, the first Israeli ambassador to Iran from 1958-1973. His memoirs spanned two volumes of over 350 pages each volume.

1996-Daniel with Meir Ezri.

I also edited his father's memoirs, Tzion Ezri, the builder of the Halutz movement of early Israel. His memoirs were only half the size of his son's, 400 pages. That job took me a half the time, a full year. While I was working on the Ezri's books I was appointed as the official editor of his quarterly, "Eastern Star." I learned a lot about the Iran-Israel connection from working for Mr. Ezri. I grasped much knowledge from my research and translation of his book about current politics and recent history between the two nations.

Later on I had a contract with the Iranian Shirazi community in Israel. I wrote a book for them spanning 600 pages. The topic of the book was about the Jewish community in the time of King Cyrus. After King Cyrus gave his blessings for the Jews of Iran to return to Israel and rebuild their Temple, many Jews opted to remain in Iran in the capital, Persepolis, several kilometers from Shiraz. This community wanted to show how their families dated back to the time of the destruction of the First Temple of Jerusalem. Unfortunately for various reasons the community could not

Daniel with members of the Iranian community in Israel.

publish the book.

Since I saw that this work was supporting me I continued in this field. I translated Mrs. Neima Teffilin-Menasheri's memoirs from Hebrew to Persian. She had been one of the candidates for mayor of the city of Ofakim. She was one of the more prominent Labor Party activists over the past fifty years. At the official launching of her book, many prominent officials of the government participated including Shaul Mofaz, Shimon Peres and Ariel Sharon.

Neima was a very heroic woman and a tremendous symbol of Iranian Zionism. In 1999 and 2000, 11 men of Mujahidin who had been in Ashraf, Bagdad fled. Many were tortured and had been condemned to death. Some of them fled to Jordan, however Jordan did not accept them as political refugees. From Jordan they went to Israel. They were in jail in Israel for eight months, because of their terrorist background.

Once their story had been confirmed and they were released from prison, Neima housed these refugees in her home for seven months. During this time she worked through the UN towards finding other countries that would accept them. Now several of them are political refugees in various countries in Europe and Canada. Two remain in Israel.

Despite all that Neima had done for them, given their training and background, they could not return even the slightest good for her. While I was editing Neima's book, she asked me to interview them so that I could include their own testimonies in her book. When I approached them, though, not one would consent to an interview with me without the payment of at least $10,000. This is the nature of people who were rejected from Mujahidin.

Neima also helped a young man named Reza Jabbari, a flight attendant. During a flight from Teheran to Dubai, Reza hijacked the plane with one hundred and seventy two Iranian passengers and brought them to Eilat. He served a sentence of eight years in jail. While Reza was in prison Neima gave him legal and political support. She and I worked to convince the legal authorities that while Reza's act was one of terrorism, his motivation was positive. He did not harm anyone and as soon as he landed he gave himself up to the officials.

Mrs. Teffilin was always interested with the Royal Iranian family. Because of my previous connections I helped her contact her majesty the queen among other right wing activists. Mrs. Teffilin was my greatest supporter to the Ministry of Interior and the Rabbinate in Israel. Today we are still in close contact.

These activities over the years had given me a very good reputation as a translator and had helped me develop connections and a network outside of Israel. For example I have edited the Poetry of Dr. V. Golshani, the representative of Zoroastrianism in England. Many times I have invited him and his family to Israel and we have successfully been able to build strong ties between the world Zoroastrian community and Israel. During this time, while I was editing and writing, I continued searching for a way to break into the profession I had chosen here in Israel – to become a lawyer.

Once, I had arranged a private tour for a group of non-Jewish Iranians from outside of Israel. This group consisted of Christian and Zoroastrian leaders; among them were several Muslims as well, people I had worked with previously in the political arena. I brought them group to Yad Vashem, Jerusalem's holocaust museum; they were moved to learn about Israel's history. While many of them had heard about the holocaust none of them had learned very much. They were sad and sympathetic.

The subject of the conversation continued to me. They asked me how I was managing here, living alone? My friend, Yossi Sivan, had accompanied me with this group. When our guests began questioning me about how I could live in Israel, alone, Yossi jumped in and answered for me: "He's not alone, he has six million brothers and sisters here."

It is amazing how one sentence can change your life. I had already begun to feel a part of the community here. But when I heard Yossi's answer I was so moved I truly felt that what he said was true. Yossi has been a wonderful friend to me, supportive and strong. And I thank him for all he has done.

Six or seven years ago I helped to establish an artists group as part of the Peace and Love International Movement. I named this group

Nil-Achtar – Blue Star. I collected 35 artists from many different fields including visual arts, performance arts, and musicians. Each artist donated funds, whatever each of us could afford, out of his own pocket in order to support our group.

One day a reporter from the prestigious Israeli magazine "Anashim" decided to write an article about us so I arranged for her to come during one of our meetings so that she could interview as many of us as she would need for her article. One of the artists in our group, Chaim Hakimi, a well-known playwright, told this reporter while she was interviewing him that I was like a candle to our group and the other artists were dancing around me. This touched me very deeply and made me feel deeply connected to my friends there.

For two years I lived in the Jerusalem neighborhood of Bet Hakerem. There, I went to the synagogue of Rabbi Shapira. He is very warm and open man and welcomed me with open arms. I became very close with David Herman of that congregation. He invited me to his home many times for the Sabbath meal. He did all he could to help me find a job. And when I was trying to get involved with the government with the case of Ron Arad, the missing soldier, David introduced me to the organization "Lost Soldiers" with the hope that they would be able to intervene as well. David is a very good friend and faithful man. I value his friendship.

I was not welcomed completely with open arms, though. One of my employers loved my work so much and was very proud of it. He had heard from several professors that I have a very professional and had unique style of writing in Persian. One day I was standing with him and two of our colleagues and this employer announced: "You have bound yourself to my nation and I am proud to call you my brother." Several years later he and I had a disagreement over financial issues. In front of the same two people, to whom he announced that I am his brother, I asked him how someone could treat his brother such. His response, sadly, was a denial that he had ever called me his "brother." It is a shame the way money can tear families apart.

After I found out from the high commissioner of the UN in Israel that I would be in Israel for a while, and after I had finished working for the International Christian Embassy of Jerusalem, I decided to look for a job in academia. I had come to Israel for her sake, and I wanted to continue my studies. I contacted several professors at Tel Aviv University and the Hebrew University of Jerusalem in order to see if they could help me find a job. However, not one could help me get my foot in through the door.

They would say how sorry they were that I hadn't found anything yet, but not one of them would help me more than offer their sympathies.

My financial needs pushed me to look for a proper full-time job. I contacted a human-resource firm run by the Israeli Social Security offices. After presenting them my background information they offered me a job working as a night security guard, completely ignoring my academic qualifications. Being in the financial situation that I was in I was forced to accept. Despite not being happy with my job I made the best of my situation. I used this time at night, while working, to study for the bar exam and expand my knowledge about Judaism.

I also took this time to contemplate how the Australian government had treated me. It was during those nights that I decided to sue the Foreign Affairs Ministry over the damages they had caused me by exiling me, again. Subsequently, I did attempt to sue them; however, the law firm that agreed to take my case insisted on a $20,000 down payment before they began with my case. Obviously, I could not afford that.

Over the course of two and a half years I worked five nights a week as a night guardsman. This position can be degrading and, unfortunately, I had my share of negative experiences. However, I did have my share of positive experiences as well. There were quite a few people who did treat me with respect and when they found out about my background tried to help me find another job.

On Friday, the 30th of May 2000, after eating a meal in honor of the Sabbath night, I stayed up reading until 1:30 in the morning and then went to bed. The next morning, six hours later, when I woke up I could not move. My left leg felt like it was stone and I saw that it had begun to turn purple. Marina became very upset, understandably so. I assumed that this had happened because of an accident I had had in Paris in 1984. My back had been broken then and had successfully healed. I thought that whatever they had done to fix me had come undone. For several weeks prior to that morning my left leg had ached slightly. Being the athletic person that I am, I thought that it was merely a cramp.

Marina called for an ambulance. I was first brought to the health clinic and from there I was sent to Hadassah Hospital in Jerusalem. Over the weekend, unless there is a special need, the hospital uses a minimal staff. I was examined by a young Russian doctor. He agreed with my prognosis and told me that there had been nerve damage in my back. He gave me medication and sent me home.

At home I noticed that my leg was not only not getting better but the purple had begun to turn grey. Marina called a close friend of hers who is a doctor himself. He looked at my leg and exclaimed that it was not nerve damage; rather, I had blood clots. He explained that I needed to see a hematologist immediately; if a clot were to dislodge from the veins in my leg it could go to my heart and kill me.

I returned again to the hospital where I remained for two weeks. They trained me how to inject myself, into my navel, with the drug "Celexon." I would need to inject myself for the next six months twice a day. I was also told that I would have to take Comadine for the rest of my life and that I would need to check my blood every two weeks in order to regulate the dosage. Every three months I would need to check with a Hematologist as well.

I had planned to travel to Europe for a conference. In order to do so I would need a letter explaining my illness. I went to Professor Edelson, the top Hematologist in the country for a letter explaining my situation. He wrote in his letter that the specific strain of my illness, Thalassemia Anemia Minor, is unique to Middle Eastern Jewry. I had never told Professor Edelson about my background and he did not know that I was not Jewish. Marina and I were in shock. God must have sent me this illness to show me how I really am Jewish.

I had met regularly with another well-known Hematologist, Professor Warren. I had to see him on a tri-monthly basis. On my return from my trip to Europe I met with Professor Warren again. I asked him about what Professor Edelson had told me. He was surprised that I even asked him such a question. When I told him that I was not Jewish he was in shock. He advised me that I ask my mother and other relatives about their health and find out who in my family has this problem. When he told me this I remembered that my mother always had to take medication for a blood condition that she had had. Then, I though nothing of it; but I am sure that no doctor in the Post-Shiite-Islamic Revolution Iran would mention the connection between this condition and Jews.

I called my brother, who at that time still was living in Iran, as I do regularly. I mentioned my condition and he told me that his son, who then was 12 years old, has the same condition. Apparently it is widespread in my family.

The Rabbinate

ALREADY AS A YOUNG teenager of the age of seventeen, for no apparent reason, I supported Israel and felt positively towards Judaism; these feelings almost got me expelled from high school. As I learned more about Iranian history, these feelings grew.

While I was studying to become an Anglican Priest a large portion of my studies was dedicated to becoming a missionary. During this period I wrote an essay about why Christians should not try to convert Jews. I wrote that Christianity is a child of Judaism; how can a son guide his father? A son who studies a field that his father has not, can advise his father in this field; but Judaism is the theological father of Christianity. I wrote that it is God's responsibility to guide the Jews to the right path, but it is not right for us to.

My essay caused waves throughout the Church. They thought that I was still too close to my Muslim roots to understand the importance of proselytizing to Jews. Yet, still today I believe just as strongly in this idea as I did then.

I remember one day during my training one of the leaders of the Jewish community of Australia was invited to discuss her beliefs with the trainees of my course. While she was there the floor was open to questions from all of the students. This interaction took place with the utmost respect; however, I felt pain for this woman. I found myself in a difficult situation. I believed very strongly in what both sides presented. And so, when I saw the other students bombarding her with questions, albeit respectfully, I could not help but feel pity for her. The guest held her position strongly, but all of the questions were like arrows penetrating her armor. It is not a fair thing to do to anyone.

I have had other negative experiences working with the Church since then. Specifically concerning my letter to Archbishop Kafity and when I discovered how pro-Palestinian the Church was in Israel. However I must mention that, for the most part, Christianity had welcomed me warmly and respectfully.

During the first two years in Israel I had many challenges dealing with the bureaucracy here: politically, socially and materialistically. I needed documentation accepting me as a citizen; I had no country in the world that would accept me. In order to earn money, so that I could put bread on my table, I needed this basic right. I could not practice law, nor even take the Bar exam, without the proper documentation. There was also no way for me to travel without proper citizenship.

My relationship with Marina was growing daily. Eventually we discovered that we could legally get married in Uruguay; however, we would never truly be considered a part of society here, in the Jewish country, if I were not Jewish. Unfortunately, Israel is known for her bureaucracy, and the religious institutions are known as not only having vast amounts of red tape but also being incredibly disorganized as well.

Seeing these difficulties I decided that the best path for me would be to convert to Judaism. Little did I know that it would certainly not be the easier path. At that time, when I had decided to convert, I did not feel the same burning desire towards Judaism that I had towards Christianity. Now I certainly do, but I did not see that as a hypocrisy. I believe in the Bible; I believe in God. I was fine with worshiping an incorporeal God rather than Jesus. And if it meant that I would be able to fit better into society here, that would be fine with me.

I had heard about one of the respected leaders of the Iranian community in Israel, Shimeon Hanassab, who had helped a woman from Iran convert and receive her citizenship here in Israel. I decided to contact him in hope that he would be able to help me as well.

When I met with him he asked me to write a letter that described why I wanted to convert to Judaism. I wrote a short three page letter, explaining my situation and why I wanted to convert.

When I met with him for a second time he told me that I had written a beautiful letter but he needed more details. So I expanded upon what I had written. I included information about my background and some of my feelings. This second letter was ten pages long. But a ten-page letter was not long enough either. Again I was sent away and told that I needed to write more.

This time I told my whole story and my whole background. I described everything I felt and what had brought me to this point. This third letter was 54 pages long. I interviewed with him several times. He asked me many questions about my background but after two years he still did not have an answer for me, neither here nor there.

Finally Mrs. Puran Farzan, one of the leaders of the Iranian community in Jerusalem, advised me that I contact the Rabbinate directly. She introduced me to Rabbi X, an American. She suggested that I contact the American Rabbinate of Jerusalem and work through the system in English since there is no Persian-speaking infrastructure set up in the Chief Rabbinate in Israel.

I met with a panel of five people: four Rabbis along with the wife of one of the Rabbis. They asked me many questions about my background, my philosophies, and why I wanted to become Jewish. When the subject of my Christian background arose, I explained why I had originally decided to become Christian. I continued to explain that I truly have no qualms with Christianity, except for a few unfortunate incidents, which I then described. But I said that I saw Christianity as the vessel, which brought me to my true roots, that helped me understand who I am and for that I am thankful. This seemed to be a problem for them. The Jewish community tends to be suspicious of Jews, or people who want to be Jewish, who also believe in the tenets of Christianity. This suspicion is probably warranted since most people and organizations, which openly accept both faiths, tend to focus a lot of energy on missionizing Jews. However, I was not familiar with the source of these fears. If I had been, I would have happily shared with them my feelings on the subject.

By that time I had many Jewish friends and they advised me that I dissimulate my feelings about the matter. But I could not, I had to be honest. Over the course of two years I met with this council four times. Finally, at the fourth meeting they accepted me to study in their program.

Over the course of a year, twice a week, I went to a course. Many times Marina joined the class as well. We had a very positive experience. The teachers of the program were warm and accepting; these were the very same people who were on the panel that had accepted me. I have very fond memories of that time. We studied many subjects including academic level biblical studies, along with many different practical applications of the material we were studying. We learned how to keep a Jewish home.

RELIGION HAS PLAYED A big part in my life. I was born a Shiite Muslim, I have lived as a devout Christian and now I am Jewish. I believe that as a result of my experiences I can present a different perspective on these religions than most scholars of comparative religion.

For the first fifteen years of my life I was brainwashed. I had been brought up to be a devout Muslim. My grandmother had wanted me to be an Ayatollah. But I was paralyzed in my faith. I did not know about anything else; I had no knowledge of other world-views. While I was practicing this life system I had no idea how anyone could live otherwise. It was the truth.

From my wanderings throughout the world I saw that many people live in this manner. They are brought up one way and they never consider that it might not be the only way through which to see the world. This is even more so in the Shiite-Islamic world. Most people are brainwashed: socially, politically, economically, and spiritually. The Shiite-Islamic world is very closed and controlling. There is a powerful propaganda machine turning out hateful messages against anything different constantly. Their religious outlook is based upon discrimination and is highly politically motivated. No one would consider looking in another direction for answers. People are closed in an iron frame and immovable.

A devout Shiite-Muslim goes to mosque twice a day: every morning and evening. Aside from that, he prays three more times throughout the day making the count a total five times a day. I was still young and did not go regularly to mosque but I did pray regularly. I went to a religious school and spent much time studying the Koran.

During two months out of the year I was religiously more active. From sunrise to sunset throughout the month Ramadan a 12-hour fast is held each day. I fasted throughout the month of Ramadan, sometimes I would even begin fasting before the month started to welcome it in. My father not pleased with this. The second month in which I was more active religiously was Muhoram, with the parades.

There are also dietary restrictions. A religious Muslim will not eat any pig or drink alcohol or any derivatives of these foods. These restrictions are similar to the dietary restrictions in Judaism; however, there are more in Judaism. But these restrictions are irrelevant when living in a theocracy, where one cannot easily acquire these products anyways.

There are many similarities between the two religions of Judaism and Shiite Islam. One big difference, though, is that Shiite Islam is corrupt. When a Jew is a faithful Jew he practices the tenets of his faith with all of his heart. In Shiite Islam, in contrast, it is all for show. I will not deny that there are Jews who practice what they do only to better their position in their community but, from my experience, the majority of the devout in Shiite Islam is corrupt and in Judaism, the intentions are pure. In Shiite Islam, in order to rise above the rest in the clergy one must be corrupt, while in Judaism and Christianity it is the opposite that is true.

There was a thirty-year gap between my life as a Muslim and my life as a Christian. Once I left my religious life behind all I believed in were science, power and money; I was a devout atheist. When I found God again I saw it as a miracle that this could happen to me. My heart shifted so quickly. And seeing this only motivated me to grow in Christianity even more.

The more I leaned the more I saw that the major difference between Christianity and Shiite Islam is that Christianity is a faith-based religion. The renaissance and reformation gave freedom of choice and democracy to the West. I felt that if there is a God, God is in Judeo-Christianity. If there is a Creator, this Creator must be a loving Creator. We are this Creator's children. Through having children I understand the idea of love for one's creation. God, having created this world, must love infinitely more. Judeo-Christianity is based upon this love as it says in Leviticus 18:19: "Love your neighbor as yourself." Holders of the Judeo-Christian beliefs are more open minded and accepting of all of God's children. They have good relationships with each other. Christianity is an open and healthy society. Shiite Islam is a closed society; people beat and cheat each other and, all in all, are destructive to all. If we all are children of God, why is it okay to be dishonest with other children of God?

Daniel, speaking with Bibi Netanyahu about PLIM. Netanyahu is the current Prime Minister of Israel.

When a Christian believes he believes in his heart. Being a part of Christianity was a different world experience.

For the first five years living in Australia, living as a Christian, I was always trying to be fruitful for my society. I was honest and clean and I followed Christian order. Every Sunday I went to church. Twice a week I went to various Bible studies classes. I organized several activities for the community. I was an active missionary. But as I mentioned before, I never evangelized Jews; mostly I evangelized Muslims. I operated hundreds of interviews both with Christians and Muslims. I taught the Christians how to share with Muslims how they are far from God.

I believe that in all three groups of people there are truly religious people. But for the most part, my experience was that the higher religious

Daniel explains PLIM to Israeli President Shimon Peres, at President's House in Jerusalem. To the left of President Peres is Rev. Fritz Porter, who represents PLIM in Atlanta, Georgia.

people would rise up in the Muslim world, the more corrupt and insincere they would become. But in Judaism and Christianity the truly religious people were pure in their hearts with God. Judaism was rationally different. I am proud to now be a Jew.

    The rabbinate truly tortured me. I forgive them; I know that their intent was not to hurt me. They made a mistake, but they were doing their jobs. I cannot believe that their intentions were truly negative. There were no diabolical intentions there. I cannot hold onto my hates. I know that they were holding, in their hearts, to the edict: "Do not be bad to your neighbor."

    But I cannot forgive my Muslim brothers. The religion commands one to be dishonest with people that are not like you. All of the problems that were brought upon me, I believe, were intentional. Is this God? Does God, the father of this beautiful creation hold a grudge? There are countless examples of cases where the Koran says to do things specifically against Jews and Christians.

    I am not angry at Shiite Islam. I have a responsibility to my readers. God is not bad. A billion people are not all bad and terrorists. They are not reading the Koran correctly.

    The Koran is called "Kalamallah", the last word of Allah. Muslims will not read the Bible. The Koran claims to include in it the messages of the Bible. But one cannot truly compare the two and believe that they are the same.

    In Judaism and Christianity our Heavenly Father has a direct relationship with us, the children of His creation. In Islam this is not so. Allah is so far removed from the creation that according to Islam it is impossible for man to have a relationship with God.

There is a concept of a messiah in Shiite Islam, similar to the concept of a messiah in Judaism and Christianity. In Judaism there is a messiah, and when he comes he will bring world peace with him. Christianity believes that Jesus was the messiah and he will return and bring world peace with him as well. In Shiite Islam there is a messiah too: "Emam-e Zaman." When he comes, according to their tradition, his horse will be up to its knees in blood as a result of the slaughter that his rider will bring with him. Does a father treat his children in this manner? Can you believe that God is the Creator of this world and believe that He treats his creation in this way?

I was born a Muslim so I had no choice in the matter. It had been passed down through the generations. I became a Christian because of feelings. For me, my reawakening was a miracle and it filled my world with goodness. I converted to Judaism because of wisdom. I felt a strong connection to the people. And as I learned more, I was stimulated and grew in belief of her wisdom. But it was more than that. Judaism is in my blood.

THROUGHOUT THE YEAR THAT I was studying to for my conversion, I prayed regularly in the Great Synagogue in Jerusalem. I became very close with all of the members of the community. It was there that I found a place to do my clerkship while I was studying for my Bar exam.

At the end of the course, I took a test and passed. I went to the rabbinate to complete the process of conversion. They wanted various documents and papers, including a letter of certification from the synagogue in which I prayed as well as a letter from a well-known Jewish family that we had been in contact with us throughout the year, to make sure that we were progressing properly. Edward Cohen and David Herman were very supportive of my progress and they wrote me letters. I also gathered letters from various Iranian leaders and thinkers in the Iranian community here.

They also requested the get, Jewish divorce contract, from Marina's previous marriage. It was not only an expensive ordeal, the special notarization needed cost $2,000, but also it was an extremely sensitive issue to arrange. She had been divorced for 19 years and they had not spoken that whole time, but now she had to call him up and ask him for divorce papers all over again; it was very difficult.

The process with the rabbinate took two and a half years. I went for interviews three separate times with Marina. Each time needed different papers, and each official that we met with requested a separate payment.

Finally Rabbi Mamo accepted us. We passed the panel of rabbis on the third time and he told me that when I receive my Israeli identification papers, my ezrachut, I should come back to receive my certificate from him.

This never happens. In fact, converting in Israel, for many cases, is a prerequisite for receiving one's citizenship. I debated this point with him but it was useless.

It took me another three years to receive my ezrachut. Many friends intervened. Rabbi Dahan, among many other rabbis, tried to sort out my story with the rabbinate.

After 12 years living in Israel and seven years working with the rabbinate I received my citizenship. I was looking forward to finishing the conversion process and I wanted to arrange a huppah, a Jewish wedding ceremony, with Marina. I went to Rabbi Mamo's office with my citizenship papers.

When I got there I found out that he had been expelled from the rabbinate because of financial corruption. Someone else had taken over for Rabbi Mamo. I told him my story and what Rabbi Mamo had said but this new rabbi couldn't find my file. He told me to come back.

I had to come back three times, each time with the same story. On the third time he told me that they had lost my file and I would have to go through the entire process of converting again. It is notable to mention that Marina hadn't made a copy of her get, divorce papers. She had trusted them that they would not lose such a valuable and expensive document. We did not know at that time how irresponsible they could be. Not to mention all the other papers and documents. And the process on top of all that! To go through it all again was beyond me.

I was fuming. I took my kippa off and threw it on the floor at this rabbi's feet. I exclaimed: "I am more Jewish than you are! It is running through my veins. I am more of a Zionist than you will ever be." But there was nothing I could do. Since then I have not worn a kippa again. Despite this, I feel more and more connected with my true Jewish roots than ever before. My roots that go back thousands of years to the time of King Cyrus and beyond.

Epilogue

WHEN I RECEIVED MY citizenship, I changed name to Dana from Hassani. Dana had been my grandfather's name from my mother's side. This was the same grandfather who had come to Iran from Azerbaijan. Most probably he came to Azerbaijan from the Jewish community of Mashad. He was the official Persian-Russian translator for the government in the city of Baku in Azerbaijan. His family name had been Abayef, as Khalu-Muossa had told his daughter. But when my grandfather reached Iran the officials told him that to be accepted into the community it would be better to take on a more Persian-sounding name. Abayef was "too Jewish" so he adopted the name Danadeh, which means wise man. This name was his nickname in Azerbaijan.

The feelings that I had had in Australia drove me to create the Peace and Love International Movement (PLIM). I wanted to evangelize Shiite-Muslims back to our Iranian roots. When I moved to Israel, I continued developing the movement. Because of my relationship with the Iranian opposition, PLIM shifted from a religious platform to a more political platform. I recognized that the ideals and goals of PLIM were relevant for all walks of faith around the world. I saw that it was a much larger task than I had originally envisioned.

Daniel, speaking in Japan in 2008 to large audience supporting PLIM.

Fourteen centuries ago the Iranian faith had been Zoroastrianism, the faith of King Cyrus who was the only non-Jew in the Bible to be called "messiah." I have a close relationship with Zoroastrianism all around the world. I have close ties with Christianity and now being Jewish, I am close to this community as well.

As a bridge builder between faiths, I recognized that these three religions should work together to. These three groups suffered for 14 centuries as second-class citizens in Iran. They had been the entire population and should not be secondary citizens.

Peace and Love International is working together from all these groups of people. We see ourselves as the children of King Cyrus and we want to reform Shiite Islam. We want equal opportunity and rights for everybody, as King Cyrus had offered in his empire. This is the greatest dream of Abayef.

Appendix I

Shiite Reformation in Iran
Dr. Daniel Dana

CHRISTIANS IN THE WEST have paid a heavy price for their infidelity to their Lord through an excess of 250 years of Crusades and still their Holiest site still needs to be cleansed. The second heavy price was paid during the Inquisitions. The negative consequences of the first test brought them a terrible reputation. The second price, despite its horrible nature, motivated many leaders of Protestantism, including Luther, Swingy, Berkley, Calvin and many others to facilitate the Reformation atmosphere, French Revolution, new technology and the western social democracy. What could be a third heavy price? I believe that a third price paid is the ignorance of new changes in the Church and the recent face of the Islamic migration to the West.

Today there are different forms of corruption inside and outside the Church. It causes a lot of problems when millions of Muslims, either Shiite or Sunni, are moving to the West, not to be as Westerners, rather to make Westerners like themselves. What are the results of such policies? It is none of my business and this is a Church problem or a case for political leaders in the West. But, whatever has motivated me to share my experience with my Christian and Jewish families, is only the notion of obedience of my Lord and to help people know His glory as much as I can in answering the above question: "What could be the third heavy price of Judeo-Christianity?"

To give an analytical comparative study between Shiite Islam and Judeo-Christianity would be an academic work, and not for here. Therefore, I will attempt to help brothers and sisters to realize deep changes in Iran. Whatever you are reading is based on my own academic or practical experiences as an ex-Muslim lawyer and well educated in Judeo-Christianity and Zoroastrianism.

Basic Reforms

MOST OF THE CURRENT Shiite leaders today were borne in Iran. Despite this, many Iranians hesitated to call them Iranian citizen. According to the mass media, they have a great portion of responsibility for the large numbers of terrorist attacks over the past three decades since coming into power in Iran.

As an Iranian believer, I am convinced that God is with us and we have to help more people to increase a true peace amongst the 75 million Iranians who have reasonable expectations to live in peace. Only a deep reformation in the idea of Shiite Islam, though, can help the world in minimizing the terror. Prior to the Islamic revolution in Iran in 1979, Islamic terrorism was not as severe as it is today.

If we are looking for a fundamental reform of a nation, we need to know people, their culture and the history of their country. Much of the mass media in the West today are filled with news of the illegal atomic activities of Shiite Muslim leaders in the country of my birth. I have not seen that any of these journalists have a basic, accurate, cultural analogy of the reasons for this situation, nor do any of them propose any practical solutions. My fear is that the UN Security Council's decisions and its international sanction on Iran, in the end, will create another Iraq, but of greater power and proportions, creating long term and lasting terrorism.

DURING THE LAST 29 years of the Islamic Revolution in Iran, over half a million Iranian Shiite Muslims converted to Christianity and have found Jesus Christ as their only savior. This record is based on data from Iranians in exile, but whatever is happening in the country in this regard, could be a complicated question, which we will find the answer to in the future, after national liberation. This desire to change religions is an expression of their readiness for a major reformation of their ideas.

It is notable to be added that under the Koranic teaching, "Towzih-ol-Massael" by Ayatollah Khomeini, and the other major sources, such as Hadith by Al-Bukhari, that legal conversion from Shiite Islam to the other religion is not accepted, however there is a legal proceeding resulting and finally a death execution. The proceeding is as follows:

1 – First punishment: As soon as the clergy leader of the area, in which a converted man is living in, becomes aware of the convert, he will be invited to confess to his mistake and to remain a Shiite Muslim. If not, after a specified time, he will lose all of his property.

2 – Second punishment: A converted man will be invited, again by the same or another clergy leader, to be shamed publicly and return to his real religion. If he refuses, his wife and his family will not belong to him anymore.

3 – Third punishment: If the above two notices and kind proposals are not accepted by the new believer, he will be immediately hanged to death in front of his family.

This is the main reason that over the past 14 centuries, since the Arab Islamic Invasion to Iran (638), never officially has it been recorded that anyone converted to Christianity.

We have never seen or heard any written, oral, or other historical record, that during such a short period of time (1979-2007), a huge group of Shiite Muslims has converted to become Christian. In any Muslim country such a fundamental change could be seriously considered a social catastrophe. We interpret it as an absolute act of God among Iranians. Why Iran? First, we have to look at our Bible and secondly, we have to read something about Iranians pre-Islamic culture and their religious tolerance. This kind of reaction will help us understand why the Shiite-Islamic Reformation in Iran is deeply and very clearly foreseeable and how this notion should not be so strange.

Background

IRANIANS IN THE PRE-ISLAMIC period of time were Zoroastrians. They were kindly and tolerant towards religions and ideas of others. They also always had a close relationship with Jews and Christians. We can look at several Biblical and historical examples: Cyrus, the Zoroastrian King of Persia, offered freedom to Jews from captivity by Nebuchadnezzar in 558 BCE. Xeroxes, another Zoroastrian Persian King, also offered freedom to Jews in the book of Esther. Darius was another Zoroastrian Persian king, while Daniel was one of his three administrators of the 120 Satrapies.

During King Farhad, the 5th king of Parthian dynasty, the three Magi, Zoroastrian Priests, came from Iran, as indicated in the book of

Acts. Iranian Christian missionaries were the first group of believers who brought their message to China 1,600 years ago. Even today, there are some old churches in China that the local people call "Persian Temples." The greatest Jewish Yeshivot, study houses, outside of Israel were in Iran during the reign of Sassanid Dynasty (221-638).

All these popular kings and wise administrators were Zoroastrians. Millions of Iranians today are extremely sympathetic towards their ancient civilization, and see it as a great symbol of peace and they challenge to stop the Shiite barbarism.

It is not only their Iranian rich cultural background that has motivated so may Iranians to convert from Shiite Islam, nor is it the Shiite leaders' shameful attitudes during the last 14 centuries, from a historical point of view, and their harsh behavior during the last 26 years, from social and international points of view, that motivated Iranians to think about Shiite reformation, but it is also the lack of a sense of Divinity in the Shiite ideology, theology, theory and philosophy that cause Iranians to be more serious about the coming reformation.

Undivine Theology

LET US ASSUME THAT Islam is a monotheistic religion, Muhammad is a Muslim prophet and the Koran is their holy book, which has come from Allah. According to the Islamic Sunni theology, there are three major principles in this religion:

1 – **Towhid** – Acceptance of the unity of Allah.

2 – **Nabovvate** – Acceptance of Muhammad as a true prophet.

3 – **Moa'ad** – Acceptance of returning all Muslims to Allah on the day of judgment.

One of the main basic cornerstones and crucial concepts in any monotheistic religion is a Divine connection, a relationship with Heaven. If we assume that this relationship exists in Sunni Islam, in the Shiite sect it obviously does not exist. Why? Because Shiite theology has added two more principles to those three:

1 – **Emamat** – Acceptance of the succession of an Iranian citizen as Imam, instead of Caliph in the Shiite-Islamic state.

2 – **Adl** – Acceptance the social justice equality between a Persian and an Arab Muslim in the eyes of Allah.

Not only does that lack of theological principles show that Shiite Islam is not a religion, rather a man-made ideology, but also historically we have many references that prove how it is an Iranian politico-religious creation geared to deceive the Arab Muslim invaders. Shiite Islam has been the result of the Iranian national resistance against the invaders, while the army was defeated in the battlefields. The real desire of our forefathers in using the Islamic false theology was to create a strong political party as a social separation from the invading Arabs. They wished that the next generation could divide this new ideology into more sects and that in the long term become intertwined with Iranian culture and finally, the society could be free from the harsh anti-Iranian doctrine.

For this same historical reason, over one billion Sunni Muslims in the world claim against less than one hundred million Shiite Muslims, that they are unclean, hypocrites and infidels (Ajam = ignorant – Mavali = slave or second class citizen). Why? Because in fact the builders of Shiite Islam were the first group of Muslims to cut Islam in two pieces and caused a long period of wars. For the first time in the history of Islam, there are millions of Iranian Shiite Muslims who want to say to all their Sunni brothers and sisters in the world: "You are real Muslims, not us. You are the only children of the Koran and Muhammad, and not us. We give our apology that our forefathers divided your religion into 176 parts (the number of the sects in Shiite Islam). Now we are aware enough to choose the principle of freedom of choice in religion in our country without any force or any punishment if one of us preferred any other religion. We will certainly try to reform the Shiite idea in Iran, to introduce to this nation the eyes of modern civilization as a non-Muslim country, after 14 centuries of Islamization. Because of a daily force of the bloody swords of Arabs, we became Muslims, today in the name of our Lord, we want to be free from any sort of strange power."

Benefits of Reformation

THE FIRST PRACTICAL BENEFIT of this reformation goes to all Muslims in the world, while we reform Shiite Islam to stop the 14 centuries of war with Sunni Muslims. This will change the ugly face of the Middle East to one of peace and will minimize the power of terrorism and maximizing the possibility of harmony, tolerance and mercy of the real God. This could be truly helpful for millions of people in this area.

The other major benefit of such a reformation goes to the Iranian

Christians, Jews and Zoroastrians. During the last 14 centuries these three groups of Iranian citizens have been called a "minority," while in fact they have been the real owners of the country. As a matter of fact, all Shiite Muslims in Iran, either Arabs or the fiddle servants to those serious enemies, are strangers, infidels to true Iranian nationalism and rationally must be the minority in this country, but not the Christian, Jews and Zoroastrians. On the other hand, the Arab Muslim invaders destroyed the most civilized country in the world, massacred millions and millions of our last generation and called us a "minority," or second class citizen in our own homes.

Becoming Iranian liberal constitutionals after the fall of the Shiite-Islamic government, the first practical operation of P.L.I.M in Iran will start by correcting this ugly point of the future Iranian constitutional law. There are many other positive results that must be discussed and I categorized them as follows:

- Ceasing the 14 centuries of Shiite-Sunni war.
- Minimizing the power of terrorism in the world.
- Changing the face of the Middle East.
- Promoting the idea of freedom of choice and equal opportunity in Iran.
- Iranian opposition leaders who are seeking for liberal democracy and/or plural socialism based on secularism will understand the impossibility of joining these nice ideas under the Shiite ideology.
- Iran potentially could be a good friend of Judeo-Christian communities in the world with bilateral mature relationships.
- The chance of hearing Good News of God for millions of thirsty and hungry people will certainly be increased day by day.

Appendix II

Shiite Law and the West
Bozorg Omid

SHIITE LAW HAS BEEN alternatively described as a divine law and as jurists' law. These apparently contradictory descriptions reveal the basic tension that exists in the system between divine revelation and the human reasoning of jurists. The comprehensive system of personal and public behavior, which constitutes the Shiite religious law, is known as the Shariat. The goal of Shiite Islam jurisprudence was to reach an understanding (Fiqh) of the Shariat (1). The Islamic Republic legal system in Iran is based on the divinely-ordained precepts of Shiite Law, and is not subject to the provisions of international human rights standards (2). The nature of Shiite Law is to a great extent determined by its history, and its history is dominated by the contrast between theory and practice. The remarks that follow are intended to complete from a systematic point of view the historical account of the subject.

Shiite Law does not claim universal validity; it is binding for a Shiite to its full extent in the territory of the Shiite states, to a slightly lesser extent in enemy territory, and for the non-Shiite only to a limited extent in Shiite territory (3). The development of modernist legal thought in Iran has remained under the shadow of the problem of Ijtihad. This is not surprising, because the concept of Ijtehad has much exercised the minds of scholars in that part of Shiite world for the last few hundreds of years (4). Shiite Islam had already experienced a considerable breakdown of the barriers that geographical division had erected between the different schools of law in medieval times (5). Modernist Muslim legislation therefore often appears somewhat haphazard and arbitrary. In Jordan, for instance, a law of Family Rights, based mainly on the Ottoman law of 1917, was enacted in 1927, but a law of 1934 replaced it in favor of the traditional doctrine of the law of family. This, in its turn, was replaced by the Jordanian Law of Family Rights of 1951, some provisions of which, inspired by previous Egyptian legislation, anticipated those of the Syrian Law of Personal Status of 1953 (6). But Shiite clergymen stagnated in 14 centuries of history and are not ready to move.

Interpretation

THE JUDICIARY IN A democratic system is not directly responsible to the government. But in Shiite law, the judiciary is an indisputable agent of government. Judges who step outside these interpretations suffer severe consequences, often death. In a Shiite country, fundamentalist groups are pressing for the Shiite adoption of religious law (Shariat). The Islamic Republic in Iran has conceded at least some role to the Shiite clergy. In many cases, the judges are the religious leaders. The qualifications of the judges are frequently more religious than legal. Hence their religious sources rather than the constitution becomes the basis for legal decision.

In a pluralist Western democracy, power is dispersed, opinions are various and there is ample room for differences. A variety of freedoms allow this – the freedom of expression, of belief, of religion, of travel, etc. A person need not conform to the official and public line. He can hold and live out his own beliefs without a great deal of restriction. In order to allow maximum freedom, the restrictions often focus on preventing the negative effects of beliefs being enforced upon others by the majority within that society. Consequently a great deal of tolerance and flexibility is usually allowed. In this socio-political system the legislature, executive, public service and judiciary each have a limited and highly defined area of power, which is strictly circumscribed by law. As much as possible is therefore done to determine their powers so that excessive restrictions are avoided. Freedom is maximized rather than minimized.

The ideal for a Shiite government, however, is very intolerant and inflexible, where all is Shiite Islam and nothing is without. All must be believers of their leaders (Mojtahed) and there is no freedom to change belief, to criticize it, or to even to think outside of it (Moghalled). This thinking can be seen in their constitution. The notion of truth is not the same as that with which we are familiar. Truth for Shiite Islam is absolute or unchanging as it for Christians, Jews and Zoroastrians but the truth is quite different under Shiite law. And the truth is open to question in non-Shiite societies, but not in Shiite society. The Shiite law itself does not allow men to question or to inquire about it. It must be accepted as it is, without further inquiry. Consequently, the history of Shiite Islam since its rise has usually been a series of tyrannical leaders whose rule is above the law. The leader and often also the chief high priest (Imam) are at the top of the political pyramid. Through a hierarchy they rule the masses at the bottom of the pyramid. In Shiite country today, the constitution and its consequences are crucial instruments in the hands of the ruling party. The opposition party generally cooperates with the government. Following are excerpts from the constitutions of Shiite nation, which demonstrate the obstacles to the alignment laws, and to the introduction of democratic rights and freedoms.

This law was brought in to discriminate against the others. Even deviation from the mainstream of Shiite belief is not permitted. In Iran, violent killings often take place against another Muslim sect, Sunni or the Bahai. As a result, many have migrated to the west. On the other hand a democratic community and its judiciary share a mutual and indispensable need for confidence and good will. People will not have confidence in their law unless the judges have confidence to the community. So this bilateral confidence is a pillar of democracy.

In the West the constitution is not just a piece of paper. It guides and directs the whole pure legal system. It is the written foundation for the establishment and outworking of Western laws; among, the constitutional amendments adopted by referendum. In July 1979, in the Islamic Republic was the establishment of a new post, Head of the judiciary. This new authority took over the role of the Supreme Judicial Council – that is, to bear responsibility for the appointment and dismissal of judges, the drafting of bills of law to be considered by the Shiite Consultative Assembly, and the drafting of guidelines for the enforcement of legislation by the courts. This first incumbent of this post, appointed directly by the Leader of the Islamic Republic, was Ayatollah Muhammad Yazdi. The Head of the Judiciary appoints the Prosecutor General and the President of the Supreme Court. The judicial is independent of the Minister of Justice, who is in charge of the administrative organization of the courts. The Minister of Justice responds to questions about the judiciary in the Shiite Consultative Assembly, providing a constitutional shield for the judiciary against political pressure from the legislature (7). Thousands of former political prisoners have described the extremely summary nature of their trails by Shiite-Islamic Revolutionary Courts, which usually last only a few minutes (8). There are a number of less frequently used execution methods, including stoning to death, beheading and being forced to jump from a high place, which is scribed by Shiite Law (9). Article 119 of Shiite Penal Code described as follow:

"In the punishment of stoning to death, the stones should not be too large so that the person dies on being hit one or two of them; they should not be so small either that they could not be defined as stones."

Mr. Khoiniha on April 5, 1989 the Islamic Republic prosecutor general reported on Tehran Radio as follow:

"The implementation of this law has been very successful up to now." (BBC Summary of World Broadcasts, 6 April 1989).

The relationship between judges and the legal professions are very fragile. In some courts the lawyers have no right to participate and represent their own clients. The president of the Supreme Judicial Council of the Islamic Republic described a system whereby a representative of the Leader of the Islamic Republic "from outside the maze of the judicial system "could hold an immediate trial" and bring cases to an end "in a matter of three, four or five days"(10).

There is no independent Bar Association. Lawyers were among the first to be imprisoned as prisoners of conscience and forced into exile as political repression grew in 1980 and 1981 (11).

The question of applicability of international human rights standards to countries seeking to implement a system of Shiite Law appears to be a subject on which there are differing views within the clerical leadership (Keyhan Islamic Republic official daily newspaper, Tehran, 28 November 1989). General policies of the judiciary are based, as far as possible, upon eliminating the interval between the committing of a crime and the punishment of the convict, so that the convict is punished as soon as possible, the head of Islamic Republic Judiciary (12). It is of course impossible to argue against assertions, such as that made by the Permanent Mission of Islamic Republic to the UN in New York in a letter to Amnesty International received on August 9, 1989, that "there is no doubt that the divine faith of Shiite Islam, more than any other man-made ideology, is responsive to human society in question of legal adjudication" (13). The special representative of the UN Human Rights Commission in his February 1990 report described in paragraph 213 his meeting with "an experienced lawyer." The lawyer said that in cases where death sentences were passed by Shiite Courts "the defendant was never informed of his condemnation" (14).

Forces Leading Towards Alignment Of Laws
- Secularism and Religious Revival
- Migrations
- New technology
- Warfare and Diplomacy
- Constitutions

- International Court of Justice and the other international legal organizations

Specific Legal Issues
- Family law
- Inheritance
- Rights and obligations
- Trusts
- Nationality
- Torts
- Litigation
- Arbitration

Solutions for handling the conflict of laws
- Connecting Factor
- The exigencies of new generations
- Methods
- Renvoi
- Koranic Law
- Tolerant jurisdiction
- International Court of Justice and the other international legal organizations

A DEMOCRATIC AND LIBERAL WESTERN country with a typical Common Law system, conflicts exist between the various Federal and State legal systems. The legal system in Shiite law in Iran and the majority of Middle-Eastern legal systems are patterned on the French Codified system, which is combined with the Shiite law. Fields of law where this combination can be seen are civil and criminal codes and procedures, prescriptions, tribunals, expertise, delays, inheritance, executions, the criteria of prisons, contracts, torts, family, trusts, litigation, and arbitration. Internal laws are strictly measured against Shiite legal sources interpretations. But foreign commercial law and international private and public laws are much more loosely viewed.

Our personal enthusiasm, educational background, and professional experiences and the recent aggressive Shiite revolution in Iran, fundamentalism and its subsequent flood of refugees have international repercussions that even West is not immune from, caused us to this research. The increased immigration of people from Shiite backgrounds into the West are increasingly facing people with a vastly different value system with widely different views of authority and what is right. A better understanding of each perspective can minimize the resulting conflicts where they occur. What would be the long-term legal implications for the huge numbers of Shiite migrants who have flowed to the Western countries during the last few decades? Do they need to know more about the Western legal system? How can we find reasonable solutions to reduce the conflict of laws, which may apply to them externally? A logical response to the needs of both the Western and Shiite nation as they interact on a commercial, legal and social basis in order is to build a workable cultural bridge between these two sides. There will be in the future an increasing need for non-Islamic countries all over the world to negotiate with Shiite countries on a multitude of matters ranging from question to war and peace to mercantile contracts. Such negotiation will require more understanding of Shiite attitudes, history and culture. An excellent example of an opportunity lost though lack of such understanding was the hostage crisis in Iran. The U.S.A, asserting the well-accepted principle of diplomatic immunity and right to protection, kept referring continually to the formulations of this rule in the Western law books (15).

During the past century pragmatist Shiite Islam has tried to change the face of Shiite law in the Middle East and especially in Iran. Now is the right time for judicial evolution in the region. Modernism in the area of law has to run parallel with other social developments. The new doctrines of law must help to minimize the conflict of laws. The negative reaction to the Islamic revolution in Iranian society is gradually increasing; there are many people who hate Shiite Islam both in legislation and jurisdiction, and both in theory and practice. From the 19th century onwards there grew up an increasingly intimate contact between Shiite and Western civilization, and legal development was hence-forth conditioned, almost exclusively, by the novel influences to which Shiite thus became subject. Politically, socially, and economically, Western civilization was based on concepts and institutions fundamentally alien to Shiite tradition and to the Shiite Law, which expressed that tradition (16). Interesting reflections on the similarities between the Shiite jurists and the jurists of Rome are to be found in the writings of outstanding European scholars. Assign Rome, officially licensed jurists, called "Imam" could be called on for their opinions. There were authoritative and no reasons need be given. They were an element in adding to the complexity of the law, as opinions could vary from jurist to jurist (17). We have observed the various techniques by which the jurist made his contribution to the development of Shiite jurisprudence. As this contribution has an important bearing on international law and human rights it becomes necessary to compare the role of the jurist in Shiite systems with the jurist's position in comparable systems. The jurists in Shiite Islam never had the authority to make law in their own right. Their function was to discover the law and expound it, but Allah made all law.

It is true that the consensus of the Shiite community was also a source of law but this was regarded as the product of divine guidance given to the Shiite community. The Roman lawyer's "Auctoritas prudential" was a source of law in a different sense, for the lawyers who had this privilege by special recognition from the Emperor were, within limits, law-makers in their own right (18). A legal profession in the source of a skilled body of people appearing for litigants thus appeared quite early in the Shiite system, antedating in this regard the appearance of a legal system in any European tradition except the Roman (19). Shariat Law had come into being as a doctrinal system independently of and essentially opposed to current legal practice (20).

Enough has now been said to indicate that Shariat Law, however strong its religious force as providing an ideal and comprehensive code of conduct for the individual, can form only a part of the Shiite legal system. The doctrine of Siyyasat-Shariat, based on a realistic assessment of the nature of Shariat Law and the historical process by which it had been absorbed into the structure of the state, admitted the necessity for, and the validity of, extra-Shariat jurisdiction, which cannot therefore be regarded, in themselves, as deviations from any ideal standard. Shiite government has never meant, in theory or in practice, the exclusive jurisdiction of Shariat tribunals (21).

Among some communities the force of indigenous custom was strong enough to deny the Shariat any influence at all in the regulation of their family relationships. However since their profession and practice of the faith may have been, they accepted Shiite Islam as a religion but not as a way of life, and consequently remained, from the standpoint of strict orthodoxy, only superficially Shiite Islam (22). In the Indian sub-continent the administration of Shariat Law by British or anglicized courts, subject to the supreme authority of the decisions of the Privy Council, led to a remarkable fusion of the two systems. This is aptly termed Anglo-Mohammedan law, because, through the introduction of English principles and concepts, the law applied by the Indian courts came to diverge in many particulars from traditional Sunni law (23). Anglo-Mohammedan law, then, is an expression of Islamic law unique not only in form-for it is genuinely applied as a case law system through a hierarchy of courts which observes the doctrine of binding precedent- but also in substance, inasmuch as it has absorbed English influences, particularly those of Equity, in as generally facile a manner as nascent Islamic law had absorbed Roman influences in the earliest historical period (24).

Personal, family, and financial laws are the most commonly litigated and disputed in both societies and are therefore given priority in this study. The idea of law, the obligatory rules of human behavior, alone make society possible. Its ultimate basis is therefore pure necessity, whatever secondary function law may also be called upon to perform. Within this basic unity of the idea of law comes diversity in the substantive rules of law in different societies. This diversity in the course of evolution in turn gives rise to system of private international law, in mechanical terms a sort of universal joint of the international community (25). The American Declaration of Independence and the French Declaration of the Rights of Man proclaimed that all men were created equal. Such pronouncements were all the more ringing because they announced ideals rather than described reality. Sex, social position, wealth (perhaps earned but better if inherited), education, occupation, race, and a myriad of other factors conferred special status in dealing with government as well as fellow citizens. But the leaders of the French and American revolutions realized that a democratic political system that was consistent with its basic premises had to provide at least equality before the law for all its male citizens – few were so radical as to include women as full participants in the polity (26). The Shiite men struggle against adversaries, which depleted the male members of the community leaving many scores of widows and orphans, inevitably interfered with the customary transfer of property on death. It was paramount to introduce generally a more extensive distributive system around the wider family circle, and, in particular in the main source in the legal field is contained in the verses which provided a series of fixed fractional inheritance rights to certain relatives of the deceased who, in the pre-Islamic customary law, may not have received any part of the estate. The result of this innovation is to transform the old tribal bond of pre-Islamic Arabia into an extended family bond of Shiite community, politically allied by religion and legally allied by inheritance (27). Because of this and thousands of the other reasons, such unfair legal ideas must be reformed.

Endnotes to Appendix II

1 – C. G. Weermantry, Islamic Jurisprudence, An International Perspective, US, Nash, 1988, ISBN 0-312-01204-7, P 3.
2 – Amnesty International Report, Violations of human rights, Iran, 1987-1990, A. I. Publications London, December 1990, P 55.
3 – Joseph Schacht, An introduction to Islamic Law, Oxford Clarendon Press 1964, P 199.
4 – Ibid, P 104.
5 – N.J. Coulson A history of Islamic law, M.A, Edinburgh University Press, 1964, P 182.
6 – Joseph Schacht, P 105-106.
7 – Amnesty International Report, P 42.
8 – Op Cit, P 28.
9 – Op Cit,, P10.
10 – Op Cit,, P10.
11 – Op Cit,, P15.
12 – Op Cit, P 50.
13 – Op Cit,, P 56.
14 – Op Cit, P 28.
15 – C. G. Weermantry, Islamic Jurisprudence, P 189.
16 – N. J. Coulson, A history of Islamic law, P 149.
17 – Joseph Schacht, An introduction to..., P 116.
18 – C. G. Weermantry, P 56.
19 – Op Cit,, P 77.
20 – N. J. Coulson, P 102.
21 – Op Cit, P 134.
22 – Op Cit, PP 135-136.
23 – Op Cit,, P 164.
24 – Op Cit, P 171.
25 – R. H. Graveson, Comparative Conflict of Laws, North Holland Publishing Company 1977, ISBN 0-7204-0486-X, P 306.
26 – W. F. Murphy, Comparative Constitutional Law, Cases and Commentaries, Joseph Tanenhaus, Copyrights, Martin's Press, Inc, New York, 1977, ISBN 0-333-231082, P 388.
27 – David Pearl, A textbook on Muslim Law, 1979, Croom Helm publication, London, ISBN 0-85664 959-7, P 2.